The Music of
ISRAEL

Its Rise and Growth
Through 5000 Years

By PETER GRADENWITZ

W · W · NORTON & COMPANY · INC · New York

The Music of
ISRAEL

TO
LEONARD BERNSTEIN
as a token of friendship
and sincere appreciation

Contents

8 CONTENTS

Illustrations

Text Illustrations

Music Examples

Introduction

MANY BOOKS AND ESSAYS have been written on the music of the ancient Hebrews as described in the books of the Bible and in the commentaries of rabbinical scholars, and some writers have studied the role of the Jew in the general history of the civilizations and the arts. Theologians, historians, sociologists, and literary and musical scholars have tried to analyze various aspects of Jewish history and to explain the singular case of a people who, after enjoying a few centuries of cultural prosperity, and giving to the world a high code of laws and ethics, its greatest book, and some of its most magnificent poetry, were then dispersed among the nations of the globe and subjected to oppression and persecution for two millennia. Jewish history, it has been said, reads more strangely than fiction, and many writers, swayed either by affection and compassion or by intolerance and agitation, have found it difficult to let the undistorted facts speak for themselves. In the field of music, too, the reader has hitherto

11

had to choose between extremes of superlative praise and of vilification; only a very few aspects of Jewish musical history—among them the music of the Bible—have been studied by scholars in a detached and truly scientific spirit.

The serious student of the music of Israel is confronted with various difficulties. It is never easy to write the musical history of a particular nation or people, for the national character—like that of the individual personality—is composed not only of distinctive, seemingly inborn features but of a considerable number of foreign influences absorbed in one way or another. In the case of the Jews there is added the peculiar fact that throughout history their fate has been linked with that of other peoples. The ancient Hebrews had wandered from country to country before they were able to found their theocratic state in a land of their own, and on the way they adapted many foreign customs to their own way of living. Later, in the two millennia of their dispersion among the nations of the world, they were in close contact with the life and art of many different peoples, and though preserving their own ancient belief and spiritual values they could not but keep up with the spirit of the times and assimilate themselves to European thinking and ways of expression. In modern Palestine, at last, Jews are again assembling from all corners of the globe, and from each country they bring different customs and different standards of culture to the land they are building anew.

It was the ancient Torah—their religious, legal, and moral canon—together with their prayer chant that kept the Jews united throughout the world and allowed them to maintain some of their ancient Oriental character, however extensive became their westernization in later centuries. Law and music have been the fields traditionally cultivated by the Jews throughout the ages, and it is not to be wondered at that they excelled in these professions when European civilization permitted them to take part, like other citizens, in public and social life. The Jewish love for music and their specific musical talent are evidenced all the way from the earliest pages of Genesis—where the invention of music is attributed to the seventh generation of men—down to the era of high European cultural development, to which Jewry contributed many ingenious creators and performers of great music. In the musical as well as in other fields the Jew always held a position between tradition and progress; but it is not always easy to distinguish the Jew in his general works of art, and in the case of emancipated composers it is well-nigh impossible.

Jewish musicology labors under difficulties. The ban on worldly science on the part of the rabbinical authorities—particularly in the early periods and in the eastern European sphere —forbade a detached study of the Biblical sources and the notation of actual melodies. Moreover, the ancient commandment to refrain from the creation of images denies us a close knowledge of the music of the ancient Hebrews; no representation of musical instruments and no original Biblical melodies have come down to us, and the very names for the instruments used in Biblical times have not all been completely explained as yet. The wholesale burning of Jewish books in the Middle Ages and again in modern times robbed us of a great many important theoretical sources and ancient manuscripts and added to the scarcity of material prevailing in our field. Comparative study and conjecture thus reign foremost in all investigations into the history of the music of Israel.

The present book is a survey of the music of Israel from the times of the ancient Hebrews to the new music of modern Palestine; it attempts to show the function of music in the ancient Temple and in Jewish life in the various centers of the Diaspora as well as the influence the ancient Hebrew culture and later Jewish achievements exerted on general music history, and to fix the historical position of the Jewish composers whose works have become part of the treasure of world music. The author has tried to keep the narrative as clear and as comprehensible as possible and not to burden the reader with more than the most necessary references. The historical and general cultural background for all periods of musical development is provided, and the mutual influences shaping the music of the nations and of the Jews living within their midst are always examined.

The reader will note that the present book often varies from the generally accepted texts in its translations of well-known Biblical sources and of Talmudic passages; it must be understood that these variants constitute part of our research.

The author—who presents in this volume the fruits of fifteen years of research and preparation—has been able to draw on a great many sources and monographs (listed in the bibliographical appendix) and feels that he can offer a comprehensive study of all aspects of his theme. In his investigation of the ancient sources—Biblical and Talmudic—the author was greatly assisted by Mr. Ephraim Trochae (Dror), with whom he collaborated on a first short survey of this vast subject which was published in Jerusalem (in Hebrew) in 1945; but he has since been able substantially to enlarge the scope of his knowledge and insight and to add several chapters to the original book.

A great many colleagues and friends have assisted the author in his research in many countries, and a number of composers and their publishers were good enough to make available their manuscripts and printed editions and permitted the quotation of musical excerpts. I hope they will all accept the author's sincere thanks for their valuable help in this way—collectively, as individual acknowledgments would fill many pages.

But I must mention a few to whom I am particularly indebted for their active interest and assistance while I prepared this book for publication. My sincere thanks go to Dr. Paul Henry Lang, whose valuable suggestions and queries set me thinking anew about many historical problems. I am also grateful to Dr. Paul Landau, who checked the general cultural aspects of the book, and to Dr. Curt Sachs and Dr. Eric Werner, the two great scholars of the music of the ancient world whose work laid the foundation for all subsequent research, for their pertinent suggestions, and for their reading of the book in proof; to Dr. Werner also for making available to me the fruits of his most recent researches and for permitting the reproduction of his photostat and transcription of a newly discovered Judeo-Spanish manuscript. To Dr. Edith Gerson-Kiwi I am thankful for her permission to use her transcriptions of Oriental music, only recently recorded by her and published here for the first time prior to her own book, *Music of the Orient—Ancient and Modern,* and for her valuable recommendations after she had read the book in proof. I also gratefully acknowledge the help given to me at various stages of my work by a number of libraries and institutions, especially the Hebrew University, Jerusalem; the British Museum, London; the Bibliothèque Nationale, Paris; the San Marco Library, Venice; the Music Room and the Jewish Division of the New York Public Library; the Hebrew Union College, Cincinnati, Ohio; the Jacob Michael Collection of Jewish Music, New York; and the National Jewish Music Council, New York, whose chairman, Mrs. Frank Cohen, was always ready with advice and encouragement. Rabbi Israel Goldfarb has obliged me by supplying valuable information about the poet of the Jewish National Anthem (Appendix Three), and I gratefully remember the interesting exchange of ideas on my subject with M. Leon Algazi of Paris, the late Mr. Samuel Alman of London, the late Mr. Arno Nadel of Berlin, Mrs. Alice Jacob-Loewenson of Jerusalem, and Mr. Joachim Stutchevsky of Tel-Aviv.

Finally, I must express my sincere thanks to the staff of W. W. Norton and Company, particularly to Miss Katherine Barnard, for the kind assistance, the good will and understanding, and the wholehearted co-operation extended to me in the last, and decisive, stage of my work.

PETER GRADENWITZ

Tel-Aviv, Israel

PROLOGUE

The Eternal Land

*U*NDER A SOLITARY PALM TREE on the edge of the wide desert of the Southland a shepherd boy dreamily plays his pipe. Soon he will leave the dry sands of the Negev for the friendlier North, once the oasis has yielded its sparse treasures to his patient and placid flock. The hollow yet piercing tones of his serene pastoral resound over the endless plains and from somewhere an echo faintly answers; is it another shepherd far away in the desert, is it a camel driver's plaintive song, or is it just his own tune that returns to the friendly oasis from a futile journey across the sands? We cannot tell, and the shepherd does not care. He is engulfed in his own world, which is the welfare of his flock and the eternal question whither to go next in search of pasture and food. His meditations, his joy, and his sorrow ring through his tune. . . .

Over the rocky Judean mountains reverberate the mighty sounds of a many-voiced chorus and an orchestra composed of a colorful variety of instruments. You can hear their solemn music far across the stony desert down to the lowest valley of this earth, where the Jordan rushes its waters into the Dead Sea, and it resounds in the olive and cypress groves on the hills as well as in the lanes and alleys of the Holy City. You listen spellbound, and the magnitude of the Jerusalem scene and the loftiness of the music inspire you with awe. . . .

A light breeze carries the exquisite music of a small group of instruments over the gentle waters of the Sea of Galilee. In the cool night following a scorching day sweet chamber music refreshes and delights the company stretched out on the lawns adorning the shores of the beautiful lake. You can distinguish the flute and the violins singing a song of yearning and love, and again sounding a lively tune of hope and of joy. . . .

This is the country holy to three great world religions, a land full of bold contrasts—the fertile valley bordering on barren desert, the sounds of feasts and rejoicing next to solitude and austerest calm. The time—some nine hundred years before a Nazarene rabbi preached a new ethos to the Jews of Galilee and Judea and ushered in a new era of history, some nine hundred and fifty years before the splendors of King Solomon's Temple fell under the blow of the Romans, the mighty conquerors of Israel whose victory opened two millennia of Jewish dispersion and misery among the peoples of the world. The shepherd playing his tranquil tune in the southern desert knows little of the prosperous life of his northern brethren, the Israelites, feasting and dancing on the shores of the Sea of Galilee to the accompaniment of exquisite music. Perhaps he will be able to join the pilgrims this autumn at the gigantic festival in Jerusalem. For then the children of Israel will commemorate their sojourn in the tabernacles put up in the wilderness, and then the fruits of the year will be brought in to the Temple in Jerusalem. Then the chorus and orchestra will raise their voices to the Lord of hosts. . . .

But wait—is that really the Palestine of three thousand years ago? The shepherd has abruptly stopped his playing and hurries to soothe his flock, which is frightened by a loud noise and by clouds of dust whirled up from the desert. The boy rubs his eyes and looks around—and here it is, the four-legged monster that has disturbed the calm of the oasis. It is a motor truck laden with young people, singing and laughing gaily as their car struggles its way through the dry sands and speeds them home from a hard day's work. They have built houses and huts in the midst of the desert, and the shepherd has often rested and refreshed himself in their spacious dining hall. Their song has little of the melancholy strains of his own plaintive pipe, but strange as it sounds to his ears he finds that theirs, too, is a song of the desert, a song of the common land.

So this is the twentieth century, with the motorcar usurping the camel's place and with the desert yielding soil and fruit to the Jews returning to their land of yore? Then what are the sounds ringing over the mountains of Judea, the music heard on the shores of the Sea of Galilee? The Temple has not been rebuilt, and old memories deny to the Jews the use of music in the house of worship. But on one of the hills overlooking the Holy City there has risen a center of learning and study, the Hebrew University, and in its amphitheater there plays a symphony orchestra assisted by a large modern chorus. And music rises over the mountains just as it did when the trumpets of the Lord made the walls of Jericho crumble.

On the shores of the Kinnereth new life has risen from ancient ruins as well. The lake is surrounded by agricultural settlements, and the one most favored by natural beauty, Ein Gev, on the slopes of the Susita hill opposite the ancient city of Tiberias, has become a mecca of music lovers all over the country; here occasional concerts are given, and once a year a one-week music festival attracts thousands of visitors. And today, just as three millennia ago, there is singing and dancing on the romantic shores of the Sea of Galilee.

Time seems to have stood still in the Holy Country. Elsewhere empires have risen to mighty power and have rotted and perished. Men have loved and hated, succeeded to fame and vanished, have usurped power and were brought low. Genius has given to the world immortal treasures of thought, art, and music, and built magnificent edifices of marble and stone. Mankind has learned to traverse the wide world on land, on sea, and in the air, and magic machines have been created that allow us to watch and to listen to fellow men speaking, acting, or singing hundreds or thousands of miles away. In Palestine many armies and nations have fought for possession of holy places and strategic positions, have devastated and again rebuilt the country. Little was left of the Holy Land's ancient glory, and few are the monuments telling of the splendors of old. Today the Jews have come back to the country they had made great in olden times; they are bringing with them the experience and the knowledge they gathered in the two thousand years of their contact with the western world, a world whose ideas are diametrically opposed to those of the Orient but which has also absorbed much of Oriental custom and thought. The reclamation of the soil and the renaissance of art are a fascinating chapter in the long and exciting story of the fight between desert and land of plenty, between the unsteady and the settled, between a life of thrift and a life of luxury.

Thousands of volumes are necessary to record all the events of historical significance which have changed the life of men since the Temple was erected in the heart of Jerusalem, but the Palestine of modern times is still the country of old. Its music mirrors continuity as well as change: it has not fundamentally changed in character as it still sounds over the plains of the South, the Judean hills, and the waters of Galilee. The shepherd's song, played on the thousand-year-old pipe, is the calm and austere tune created by the son of the wide deserts; the sonorous music of the orchestral instruments belongs in the prosperous towns and the fertile valleys. These are the very same opposing forces acknowledged by ancient Greece, where they find expression in the temperate art of the Apollonian cult—with the soft-voiced cithara as the favorite instrument—and the orgiastic music of the worshipers of Dionysus who accompanied their song on the shrill-sounding aulos. Just as in classical Greece, geographic conditions created the life of the inhabitants of ancient Palestine and their social development; their music was a direct and simple expression of their soul in their life with nature, while in the wealthy urban centers it developed into an exuberant art. Today the soil of the desert is being reclaimed and forced to yield fruit, but the song of the plain is still shaping the tunes sung by the settlers. In the towns the chorus and orchestra created to sing and play unto the Lord have been replaced by choruses and orchestras serving the community of citizens, elevating their souls and adorning their hours of leisure just as they do in the great urban centers of other civilized continents. But the characteristic aspect of the country has not changed at all: the shepherd—Jewish or Arab—plays his flute just as he did in King Solomon's time, the Judean mountains reverberate to the sounds of a many-voiced chorus and orchestra, and the light breeze carries over the Sea of Galilee the exquisite music of a small group of flutes and violins. . . .

Chapter
ONE

Music of the Desert

FROM THE DAWN of its history down to the beginning of the first millennium of the pre-Christian era Israel was a people of nomads and shepherd tribes; their patriarchs, their judges, and their first prophets and kings were sons of the land. It is only with the rise of their kingdom that urban civilization begins to develop and that pastoral poetry and song is rivaled by courtly art and music. But the parables and the proverbs, the verse and the song of Israel are living witness of the people's origin; they come forth from the mind and the heart of shepherd poets and singers, and it is the peasant and the shepherd whom they still glorify in their song:

> The Lord is my shepherd [sings David, the royal shepherd
>   boy]; I shall not want.
> He maketh me to lie down in green pastures;
> He leadeth me beside the still waters.

He restoreth my soul;

He leadeth me in the paths of righteousness for his name's
sake.

Yea, though I walk through the valley of the shadow of
death, I will fear no evil:

For thou art with me; thy rod and thy staff they comfort me.

Thou preparest a table before me in the presence of mine
enemies:

Thou anointest my head with oil; my cup runneth over.

Surely goodness and mercy shall follow me all the days of
my life:

And I will dwell in the house of the Lord for ever.

David's Psalms and the Song of Solomon are sublime examples of shepherd poetry and song. To grasp their spirit and to
get an idea of what pre-monarchist Israel's music may have
been like, we must turn to the peasant and nomad past of Israel.
No pictorial sources and no written music are there to help us
in our endeavors to reconstruct the picture of ancient Hebrew
playing and song; we must rely on comparisons with the culture
of the neighboring countries and on the few actual hints contained in the early books of the Bible.

We know little about the musical instruments and the songs
of Israel in its early history. The Hebrews, who constituted one of
the many Semitic tribes which led an unsteady life of migration
between the Arabian Peninsula and the northern parts of Asia
Minor but who seem to have separated from the other groups
during the twentieth century B.C., presented a strange mixture
of nomads and peasants: they were restless wanderers longing
for a secure place of permanent settlement. The country through
which they drove their herds of cattle and their flocks of sheep
was undeveloped and bare, and no place seemed inviting

enough for them to pitch their tents permanently. Highly civilized countries lay to the north and south of their lands: the Sumerians—a non-Semitic people of eastern Asiatic origin—ruled in the fertile plains of Mesopotamia, while in Egypt there flourished the culture of the Old Kingdom. Abraham had come to Canaan from Ur, capital of Sumeria, and his wanderings had led him to Egypt, too; indeed, in his days the first contacts seem to have been made between the two great civilizations after more than seven hundred years of isolation. Musical archaeology actually helps us to examine the cultural relations between Sumeria (and later Babylon) and Egypt, and it also proves that Israel here began—at the earliest stage of its history, and in the days of its oldest patriarch—to play the role it was destined to fill throughout the ages: the role of a mediator between peoples and civilizations.

The ancient Sumerian civilization has provided us with the oldest records of musical systems and musical organization; these records go back to the third millennium B.C. For the Sumerian Temple professional singers and players were trained by an appointed officer; music schools were founded for this purpose in various centers and were later kept up by the Babylonians, successors of the Sumerians as rulers of Mesopotamia. Clappers, cymbals, bells, rattles, and drums are known to have been used in Sumeria; pipes, blowing horns, and trumpets are mentioned occasionally; but it seems that the Sumerians most favored the softer stringed instruments: a large type of lyre, harps, and the lute. It is of special interest for us here that most of the surviving specimens of these musical instruments were found in the royal cemetery of Abraham's native town, Ur.

The Old Kingdom of Egypt knew the same instruments as ancient Sumeria, but it appears that there was no contact between the two countries from about 2700 B.C. to the time of

Abraham (ca. 2000), for the favorite Sumerian instrument of the later third millennium, the lyre, is shown on an Egyptian painting for the first time in that period. Semitic nomads—very probably Hebrews—are there depicted offering presents to the Pharaoh of Egypt, among them a lyre; it has been assumed that the Semites of the picture are none other than Joseph's brethren coming before Pharaoh.

Sumerian musicians. Vase fragment of the fourth millennium before the Common Era. The two lyres depicted have five and seven strings respectively. (After Curt Sachs: *Musik der Antike*)

If it seems certain that the Hebrews (from whom in the meantime a new group had detached itself, the Sons of Israel, who on their part were divided into twelve tribes named after the sons of Jacob, or Israel) acted as a link between the highly civilized Sumerians and Egyptians at the time their own history actually opens, the development of a civilization of their own was still hampered by their unsteady nomad life. Organized musical practice, the evolution of tonal systems, and the development of musical instruments—such as those developed by the ancient Hebrews in the neighboring countries—are impossible without the creation of an organized community and of a cultural center—temple or court. The tribes of Israel lived and wandered about in different regions and under different climatic and geographic conditions, and their standard of life depended on the yield of their soil. It was hunger and want that drove some of them—a small fraction, it is true—to the fertile Nile valley, the destination of many Semitic tribes in search of pasture. The cattle drivers and shepherds of Israel eased the boredom of their wanderings by singing and piping their songs or strumming the lyre, giving free rein to their emotions and feelings; they used the instruments and remembered the tunes known all over the Near East—some of them going back to the same central Asiatic cradle from which the Far Eastern civilizations also sprang—but they could not develop a systematized art without first creating a communal and cultural center of their own. And this was not achieved before the times of the Judges and the Kings, a millennium after Abraham had settled in Canaan.

Still, it is certain that the ancient Hebrews loved singing, playing, and dancing as much as did the Sumerians and the Egyptians; the early books of the Pentateuch prove that music was regarded as indispensable by them in joy and in sorrow, at the feast and in the fields. Most ancient peoples attribute the invention of music to a legendary national hero of their own; the writers of Israel's history ascribe the first use of musical instruments to the seventh generation after the creation of the world, when no Hebrews could, of course, be spoken of as yet: Jubal (son of Ada and Lamech, offspring of Methusael, son of Mehujael, son of Irad, son of Enoch, son of Cain, Adam and Eve's first-born) "was the father of all such as handle the harp and pipe" (Gen. 4:21). Arab legend, which goes back to the same treasure of ancient Semitic lore as the Biblical stories, credits Jubal, son of Cain (Qain), with the first song—an elegy on the death of Abel; Lamak (the Hebrew Lamech) is called the inventor of the lute (a European word actually derived from the Arabic *'ūd*), while his son Tūbal (Jubal's stepbrother in Biblical history: "Tubal-cain, an instructor of every artificer in brass and iron," Gen. 4:22) is credited with the introduction of drum and tambourine. The same Arab source claims that the *tunbūr* came from the people of Sodom (*Lūt* = Lot); this instrument was in fact the Sumerian lute, the ancestor of most later stringed instruments; the Greek word for it, *pandura*, points to its having been imported from Asia Minor, as in Sumeria the lute was called *Pan-tur*, which means "bow-small" and indicates an origin in the most ancient of stringed instruments, the musical bow.

Another ancient tradition—mentioned in the thirteenth century A.D. by Bar Hebraeus, the Syriac patristic writer of Jewish parentage—has it that the daughters of Cain invented musical instruments; the singing-girl, who played an important part in Arabic music, was called *qaina*, and a similar word describes musicians and singers in the Persian language. This is particularly interesting with regard to the place ascribed to women in early music. Though women were probably banned from Temple music, they were always found in the spheres of popular musical practice: this, too, is a phenomenon common to all Oriental cultures. In ancient Japan women were not permitted to sing or play the religious music of the educated musicians, nor could they join in the music making of the less educated merchant classes; they were confined to the lowest style of music and forbidden to use the tunes and styles of higher classes even if they had enjoyed a higher education. The student of ancient history can thus find in the women's music of early civilizations the most primitive stages of musical development. Singing and dancing still went largely together in the women's music of the ancient Orient; simple melodic patterns and rhythmic accompaniment on instruments characterize their songs all through the ancient East. In some places in our contemporary world we can still study at first hand the singing and playing that must have been practiced by the women singers of old. Jewish women on the North African Isle of Djerba have been found by a modern scholar, Robert Lachmann, to constitute living relics from Oriental civilization of thousands of years ago. Their songs depend on a small store of typical melodic turns; the various songs reproduce these turns—or some of them—time and again. Their tone relations reveal one of the many kinds of practices of vocal music before its subjection to a rational scale system as understood by theory. The women's songs of this island, isolated from the cultural development in the past millennia, belong, says Lachmann,[1] to a species whose forms are essentially dependent not on the requirements of the text but on certain processes of motion. Thus we find here, in place of the free rhythm of cantillation and its very intricate line of melody, a periodical up-and-down movement. This type of song, like the recitation of magic or liturgical texts, goes back to prehistoric times. In the Jewish communities, not only in Oriental-Sephardic districts, but also, for example, in Yemen, the women accompany their songs on frame drums or cymbals which they beat with their hands. The beats follow at regular intervals; they fall on each period of the melody. They give the length of the unit of line, but they do not divide the melody into bars, nor do they bring it within the limits of a systematic rhythmic pattern.

Lachmann's description of ancient women's singing as preserved down to our own days provides us with a fitting picture of how the people sang, played, and danced in ancient Israel;

[1] Robert Lachmann, *Jewish Cantillation and Song in the Isle of Djerba.*

Miriam and her women responding to Moses' hymn of triumph and praise (Exod. 15), Deborah proclaiming victory and joy (Judg. 5), Jephthah's daughter welcoming her father (Judg. 11:34), and the women of Israel coming to greet King Saul after David had slain Goliath (I Sam. 18:6 f.) certainly sang and played in a way not far remote from the style of these living relics, the women of the isolated North African and Yemenite communities of today.

Early sources tell us that singing was always accompanied by instrumental playing, but the instruments actually mentioned in the Pentateuch in connection with Israel's earliest history are very few. The primitive and emotional character of ancient Hebrew music is confirmed by what we know about them—from etymological study, from the sparse descriptions offered by the Bible and by Talmudic commentaries, and from comparison with Sumerian and Egyptian types, for no pictorial relics are available for the ancient Hebrew Orient. The six instruments named in Israel's nomadic period are the 'ugab, probably a shepherd flute of some kind; the kinnor, a stringed instrument used for accompanying the singers, a small rounded lyre which may have stemmed from the larger Sumerian prototype; the tof, a frame drum; the pa'amon, a bell or jingle; the shofar, the ram's horn; and the hazozra, the loud trumpet.

The flute, the lyre, and the drum—none of them strong in sound—were the instruments of the people and were used to accompany their songs. The ram's horn and trumpet, on the other hand, were the shrill and resounding instruments of Israel's cult: they point to a still primitive stage in the worship of the Lord. The trumpet, used in pairs in accordance with a most ancient belief in the power of symmetry, fulfills the task

ascribed to it in all primitive communities, namely to remind
God of his people in worship as well as in war (Num. 10:1–2,
9–10). The bell—"it should be upon Aaron to minister: and
his sound shall be heard when he goeth in unto the holy place
before the Lord, and when he cometh out, that he die not"
(Exod. 28:25)—is a relic of magic belief; it protects the priest

Lyre player, from Egyptian wall painting at Beni Hasan. The lyre depicted
is somewhat different from those seen on other paintings of the period; it
is probably the Biblical "kinnor," played with a plectrum.

against evil spirits while he is outside the holy place. The
shofar, finally, the only instrument still used in the worship of
the Jews on their holiest days, most eloquently proves the sur-
vival of ancient magical associations; not only is the ram's horn
—which has purposely remained primitive in form and in tone
—blown in times of danger or repentance, but it is covered so
that the worshipers may not see it; in many primitive civilizations the sight of sacred objects is denied to the people. The
magic power of seven shofarim, blown seven times on the
seventh day of the siege of Jericho (the recurring number

seven indicates another remnant of ancient sacred belief) makes the wall of the city fall down flat (Josh. 6:20); Gideon the Judge frightens his enemies, the Midianites, by the sound of the Lord's horn blown by three hundred of his men (Judg. 7:16–22); Zechariah believed that "the Lord God shall blow the horn" himself on the day of Israel's salvation (Zech. 9:14); and the belief in the shofar's magic powers still lives on in the people's minds—one need only remember the "Dybbuk" legend.

While the musical instruments used in the service of worship had the shrill or loud sound proper to their purpose, it is doubtful indeed whether the worshipers themselves were really "crying unto God." Though in primitive belief only the fervent and clamorous prayer will be heard and eventually granted, it seems certain that the Jews were more reserved in the cantillation of their prayers than other Orientals. A sweet and expressive rather than a strong and loud voice is still favored today in archaic Jewish-Oriental communities, and only at the climax of a prayer is the singer required to raise his voice. At the nomadic stage of Israel's history there cannot have been a great difference between the tunes of the shepherd in the fields and those intoned in prayer; they are the fluent, continuous melodies moving within a narrow range of four or, at the most, six notes and based upon ever-recurring melodic formulas. It is only with Israel's return from Egypt that definite forms of singing and playing began to take shape under the influence of a richly developed foreign culture, though the full impact of the Egyptian—and other neighboring—practices was only felt three centuries after the Exodus, at the time of the Kings. Biblical narrative, poetry, form, and signs are helpful in drawing a picture of Israel's music between the time of the Egyptian exile and the erection of the Temple. But before attempting to describe the state of music in this second great period of Israel's ancient history, we must cast a glance at the music of Egypt under the New Kingdom; the Israelites were slaves and servants in Egypt after a short period of prosperity and wealth, yet they had full opportunity of getting acquainted with the high civilization and flourishing culture of their oppressors.

The Old Egyptian Empire of the third millennium had had a music similar to that of Sumeria, all the musical instruments known in Mesopotamia being in use in Egypt as well. It has already been stated that the contact between the two countries had been interrupted for some seven hundred years and that a new Asiatic influence had made itself felt with the beginning of the second millennium, the time Abraham came to Egypt. The character of Egyptian art had greatly changed with the steady influx of foreign artists in the period of the Middle Kingdom. The kings of the southwest Asiatic countries subjugated by Egypt had sent singers and players as part of their tribute; the dancing girls and their instruments, new and strange to Egyptian eyes and ears, are a prominent feature of Middle Kingdom paintings. The sweet-sounding vertical flute and the soft double-cane reed pipe were replaced by shrill oboe-like instruments; new kinds of harps were introduced, and the ancient small harp was enlarged in size and given more strings; lyres, lutes, and drums appeared in the Egyptian orchestra for the first time. The quiet and mild music of the Old Kingdom was superseded by a noisy, exciting, and many-colored tonal art, just as the dance scenes depicted in the wall paintings show a sensuous emotion unparalleled in earlier sources. The singing girls imported from southwestern Asia brought about a change in the social status of music in Egypt, too; Egyptian women also began playing musical instruments and did away with the restriction of professional singing and playing to the upper ranks.

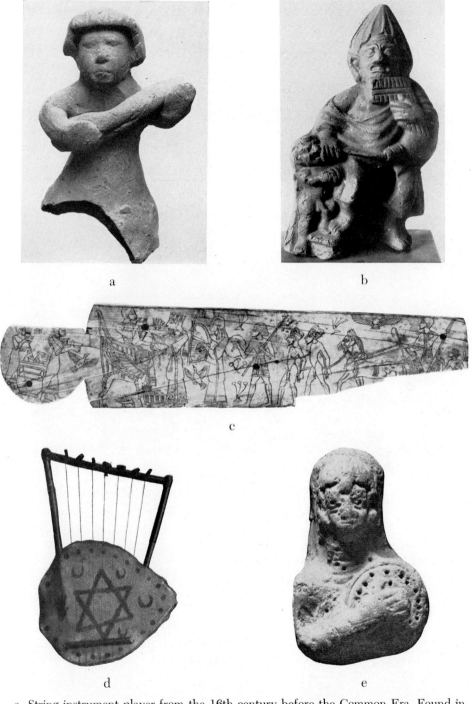

a. String-instrument player from the 16th century before the Common Era. Found in Tell-el-ajjul (ancient Gaza) in Southern Palestine. b. Syrian piper, with panpipe-like instrument, an ancestor of the organ ("magrepha"?). Alexandrian terra cotta from first century before Common Era. c. Phoenician ivory plaque, 13th century before the Common Era, with incised scene depicting musicians. Found at Megiddo, northern Palestine. d. Seven-stringed Abyssinian "kissar" with Islamic half-crescent and Jewish shield of David. e. Figure with drum. Found at Megiddo. (*a,b,c,d: Palestine Archaeological Museum, Jerusalem. e: after Curt Sachs*)

Musicians of the Elamite Court Orchestra greet King Assurbanipal on his victorious return to Susa in 661 before the Common Era. *From a relief at the British Museum.*

And with the new instruments introduced into Egypt a change occurred not only in the character and sound of orchestral combinations but in melodies and rhythms as well.

In the eighteenth and seventeenth centuries B.C. the civilization of the Middle Kingdom, in which ancient tradition and new trends reigned side by side, was completely destroyed by the Syriac-Semitic Hyksos tribes at the same time as the Kassites conquered the Babylonian Empire. The New Kingdom, whose history opens about 1580 B.C., shows a greatly different scene. Though it seems that the dignity of ancient ritual music was preserved in the temples and schools, public life resounded with the new music and the still noisier and more sonorous instruments brought to Egypt from Asia Minor. The traditional music, which had developed some distinct national trends, was regarded as old-fashioned and artificial, while the cosmopolitan character of the newly introduced instruments and their musicians mirrored the widened horizon as well as the refinement, the elegance, and the splendor of life in the New Empire.

The Egyptians had wealthy towns in which, in the course of the centuries, an organized musical life had been developed in the temples and the secular courts alike. The graphic monuments tell us that singing, playing, and dancing were generally practiced simultaneously, and a celebration or feast is usually seen accompanied by entire bands. It is interesting to reflect, in the face of all this splendor and wealth, that of the twenty-six instruments known to have been used in Egypt at the height of its culture, two at the most can be attributed to native origin—the sistrum and the shawm. The sistrum, for which primitive prototypes can be found, was an instrument consisting of a handle and a frame with jingling crossbars. Although in ancient

Egypt it was associated with the worship of Hathor and Isis, it entered the Hebrew cult as the "mna'anim" of II Sam. 6:5, where King David and all the house of Israel are said to have played before the Lord "on all manner of instruments made of fir wood, even on lyres and harps, drums, sistra, and cymbals" (Luther's German Bible version rightly translates thus, while the English Authorized Version incomprehensibly has "cornets"; incidentally, the Hebrew word *mna'anim* is derived from the verb $nū'a =$ "shook," just as the Greek *seistron* means "thing shaken"). While the shawms are not mentioned in Jewish sources at all—they may also have lost in importance under the New Kingdom of Egypt—all the other instruments first mentioned in Hebrew history after the return from Egypt were as much the common possession of the entire large musical province round the eastern shores of the Mediterranean as were the fundamentals underlying the theory and practice of music. "Mediterranean music"—a term coined for compositions with a southern flavor in the western Europe of the romanticist nineteenth century A.D. and newly created again for one of the young Palestinian composers' schools in the 1940's—once comprised ancient Mesopotamia and Syria, Greece and Phoenicia, Italy, Cyprus and Crete, the land of Israel, Arabia, and Egypt; this unity reigned till classical Greece took over the entire cultural heritage of the Orient and preserved its highest achievements in new forms. Hellenism then united the eastern Mediterranean region again, and Islam, blending ancient Oriental culture and Hellenistic forces, became in turn the heir of Hellas.

The Jews were destined to play once more the role of mediators between ancient civilizations. In the course of a rapid ascent on the ladder of cultural development, they absorbed from the foreign civilizations about them what seemed best to them and what most fitted their specific character, and they invariably gave their practice a mark of their own. Just as most of their ancient legends and customs, religious or national, were derived from common Oriental lore but were molded and interpreted by them in a new spirit, so they created a Temple service and a poetry and art, the origins of which can be traced back to other Oriental sources but which assumed with them a distinctive individual note; just as they originated new moral values and were able to erect the greatest spiritual and cultural center of the ancient world, so they gave music new foundations on which, a thousand years after King Solomon's Temple, Western civilization could base its musical style.

Jewish history at the time of its Kings went through the same process of transition that had taken place in Egypt some six hundred years before. Foreign influx and the development of urban life did away with the pastoral calm of their music and introduced the splendor of orchestral sound and of music for dancing; more expressive and powerful instruments replaced the soft-voiced flute and lyre of old. Music became a profession practiced by a religious caste in the Temple and by professional women in the king's or the wealthy nobleman's house, and melodies became subject to systematization and to rational, as well as spiritual, theory.

But in order to be able to draw a dividing line between the two civilizations at the time of Israel's sojourn in Egypt, and again between Egypt under the New Kingdom and King Solomon's empire, we must complete our survey of Egyptian music by trying to picture for ourselves an Egyptian orchestra and to get an idea of the musical theory and practice of the Egyptian musicians. For the abundance in Egypt of pictorial and written evidence must compensate us for the dearth of scriptural sources and the complete lack of pictures that might cast light upon the music history of ancient Israel.

An orchestra characteristic of the Mediterranean civilization at the time of Egypt's New Kingdom is depicted on a bas-relief now at the British Museum. Though it dates from as late as 650 B.C., that is to say some seven hundred years after Israel's Exodus from Egypt, and though it is not of Egyptian provenance itself earlier examples confirm that its typical features were essentially those of the ancient orchestras; moreover, as Israel had in the meantime built its Temple in Jerusalem, it must be surmised that the Temple orchestra cannot have been very much different. (See illustration facing page 33.)

The relief depicts the musicians of the Elamite court coming out to greet King Assurbanipal on his return to Susa from his victorious campaign against Babylon. Eleven musicians open the procession. They are, first, seven harpists (seven was still a holy number) plucking different strings, and players on double reeds and on drums—women among them. The instrumentalists are followed by singers: nine boys and six women. One of the latter compresses her throat with her hand in order to produce a shrill and vibrating tone; this is an old Oriental custom in use to this very day in Syria and Arabia; many ancient pictures show that the singers were wont to produce nasal tones and a high-pitched voice if not necessarily a piercing and loud one.[2] It is interesting to look at the singers on the Assyrian and Egyptian reliefs in the light of a Talmudic description with regard to singing in the Second Temple: "When he (the singer) raises his voice in song, he puts his thumb into his mouth and brings his forefinger between the vocal cords, till his brethren the priests get rapidly up behind him" (Ioma—the treatise on the Day of Atonement—38). Were they provoked or irri-

---

[2] Curt Sachs has pointed to the wrinkles around the noses and mouths of the angels on the Ghent altarpiece as a proof that the nasaling style of the East was still practiced in fifteenth-century Europe (these features cannot, however, be recognized on commercial photographs). See *The Orient and Western Music*.

tated by the shrillness of the voice? Returning to the Elamite orchestra, we also note that singing and dancing were still closely allied, for some of the musicians are making actual dance movements, while the singers are clapping their hands.

The Oriental orchestra as we know it from Assyrian and Egyptian paintings and reliefs is described in one Biblical source which also throws light on the form of orchestral performance in the ancient Orient. This source—Dan. 3:5 ff.—speaks of the musicians of Nebuchadnezzar, King of Babylon, about a generation after Assurbanipal; the book was probably written in the second century B.C.—four hundred years after the events described—and its author may have known the instruments and way of performance from personal experience. The passage tells us that a herald commanded the people to worship the golden image set up by the king as soon as they heard the sound of the *keren,* the *mashrokītha,* the *kathrus,* the *sabka,* the *psanterin,* the *sumponiah,* "and all kinds of instruments." We have little difficulty in identifying the four instruments mentioned first: the keren is a horn or trumpet; the mashrokītha was a sort of pipe, as indicated by its derivation from the Hebrew word *sharok* = "to pipe" or "to whistle"; the kathrus is a stringed instrument, probably a lyre; the sabka is a kind of harp, which appears in Greek as "sambuca"; the psanterin (= psaltery, mentioned in the Book of Daniel only, 3:5, 10, 15) indicates by its name that it was an instrument used to accompany the Psalms, its Greek form being *psaltêrion.* But the most interesting term is the last: *sumponiah.* Some passages in Biblical commentaries point to the sumponiah being a musical instrument (it was once identified with the ancient 'ugab, the shepherd flute, and again described as a composite instrument on the strength of the Greek meaning of the word "symphonia" = "simultaneous sound"); while the mishna (Kelim—on the ritual uncleanness of the objects of daily use—11:6) couples the symphonia with a brass flute in uncleanness. But it has been justly argued that in the Daniel passage "sumponiah" does not mean a single instrument of music at all but must be quite literally translated as a "combination of sounds" or just "orchestra"; the Authorized Version, in fact, includes the word in "all kinds of music" (in telling the parable of the prodigal son, St. Luke—15:25—also uses the term, and the Authorized Version again translates simply "music"). Though in later times, when many Greek terms were made to change their meanings, a composite musical instrument may well have been described by the fitting name "sumponiah," it is improbable indeed that the ancient Aramaic text of the book of Daniel should have alluded to a musical instrument by a term that in the original Greek was never used in this sense. Moreover, Curt Sachs has proved that if "sumponiah" is translated by "orchestra" or "band," the entire passage could be understood to describe not the composition of the orchestra but an orchestral performance in the ancient Orient—and the context makes this entirely plausible. If we accept the Aramaic text word for word, says Sachs, the king's subjects heard the various instruments first singly and then all together—in the way familiar to all students of Eastern music. A flourish on the horn or trumpet is designed to attract the attention of the players and of the masses alike. The most accomplished musicians of the band then display their virtuoso art in solo passages, improvising upon the melodic patterns of the piece, and only then does the full orchestra combine in playing a "symphony" in the sense of the seventeenth-century Italian *sinfonia:* a short instrumental ritornello. If this interpretation is correct, the additional "all kinds of instruments" may be drums and other instruments of merely rhythmical character, which were not mentioned with the solo performers but which cannot have been missing in the ensemble; it can well be understood that they joined in the music only when the entire band played together. The people were thus advised to wait for the horn signal, followed by solos of the pipe, lyre, harp, and psaltery, after which the full ensemble of these would play together with the percussion instruments.[3]

The orchestral performance described—a kind of concerto grosso without the opening tutti, if we wish to liken it to a form familiar in western European instrumental music—has a parallel in the responsorial singing practiced in the Jewish Temple and in many other Oriental civilizations; it is substantially the same style of performance that is described in the first great piece of poetry in the Pentateuch: Moses' hymn of praise after Israel's deliverance from the Egyptians. On the shores of the Red Sea, Moses sang his song unto the Lord and was joined by the children of Israel (Exod. 15:1); then Miriam, the sister of Aaron, followed by all the women, took a timbrel in her hand and responded, taking up the refrain of Moses' song (Exod. 15:20–21).

During the centuries of their sojourn in Egypt the Jews had ample opportunity to admire the splendor of the Egyptian orchestral ensembles, and they took with them a number of the instruments which were in use there as elsewhere in the Mediterranean countries; the practice and style of Egyptian performance left their mark on their own poetry and music—the reason for our having dealt with the music of Egypt at some length. But we have still to consider another important musical heritage that must have greatly contributed to the style of Israel's singing and playing in the post-Egyptian part of their nomadic period and that also helped to shape their music in the

[3] See Curt Sachs, *The History of Musical Instruments*, pp. 83–85.

subsequent Golden Age of ancient Hebrew life and art—the time of the great Kings. This is the theory and the ethics of Egyptian—and generally Oriental—music as fully developed at the time of the Exodus. The Jews, whose first generations had experienced in Egypt their earliest contact with urban life and civilization and whose subsequent generations were largely brought up in towns, had not known before that music may be more than the immediate expression of emotional sensation or that the shaping of melodies can be subjected to rational and systematic thinking while still keeping its spontaneous character. They learned for the first time the professional aspects of music (Israel's sources in the earliest period never mention professional musicians, though all neighboring countries had music-training schools), and they also experienced the schism between the spiritual music of the highly educated and the popular music of the masses: they must have wondered at the singing-girls, just as the Egyptians had wondered at them some hundred years before when they had been introduced from southwestern Asia.

We need not go into detail here about this professional training, for it becomes relevant only with the erection of the Temple. Regarding the women's music it suffices to say that Jewish women took up singing and dancing immediately, as shown in the Exodus passage quoted above; Palestinian singing- and playing-girls achieved international fame in later days; the geographer of Jesus' time, Strabo, advises his readers to present Indian rajahs with musical instruments or pretty singing-girls from Palestine or Alexandria in order to win their favor, and two hundred years later, the Acts of St. Thomas tell how a piper came down to the place where the apostle landed in India, "stood over him and played at his head for a long time: now this piper-girl was by race a Hebrew." But the musical ideas and system of the Egyptians require some discussion for their influence upon Jewish thought and for their significance in the changes apparent in post-Egyptian Hebrew music.

It is in Egypt that composing in certain *modes* developed into a well-defined system, a practice which the Jews were later to expand and to perfect to serve their own cultural and spiritual needs and which then passed on to the Greeks. The ancient singer or player composed a melody by arranging and combining a limited number of motives. This practice prevails in Oriental civilization down to our own day. In contrast to the modern musician of the Western world, who regards each note of a complete melody individually as well as in its relation to other notes, the Oriental thinks in melodic formulas and tonal groups; he is unable to ascribe significance to a single tone out of its context—the step leading up to or away from it. When he sings or plays his melodies he also invariably improvises upon and embellishes them.

The mode is characterized by the way in which certain beginning, middle, and concluding tones are joined and contrasted in the melody sung or played; within the modes chosen the singer or player has every individual freedom of variation and of emotional expression. But the modes not only supplied the purely musical particles of the melodies. They were also associated with spiritual and ethical qualities: the particular modes had their distinct associations with certain holy days or offerings or were characteristic of definite ethical notions.

The Temple music of the Jews shows the modal system at a high stage of perfection; and though their way and style of singing has changed in the course of the three millennia of Israel's subsequent history, the present-day cantillation of the Scriptures and prayers substantially follows the modal theory of the Orient in the eastern as well as the western Jewish communities.

The melodic patterns underlying the modal melody—the Arabic *maqamat* and the Hindu *rāgas*—were in the earlier stage of development composed of motives fitting certain lines of text and in the later stage of motives for words or short phrases. Folk melodies seem to have been instrumental in the formation of these melodicles, and they also provided names for them, as we shall see when discussing the Psalms and their enigmatic headings. In the Orient the word "compose" has always been true to its original Latin meaning—"to put together"; and Western music has by no means ignored the modal technique of motive-combination—it recurs throughout history from the Gregorian chant to the art of the German Meistersinger, and from medieval composition to Schoenberg's twelve-tone system, and the spirit of improvising on short melodic phrases has been revived in modern jazz.

The systematization of music in Egypt provided the fundamentals for Hebrew musical theory, in which special modes and motives were assigned to the reading of the different portions of the Pentateuch, the Prophets, the Psalms, the Song of Songs, the book of Esther, the Lamentations, and the prayers. It is characteristic that in Hebrew theory the modes have always served the religious cult only, while the Greeks, who based their own musical system on the inheritance of Hebrew as well as of Egyptian music, ascribed to the various modal motives and scales moral powers and ethical qualities that implied their use for educational aims.

From Egypt, too, the Jews learned how best to remind the singers and players of the melodies they had to intone. Hand signs and finger motions were already employed for this purpose by Egyptian musicians in the twenty-eighth century B.C., and their early use in organized Hebrew music is proved. There is little doubt that these hand signs were largely responsible for the written signs that accompanied the Biblical texts at a time when the oral tradition seemed in danger of being forgotten and Jewish scholars in Babylon and in Palestine were anxious to preserve and to hand down to posterity the correct way of vowelizing and chanting the sacred texts.

We have to imagine the ancient Egyptian chant—and the song of the Hebrews after the Exodus—performed in complete melodic freedom within the bounds of the modes. Expression in performance was achieved by the throat-pressing device described earlier in this chapter. The rhythm of the melody was largely dependent on the rhythm of the words sung, for the content and the spirit of the words dominated the music as a matter of course; music was not performed to entertain or to elevate a lover of refined art but served the cult as a highly exalted form of speech. Rhythm proved important in nonreligious music only; it was the driving factor in work and dance, as well as in outdoor activities. But the vital impulse given to Egyptian music by the influx of foreign musicians—especially by the singing-girls and their rhythmical instruments—must have had repercussions in the religious sphere as well.

Throughout the history of Jewish civilization and culture we must attempt to understand the achievements of the Jewish people and of their great men against the background of those of other nations; for the accomplishments of the Jews are generally due to a thorough absorption and evolution of their cultural inheritance and a characteristic facility for subsequently rejecting qualities foreign to their spirit, for molding forms and styles to suit their own temper, and for raising them onto a highly individual plane. Other people have, of course, done the same in their own particular way, for no historical development takes place in geographical, social, or cultural isolation, but in the case of the Jews the analysis is of special interest because their entire ancient history is one of migration, conquest, and exile, while their modern history down to their return to Palestine unfolds itself within the empires and commonwealths of other nations.

The Hebrews came to Egypt as nomads in search of pasture, and they began their life in their own land again as shepherds and farmers when they returned from Egyptian bondage. But they had acquired a considerable standard of learning and knowledge in many branches of science as well as in the arts. Their leader, Moses, had been taught science and music by Egyptian priests (if we can believe the late testimony of Philo of Alexandria); he even lived on in Islamic tradition as patron of the pipers. The time to apply in full measure the skill and knowledge won did not at once arrive for the generations of Jews who had actually emigrated from Egypt. The decades of wandering in the desert, the struggles for possession of the promised land, and the centuries of wars against her neighbors still denied to Israel the erection of a cultural center and thus the conditions fundamental for the development of an organized art. Musical instruments were not made on Palestinian soil and of local material before the time of the Kings; for we read that King David still ordered instruments of Lebanese cypress and that King Solomon had lyres and harps made of wood from Ophir (the same that he used for the pillars of the Temple and of the royal house); and an ancient legend reports the importation of a thousand musical instruments by Pharaoh's daughter on the occasion of her wedding to Solomon (B. Sabbath 56 b.).[4] A continuous exchange with Assyria, Arabia, Egypt, and Phoe-

---

[4] This is a disputed passage which has also been interpreted to mean the importation of a thousand *musical tunes*.

nicia is evident in literary documents, too; but while the Israelites were largely the importers and mere beneficiaries in the
period leading up to their eventual rise and prosperity, they
succeeded in giving their own high civilization of the Temple
era the individual traits that made Jerusalem the spiritual and
cultural center of the entire ancient Levant. Music played its
own part in the development of Israel's cult and became a dominant feature of the Temple service. If it had not outgrown the
inheritance and importations from other civilizations it would
never have achieved the towering significance it was to assume
in later Oriental and early Occidental history; it could not have
supplied in the way it did the foundations for the development
of Western musical civilization. The music of King Solomon's
Temple reverberated through the ages, just as its sounds echoed
over the mountains of Judea, and its splendors were told and
retold by many a later generation.

Chapter
TWO

The Holy City

IN THE POETRY and art of the modern world King David
has come to be the symbolic figure of the patron of music, and
the psalms attributed to the royal poet and musician are sung
all over the civilized earth. They formed the backbone of the
musical service in the Holy Temple; psalm singing later became
popular in all the eastern and western centers of the Christian
Church, and a Greek Church Father—St. John Chrysostom,
Bishop of Constantinople, called "the golden-mouthed"—voiced
general opinion when writing, about 400 A.D.:

If the faithful are keeping vigil in the church, David is
first, middle and last. If at dawn any one wishes to sing
hymns, David is first, middle and last. At funeral processions and burials, David is first, middle and last. In the
holy monasteries, among the ranks of the heavenly war-
riors, David is first, middle and last. In the convents of vir-

gins, who are imitators of Mary, David is first, middle and last.

The Psalms have inspired a host of musical compositions throughout the ages; David playing on his lyre is a subject that has attracted the greatest sculptors and painters of the world; and among the masterpieces of contemporary music is an oratorio composed to his praise—Arthur Honegger's *Le Roi David*. Jewish popular belief and legend ascribed to David not only the organization of the musical service in the Temple and the creation and singing of the Psalms but also the invention of musical instruments proper: II Chron. 7:6 speaks of "instruments of musick of the Lord, which David the king had made to praise the Lord"; according to I Chron. 23:5, David himself said to the princes of Israel, to the priests and Levites, that "four thousand praised the Lord with the instruments which I made to praise therewith"; and the prophet Amos castigates the wanton people that "invent themselves instruments of musick, like David" (Amos 6:5). Jewish as well as later Christian belief saw in King David the musical splendor of the Temple personified, and in medieval and later paintings he is seen to play on a great variety of musical instruments. It seems a pity that the strict commandment not to make "a graven image, nor any manner of likeness" should have robbed us of ancient Hebrew representations of David and his kinnor, though we can surmise with some certainty now that this was a kind of lyre—and *not* a harp, as it is generally translated and most frequently depicted on the later paintings.

The history of Hebrew music, as well as the history of Israel's higher civilization in general, begins with King David's reign. It was David, the second king of Israel, who created a large and united Hebrew kingdom and made the Urusalim of the

Jebusites his capital, Jerusalem. The town had existed there for more than a thousand years, and the singularity of its position as well as the striking contrasts witnessed there between desert and fertile country had made its hills places of nature cult; they were regarded as domiciles of deities associated with ancient pagan worship. Jerusalem lay far removed from the principal trade routes; its strategic position was well exploited by its kings, vassals of the mighty Pharaoh of Egypt. The cosmic significance ascribed to the Jewish Temple and to some of its contents and to the garments of the priests shows that relics of the ancient cult survived in Israel. That much of the music of King David's Temple was also created under the influence of older practice is attested by the close resemblance of the forms, the ideas, and the unrestrained lyricism of the hymns preserved on ancient cuneiform tablets to those of the Hebrew psalms. The heathen origin of Jerusalem was remembered for a long time: "Thy birth and thy nativity is of the land of Canaan; thy father was an Amorite, and thy mother an Hittite" (Ezek. 16:3). It had certainly taken the Israelites long to establish their ethical and religious rule and to make the people forget their local shrines and sites of nature worship. In David they hailed the king who had taken "the strong hold of Zion: the same is the city of David" (II Sam. 5:7) and who built his altar unto the Lord on the site of Araunah the Jebusite's threshing place as he had been commanded by the Lord (II Sam. 24:16 ff.); David and his son and successor Solomon made Jerusalem the national and cultural capital of the kingdom of Israel, the "holy hill of Zion" (Ps. 2:6), "the City of the Great King" (Ps. 48:2), of the Lord "who dwelleth in Zion" (Ps. 11:11).

With the time of the kings an end was set to the nomadic period of Israel. The people had taken possession of the country; they were given time to plow its soil and to develop its resources; and they could also shape their own life and thoughts now. The long centuries of unsteady wanderings, of a nomad and warrior existence, gave way to a period of secure farming and to the establishment of an organized cultural life. Jerusalem, at first only the central place of worship and the seat of the national kingdom, soon became a center of pilgrimage as well; and though its cultural level was high above that of the masses, the Temple of the Lord and the king's house were looked to by the entire nation for inspiration and leadership. In a comparatively short time the Israelites achieved such a singularity of life, thought, and creation that they overcame their dependence upon foreign cultural inheritance and created a civilization which, in turn, exerted a far-reaching influence on the smaller neighboring nations.

As the city of Jerusalem grew in the later years of David's reign and in the times of Solomon, his son, the zone of its influence gradually expanded, too; but with the increase in the luxury of its buildings and the splendor of urban life there developed a corresponding widening of the gulf between the clerical and royal nobility on the one hand and the masses in the country on the other. We must not forget that cultural development, in the course of which music assumed its sumptuous role, was now confined to the town. The Biblical sources —which are abundant for the period of the Temple in contrast to the spare hints offered by the Pentateuch for the nomadic epoch—tell only of the music in the Holy City, of the musicians serving the Temple and the Royal Court. The Biblical scribes cared as little for the songs of the people as did later the Christian monks of the Middle Ages. We can, however, assume that popular music did not greatly change its aspect: the shepherd continued to sing and to pipe his pastoral song, and the women's music accompanied feast and dance as before. Yet the people's singing, and their instrumental accompaniment as well, must certainly have developed to some degree under the influence of the music in the Holy Temple. This music was heard by those who made pilgrimages to Jerusalem; in addition, the Levites, the bearers of musical culture from King David's days, recruited singers and players among their people in the country. There may even have existed regional preparatory schools in which the prospective Temple musicians received a training that also benefited other parts of the population.

The same development now took place in Israel that Egypt had experienced many centuries before. Music, which had once been the possession of the broad masses, which had expressed their spirit and served their life, now developed into an art reserved to a chosen few, priests and noblemen. Playing and singing had been a matter of common knowledge and common practice; whenever great happenings or overwhelming spiritual experience shook the hearts of the people, a song was intoned by the leader and the masses joined him in continuation or response. But the kings introduced professional singers and players; they, in turn, elevated music to an art and subjected it to a system. Popular music largely remained "primitive"; as we have seen, the song of women in Jewish communities cut off from the main stream of civilization for three millennia retained its character throughout the ages. In the civilized town, however, music was given an important function and place in organized life and developed rules and ethics of its own.

King David chose the Levites to supply musicians for the Holy Temple. Out of the thirty thousand they numbered at his time, the stately number of four thousand were selected for the musical service:

And David spake to the chief of the Levites to appoint their brethren to be the singers with instruments of musick, harps and lyres and cymbals, sounding, by lifting up the voice with joy. So the Levites appointed Heman the son of Joel; and of his brethren, Asaph the son of Berechiah; and of the sons of Merari their brethren, Ethan the son of Kushaiah; and with them their brethren of the second degree, Zechariah, Ben, and Jaaziel, and Shemiramoth, and Jehiel, and Unni, Eliab, and Beniah, and Maaseiah, and Mattithiah, and Eliphelech, and Mikneiah, and Obededom, and Jeiel, the doorkeepers.

So the singers, Heman, Asaph, and Ethan were appointed to sound with cymbals of brass; and Zechariah, and Aziel, and Shemiramoth, and Jehiel, and Unni, and Eliab, and Maaseiah, and Benaiah, with harps on Alamoth, and Mattithiah, and Eliphelech, and Mikneiah, and Obededom, and Jeiel, and Azaziah, with lyres on the Sheminith to lead. And Chenaniah, chief of the Levites, was for singing, he instructed them in song, for he knew it. And Berechiah and Elkanah were doorkeepers for the ark. And Shebaniah, and Jehoshaphat, and Nethaneel, and Amasai, and Zechariah, and Benaiah, and Eliezer, the priests, did blow with the trumpets before the ark of God: and Obededom and Jehiah were doorkeepers for the ark." (I Chron. 15:16–24.)

Of the instruments named here the *nevel* (harp)—mentioned for the first time in I Sam. 10:5—and the *mziltaim* (cymbals) were new to the people of Israel. They played an important role in the music academy, the institution of which is related in the passage quoted above. The nevel (which may have been of Phoenician origin—the Phoenician name was *nabla*, and the Greeks took the term over at a later date) is often mentioned together with the kinnor; it was, however, an instrument of quite different build and character and seems to have been a vertical angular harp: many traits point to its having been larger, louder, and lower in pitch than the kinnor (lyre). Josephus Flavius informs us—two generations before the destruction of the Second Temple—that the nevel had twelve strings, in contrast to the ten of the kinnor; while the latter was played with the hands, the former was plucked with a plectrum. This is confirmed by a passage in the Book of Amos, and Rabbi Jehoshua, who taught round about 200 A.D., adds to our knowledge of the instrument when he says that the strings of the nevel were made of larger animal guts and were rougher than those of the kinnor, which were prepared from the smaller intestines (Mishna Kinnim 3:6). No sure interpretation is possible for the epithets "on Alamoth" and "on the Sheminith," for the general explanation that they compare the pitch of the two instruments (the former being a "maiden" or high-pitched instrument—from the Hebrew *alma* = "maiden"—and the latter pitched an octave lower— from *shmona*, the Hebrew word for eight) cannot be accepted; the notion of an octave was most probably unknown in the ancient world, the harp must actually have been the instrument lower in pitch, and *alamoth* may sooner be connected with the Assyrian word for "wood" (*halimū*) than with the *alma* or maiden. It is more likely that the epithets refer to the modes or tunes used by the instrumentalists (or in accordance with which they tuned the strings of their instruments?), just as they do in the headings of the Psalms, which we shall discuss later on.

The harp and the cymbals were, however, not the only new instruments of the epoch. The name of the *zelzlim* occurs side by side with the mziltaim, and we also find for the first time mention of the *asor*, the *halil*, the *mna'anim*, and the *magrepha*. It would be well to try to identify these instruments before we attempt to reconstruct a picture of Temple music from sources in the Bible and the commentaries.

The asor is mentioned in three psalms, twice in connection with the harp (33:2 and 92:3) and once with harp and lyre together (144:9), and all commentators have derived from its

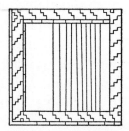

Ten-stringed psalterium (asor?) as depicted in St. Jerome's letter to Dardanus. (After Curt Sachs: *History of Musical Instruments*)

etymology (from *assara*, the Hebrew word for "ten") that it must have been a ten-stringed instrument. Curt Sachs has likened it to the Phoenician ten-stringed, rectangular zither—an instrument not found in either the Egyptian or the Assyrian civilization but known from two representations on an ivory pyxis of Phoenician origin and dating from the eighth century B.C., and from an illustration contained in a letter attributed to St. Jerome, the Church Father of the fourth century A.D.

The halil occurs in the Bible for the first time in connection with the anointment of Solomon (I Kings 1:40), but though no such instrument is mentioned as having been used in the services of the First Temple, a rabbinical commentator thought that it came from the days of Moses; in the Second Temple two to twelve halilim were used on twelve days of the year—at the first and the second Passover sacrifice, on the first day of Passover, at the Feast of Weeks, and in the eight days of the Feast of Tabernacles. Though in modern Hebrew the halil is a flute, the Biblical equivalent has been interpreted as a double reed of the oboe family; no flutes appear on any picture of neighboring civilizations at the time, and the Greek and Latin translators of the Bible were surely right when rendering "halil" by a word describing an oboe. It was probably a double oboe such as we know from many ancient civilizations; an illustration is provided by a Talmudic tractate expressly stating that the cadence marking the final verse of a scriptorial passage was marked by the playing of one pipe only—which may mean one cane of a double oboe. In later sources, especially in the Aramaic version of the Bible, there appears the new word *abub* (which is "oboe" in modern Hebrew). It is difficult to determine the difference between the ancient halil and abub, but it seems quite probable that the two terms described similar or even identical instruments. Another plausible interpretation is the rendering of *halil* by "woodwind"; in this case the Talmudic passage on the cadence being played by one *pipe* would mean the playing of a soloist out of a group of instruments of the same family.

The percussion instruments introduced in the Temple service and used (as our passage shows) by the singers do not offer particular puzzles: the mna'anim must have been sistra (as has been said in the previous chapter); the zelzlim were brass cymbals, perhaps a little different in form from the mziltaim; while *shalishim*—if not a triangle-like musical instrument—could indicate a kind of ritual dance based on three steps (*shloshah* in Hebrew = "three").

A peculiar problem is that of the magrepha. It is told that in the Temple the sound of the magrepha gave the Levites the sign to begin their music. The Mishna (completed about 150 years after the destruction of the Second Temple) says that this sound, together with that of the oboes, cymbals, and shofar

and of the singing and the proclamations, could be heard as far
as Jericho—which is quite possible in the atmospheric conditions of the Jerusalem region. A Mishna passage describes how
one of the priests *threw* the instrument between hall and altar
after the sacrifice and that it made a very loud sound; yet it
is impossible to determine from this whether it sounded while
being whirled through the air or only when touching the walls
or coming down on the floor. Mishna commentators also use
the word in its Hebrew meaning, "shovel"; the instrument can
have had this form. Three hundred years after the Mishna commentary it is argued in a Talmudic tractate that the magrepha
had ten holes and that each of them could produce ten "kinds
of song," so that the whole instrument was capable of yielding
one hundred "kinds of song." Ten holes capable of producing
one hundred sounds each—altogether one thousand "kinds of
song"—is the description offered by another, possibly exag-
gerating, source, which also adds that the measures of the
magrepha were one ell (of twenty inches) in height and one
ell in length (or width?) and that a handle protruded from the
instrument. As the holes prove that the magrepha must have
been a kind of wind instrument, it has been concluded that it
constituted some sort of organ—an instrument well known in
the ancient Orient. It cannot have been a water organ; various
rabbinical sources emphasize that no hydraulis was found in
the Temple; Rabbi Shimon ben Gamliel said (about 130 years
after the destruction of the Second Temple) that the reason
for this was that the hydraulis "disturbs [or spoils] the tune
[the sound of the other instruments?]." But the possibility of
its having been a primitive pneumatic (wind) organ is not excluded; if this is true, the magrepha was an advanced form of
the ancient 'ugab, which has for centuries been translated as
"organ" and which is reported in a tractate to have been "one

of the two instruments retained from the First Temple, but when it became defective it could not be mended" (Arachin 10, b; Sukkah 50, b). We may perhaps picture the magrepha as a row of ten pipes with the air blown in by the operation of the handle. An instrument similar to this sort of panpipe has been found by Curt Sachs on an Alexandrian terra-cotta figurine from the first century B.C. A Syrian piper is depicted on it, singing and playing.[1] He is seen holding a panpipe about one inch under his mouth and seems to sing while operating the instrument. The pipe has long bass canes which are connected with a bag that communicates by a flexible tube with a bellows worked by the man's right foot and compressed by his arm. The Hebrew instrument may have been more primitive in form and use but similar in principle, and there is no reason why its sound should not have been strong and piercing. There remains the nebulous allusion to its having been *thrown* to the altar. Who knows whether this interpretation of a rabbinical scholar was actually correct or whether perhaps the term described different instruments at different times? Or could we believe in a misunderstanding: should we read that the priest *sharak* (piped, blew) not *sarak* (threw) the magrepha? Its derivation from the 'ugab is supported by the fact that it is mentioned in connection with the Second Temple only; that its form must have been primitive seems to follow from the fact that it was used only for signaling purposes—to call the priests and the Levites to their duties— though it remains unexplained why an instrument "capable of yielding one hundred kinds of song" should have served only for signaling.

When King Solomon had finished all work for the Temple and brought in all the things David his father had dedicated, the priests and the congregation of Israel assembled before the

---

[1] See illustration facing p. 32.

ark, and the musical service was begun by the Levites. "The number of them, with their brethren that were instructed in the songs of the Lord, even all that were cunning, was two hundred fourscore and eight," and they were divided into twenty-four classes "under the hands of their fathers" (I Chron. 25:6–7). On the day of consecration "the Levites which were the singers, all of them of Asaph, of Heman, of Jeduthun, with their sons and their brethren, being arrayed in white linen, having cymbals and harps and lyres, stood at the east end of the altar, and with them an hundred and twenty priests sounding with trumpets; it came even to pass, as the trumpeters and singers were as one, to make one sound to be heard in praising and thanking the Lord; and when they lifted up their voice with the trumpets and cymbals and instruments of musick, and praised the Lord, saying, For he is good; for his mercy endureth for ever: that then the house was filled with a cloud, even the house of the Lord; so that the priests could not stand to minister by reason of the cloud: for the glory of the Lord had filled the house of God" (II Chron. 5:12–14). When the king and the people had offered their sacrifices, the Levites began to play, "and the priests sounded trumpets before them, and all Israel stood" (II Chron. 7:6).

Though certain forms of singing changed after the Babylonian exile—as will be seen later—and though some change in the instrumental part of the service seems also to have taken place (as we have already had occasion to note), the actual musical service in the Second Temple must essentially have been the same as that in King Solomon's Temple; it was most certainly the wish of the Jews rebuilding their country and the House of the Lord to do this in keeping with their knowledge of Jerusalem's glory of old. The description contained in a Talmudic tractate (Tamid 7:3–4) of Temple music in the beginning of the Common Era may thus well be applied to the earlier forms of service as well. The Talmud passage describes how the priests on duty followed up the sacrifices with benedictions and prayers and then read the Ten Commandments and some additional passages from the Scriptures. After the sacrifices the magrepha was sounded, which was the signal for the other priests to enter the Temple to prostrate themselves, and for the Levites to begin their musical performance. The high priest entered the Temple last and was solemnly received; he gave the blessing and burned the offerings on the altar. The description goes on to say:

> They gave him the wine for the drink-offering, and the Prefect stood by each horn of the altar with a towel in his hand, and two priests stood at the table of the fat pieces with two silver trumpets in their hands. They blew a prolonged, a quavering, and a prolonged blast. Then they came and stood by Ben Arza, the one on his right and the other on his left. When he stooped and poured out the drink-offering the Prefect waved the towel and Ben Arza clashed the cymbals and the Levites broke forth into singing. When they reached a break in the singing they blew upon the trumpets and the people prostrated themselves; at every break there was a blowing of the trumpet and at every blowing of the trumpet a prostration. This was the rite of the Daily Whole-Offering in the service of the House of our God. May it be his will that it shall be built up again, speedily, in our days. Amen.

The same source informs us that the Levites sang a different psalm on each of the six days of the week and on the Sabbath, and other tractates treat of the relation between choir and or-

chestra, of the forms of singing, of the training demanded of
singers and instrumentalists, and of the style of the actual performance.

The chorus, placed on the estrade, had to consist of a minimum of twelve adult singers but could be enlarged at will. (It
will be noted that the number twelve recurs everywhere: the
twelve tribes of Israel, twenty-four, or twice twelve, training
classes for singers and instrumentalists, twelve leading musicians, one hundred and twenty trumpets at the consecration of
the Temple, and twelve strings for the harp. Five and seven had
been numbers holy to the ancient Orient and to earlier Jewish
civilization alike: the lyre had ten strings and the trumpets
were seven.) The singers had passed through five years of training and usually performed their Temple service between the
ages of thirty and fifty. Boys of the Levites often joined the
choir "to add sweetness to the sound," but they were placed outside the estrade. The orchestra, on the other hand, consisted of
two to six harps, nine or more lyres, two to twelve oboes (employed only on the special days mentioned above), and one pair
of cymbals. This means that the number of musicians in the orchestra equaled that of the singers; the minimum comprised
twelve vocalists and twelve instrumentalists, and on the days
on which an "innumerable quantity" of instruments were used
(to quote the actual words of a tractate) the number of singers
was enlarged accordingly. After the Babylonian exile, however,
a decline in the appreciation of instrumental music set in. A
larger number of singers was opposed to a smaller number of
instrumental musicians, and the priests evidenced their depreciation of instrumental music by permitting non-Levites to
take up playing while singing in the Temple remained the
privilege of the Levites.

The orchestra here described was used to accompany the singing of the trained choir—with the possible exception of the cymbals, which marked the intervals. The trumpets are missing in the description of the service, which shows that they did not form a part of the accompanying orchestra but were used separately only, in the way outlined in the passage quoted earlier. Drums were also absent from the Temple; rhythm and movement are thus proved to have been of no importance in the shaping of music used for the religious service. The drums were in fact the instruments of the women, as they were in other Oriental civilizations, and the participation of women singers or players in the Temple is nowhere mentioned. Only in secular, especially Court, music were women the leaders: singing and playing servants are often mentioned in the Bible. When Barzillai the Gileadite had conducted David over the Jordan but refused to accompany him to Jerusalem, "he said unto the King: How long have I to live that I should go up with the king unto Jerusalem? I am this day fourscore years old: and can I discern between good and evil? Can thy servant taste what I eat or what I drink? Can I hear any more the voice of singing men and singing women?" (II Sam. 19:34 f.). The 200 singing men and singing women singled out from 7,337 servants and maids returning from Babylon (Ezra 2:65; Neh. 7:67 counted 245) belonged to the wealthy families. Women musicians are also mentioned in connection with the tribute demanded from King Hiskia by Sennacherib, King of Assyria, with the mourning and funeral ceremonies, and with feasts and celebrations.

The exclusion of women from the Temple service is further indicated by the fact that ritual dances are reported to have been executed by men, the most famous passage telling how "David danced before the Lord with all his might" (II Sam. 6:14); he continued dancing as the procession moved through the city with the holy ark, and it is interesting to reflect why Michal the daughter of Saul who "looked through a window and saw king David leaping and dancing before the Lord" (II Sam. 6:16) should have despised the royal dancer in her heart. This kind of ritual dance was surely well established; it had come from Egypt but seemed to have fallen into disuse at a later time, for it is rarely mentioned in connection with Temple practice. Processional dancing must, however, have lived on, as it is still practiced in the synagogue in our own days.

The dance confronts us with yet another of the many peculiar problems offered by the ancient Biblical texts. This concerns the word *machol,* used in the meaning of "dance" in modern Hebrew and in the common translation of many Biblical passages, but also often interpreted as a term for a musical instrument. It first occurs in the Pentateuch, when Miriam and her women are said to have followed Moses' song of praise with singing and playing *B'tupim uw'imm'choloth* (Exod. 15:20). The Authorized Version translates "with timbrels and with dances," and so do most European Bibles. But a rabbinical scholar ("Pirkei d'Rabbi Eliezer," second century A.D., XL, 2) comments upon this passage as follows: "And where did they get *tupim* and *mecholoth* in the desert? . . . At the time of their exodus from Egypt they made tupim and mecholoth" and thus shows that *machol* meant a musical instrument in the Hebrew tradition of his time. The same interpretation is met with as late as the fourteenth century in the commentaries of Gersonides, while Menachem b. Saruk also used it in his explanations written about 975. Psalm 150, which mentions eight different kinds of instruments and, like the Exodus passage, links the "machol" with the drum, makes little sense when we read "Praise him with the timbrel and *dance*" (v. 4), and the same is true of the preceding Psalm (v. 3). The Syrian translators of the Bible also interpreted "machol" as an instrument, and no

passage could possibly be found in the Bible where this interpretation does not fit. As "machol" is mostly mentioned together
with the drum, Ibn Ezra (eleventh century) may be right in
supposing that it was a kind of pipe ("machol" and "halil" have
similar etymological roots), perhaps one that was popularly used
for the accompaniment of dances. We would then have to add
the machol to the list of instruments discussed in the preceding
and the present chapter.

The sources provide us with quite a clear picture of the musical service in the Temple, but they have not preserved for us
the actual melodies sung and played; yet the forms of singing
discussed in the Bible and the Talmudic literature and comparisons with archaic liturgies permit us at least to form an idea
of how the singing and musical performance may have actually
sounded. What we know in this field concerns, however, almost
exclusively the post-Babylonian practice; the Levites—many of
whom are said to have remained in Palestine, especially in the
suburbs of Jerusalem, during the forty-eight years of the Babylonian exile (586–538)—reconstructed the Temple service in
accordance with the ancient tradition, but it seems that the
antiphonal singing that became characteristic for the later Jewish liturgy as well as for Christian church music was developed
only in the stricter and more systematic service of the Second
Temple.

Down to our own days the Passover Hallel and many other
hymns and songs are performed, especially by Oriental Jews, in
the form commonly known as *antiphony*—that is to say, with
the choruses alternating and responding to each other. The first
examples in the Bible of such responsorial singing are the song
of Moses and Miriam after the passage through the Red Sea

(Exod. 15:1 and 20–21), the triumph of David's victory over the Philistines ("the women sang one to another in their play. . . ." I Sam. 18:7), and the return from Babylon (Nehemiah "appointed two great companies that gave thanks and went in procession: on the right hand half of the princes of Judah and certain of the priests' sons with trumpets, and Judah, Hanani, with the musical instruments of David; and the other company of them that gave thanks went to meet them. . . ." Neh. 12:31 f. and 38). A Talmudic tractate commenting upon Israel's passage over the Jordan (Josh. 4) describes antiphonal singing as it was certainly still practiced—though, of course, on a smaller scale—in the Talmudic epoch: "When Israel crossed the Jordan and came unto Mount Gerizim and unto Mount Ebal in Samaria . . . six tribes went up to the top of Mount Gerizim and six tribes went up to the top of Mount Ebal. And the priests and the Levites stood below in the midst; and the priests surrounded the Ark and the Levites surrounded the priests, and all Israel were on this side and on that . . . and began with the blessing . . . and both these and these answered, Amen!" (Sotah 7:5).

Antiphonal singing was a common practice in the ancient Orient. It can still be heard in Abyssinia, in Upper Egypt, and in Oriental Christian communities, and the Western church has modeled most of its psalm singing on it. The use of a recurring refrain in Assyrian hymns points to their having been sung in responsorial style by the priests and the choir or by two opposing choirs in alternation; their poetry as well as their music proved a great influence on Hebrew song.

The best way of getting an idea of the different ways of performing music is an analysis of the poetical forms. The most primitive style of responsorial singing was the recitation of the prayer or psalm by a soloist and the response of the congregation with "Amen" or "Hallelujah"; at a later stage the short refrains were replaced by complete phrases such as "for his mercy endureth forever" (Psalm 118, Psalm 136). This primitive antiphony has parallels in other Oriental civilizations. An Assyrian hymn, for instance, begins:

> O Lord, who is like thee,
>> Who can be compared to thee?
> Mighty one, who is like thee,
>> Who can be compared to thee?

and Psalm 26 opens:

> The Lord is my light and my salvation;
>> Whom shall I fear?
> The Lord is the strength of my life;
>> Of whom shall I be afraid?

In the Temple service the leader and soloist usually began by singing a half-verse, and the choir repeated it; the leader than continued in half-verses, and the choir or congregation interpolated the refrain after each of them, as is particularly obvious from Deut. 27:15 ff.:

> Cursed be the man that maketh any graven or molten image, an abomination unto the Lord, the work of the hands of the craftsman, and putteth it in a secret place.
>> And all the people shall answer and say, Amen.
> Cursed be he that setteth light by his father or his mother.
>> And all the people shall say, Amen.
> Cursed be he that removeth his neighbor's landmark.
>> And all the people shall say, Amen.

In this form the "Hallel" is sung by many Jewish communities to this very day, and many popular hymns have refrains of the same kind.

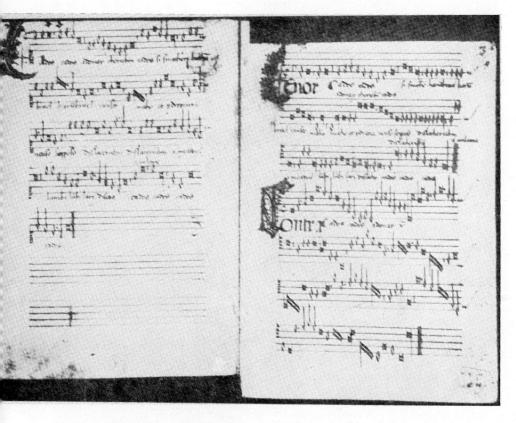

A curious Spanish-Jewish manuscript of the 13th century, a three-part "Kedusha" motet. The modern manuscript is the first page of Dr. Eric Werner's transcription of the piece. (*After Eric Werner*)

"Süsskind, the Jew of Trimberg," and a page of his songs. From the Manessian MS of the 13th century, preserved at Heidelberg, Germany.

The next step in the development of antiphony was the singing by the leader and the choir in alternating half-verses, with the choir sometimes varying the words of the first half-line:

Praise ye the Lord.
　Praise the Lord, O my soul.
While I live will I praise the Lord:
　I will sing praises unto my God while I have any being.
(Psalm 146)

In this form the children used to be instructed at school in Talmudic times.

The most developed—and truly responsive—form was the real alternation in verses; it was the form in which the "Shema-Israel" Prayer was recited:

Hearken, O Israel:
　The Lord our God is one Lord.
And thou shalt love the Lord thy God with all thine heart,
　And with all thy soul, and with all thy might.
(Deut. 6:4 f.)

This developed form of responsorial singing still characterizes the practice of Babylonian Jews, especially their singing of the Hallel for Passover. A Talmudic tractate (Sukkah 38:2) informs us that all three forms—the answering in refrains, the repetition of half-verses, and true responsorial antiphony—were in use in the later Jewish liturgical service. They have all been preserved both in the Jewish liturgy and in the Catholic Church (which took them over from the Temple service) and contributed much to the evolution of Western art music. Their origins point back to universal Oriental custom and ancient Jewish practice; their systematic cultivation must be ascribed to the Levites serving the Second Temple.

It remains for us to try to gain an insight into the way the melodies were formed and sung and thus to divine how the Temple music—with the style of whose performance we are now acquainted—actually sounded. We have already discussed the modal system of the Orient and the influence the Egyptian practice of singing in modes had had on the Jews. It must have been in the Temple service that the use of the different modes was systematized and that they assumed definite characteristics. Early instrumental music and popular singing seem to have been pentatonic—based on scales or chords of five tones—and strict in rhythm; but the vocal music that dominated the liturgy was rhythmically free and followed the irregular rhythms of the words, setting the text to music by the use of carefully chosen modal motifs. The scales in which the modal motifs moved were not pentatonic but apparently diatonic-tetrachordal; though the melodies themselves, as they were preserved by the secluded communities of the Yemen, of Babylonia, and of Persia, rarely have a range exceeding that of the fifth or sixth interval. The ancient singers did not ornament their melodies with virtuoso coloraturas, as do the cantors of modern synagogues; the coloratura embellishment, often improvised, developed with the rise of the professional precentor in the Christian Era. Nevertheless, the necessity of adapting modal motifs to words or lines of different length obviously called for melismatic treatment. The singer's melisms were born of an inner urge and not of a wish to exhibit virtuosity.

The development of Hebrew language, thought, and ideas offers distinct clues to the student of ancient Hebrew music. Comparing the earliest examples of Biblical poetry with the poetical lyricism of the Psalms and the Song of Songs, or the language of the Pentateuch in general with that of the Prophets, we notice an evolution from the expression in simple verse of a driving urgency and sweeping passion to a highly developed emphatic and eloquent language in freely shaped rhythm. The characteristic traits of the Hebrew language—its abundance of hard consonants and gutturals, of explosive sounds, and of doubled letters—were exploited to the full, and there are in the Bible many instances of actual tone-painting by means of words.

Though in its lyricism ancient Hebrew poetry has, as we have already seen, parallels in Oriental literature in general, it was unequaled in the fervent force of its expression. The very language of ancient Israel was musical in the highest degree, and various Biblical passages say that music actually inspired the songs and the visions of the leaders and prophets: "And it came to pass, when the minstrel played, that the hand of the Lord came upon him," says the chronicler of II Kings 2:15 of the prophet Elisha, and the spirit of the Lord came upon Samuel when he met a company of prophets descending from a hill accompanied by players sounding their musical instruments (I Sam. 10:5 ff.). The highly emotional character of ancient Hebrew music is thus attested by the poetry and prose of the Bible; but just as the prophets subordinated expression and form to the moral and ethical demands of their speech, so did the musical expression emphasize a higher ethical value.

The character of Hebrew verse did not allow of metrical rhythmization; Hebrew poetry was rather poetical prose, free from rhythmical accentuation and dynamic in its expression, and the musical motifs closely followed the word accents. When Jewish scholars early in the Christian Era added their interpretative symbols to the written Biblical texts, they intended both to hand down to posterity the correct vowelization and accentuation of the words and to remind the reciters which appropriate motifs to use for the chanting of the passage. These accents prove the existence of a theory and system in ancient Hebrew music;

but not all details of the system have been sufficiently explored and explained by later generations and by modern scholars. The theory concerned itself especially with the intervals characterizing the melodic patterns, each of which started from or moved around a basic note in a characteristic way.

In trying to reconstruct the melodic particles (or to analyze them from the remainders that have come down to us by way of the archaic Jewish liturgies and the early Christian chant), we must be careful to note that "high" and "low"—and accordingly "up" and "down" (used often in interpreting the accents)— meant in ancient Semitic usage, as later in Greek musical theory, the opposite of what they stand for in music today. *O* and *U* were called "high" vowels by Jewish grammarians, and in Hebrew script they are indeed depicted by a dot *above* the consonant after which they are sounded; while the vowel *I* is regarded as "low" in sound and indicated by a dot *below* the consonant. (Compare this with the dot above the *I* in modern Occidental languages, in which the *I* is regarded as a high sound and the *O* and *U* as low or dark sounds.) Here again, language and music go hand in hand in the ancient Orient; it was not the actual sound that was described by the notions of "high" and "low," but the way the sound was produced: a "high" or "tall" pipe or string produced a low or dark sound, while the "short" or "low" instrument gave out a sound we call high today. Thus when in Oriental music a melody is said to "jump up," it means that its melody sank, while a step "downward" must be rendered by a melodic ascent.[2]

The ancient Temple liturgy ascribed special melodies to each portion of the Holy Scriptures that figured in the service, and each melody was composed of either two modal motifs or of three or four motifs sung in alternation. The motifs were flexible

[2] Compare Curt Sachs, *The Rise of Music in the Ancient World*, pp. 69–70.

enough to permit their use for texts (words, half-lines, or verses) of different syllabic lengths; and most of them seem to have been given descriptive names in order to enable the singers and players to intone the right mode at once if the name was indicated. It must be surmised that all or most of the motifs and melodies used in the Temple were folk songs (some of them may even have been of foreign origin) and the Levite music leaders only modified them and sanctified their use; this was the practice followed by clerical authorities throughout the ages, down to the Lutheran Protestant Reform. And—likewise in accordance with historical experience in most civilizations—the Temple melodies exerted their influence on the people in turn; the *An'she Ma'-amad,* who represented in turns the districts and settlements of the country at the offerings and prayers of the Temple, brought the knowledge of Temple music back home with them after their two weeks' service.

With our knowledge of the origin of Temple music comes enlightenment about the hitherto enigmatic headings of the Psalms; they were erroneously translated by most Biblical scholars and almost invariably associated with the names of musical instruments. It did not strike the commentators that none of the instruments known—and occurring frequently in the Psalms themselves—are mentioned in these headings. Most probably the headings—such as *al mût lab'ben* (on the death of the son), *ayelet ha'schachar* (aurora), *schoschanim* (roses)—indicate the folk songs used for the modal melodies, in the way we might write a community song to be performed to the melody of a current hit. The descriptions preceding the Psalms have parallels in Arabian maqamât and Hindu râgas, where not only actual tunes (like the above) but also numbers (like *haschminith* = the eighth in the psalms), geographical places (the Hebrew *gittit* may mean "wine press" or "from the town of Gat"), and even combinations of two modes are named in the headings. Curt Sachs had the logical idea of testing this interpretation by the comparison of moods of psalms that have similar headings.[3] The investigation indeed shows that the six *n'ginoth* psalms (4, 54, 55, 61, 67, 74) are all prayers for escape, based on confidence in God and his power and magnificence; that the three *gittit* poems (8, 81, 84) are gay and mirthful in character; and that the three *jeduthun* psalms (39, 62, 77) show a common mood of resignation. The word *selah,* so frequently used in the Psalms and not satisfactorily explained to this day, must have something to do with the musical rendering as well; but we do not know whether it marked a pause or cadence, or whether this too pointed to a definite melodic mode or to a change or modulation.

We have attempted to draw the picture of Temple music from the available sources and have found it to be many-colored indeed. The urge and passion of its vocal expression, together with the impressive orchestral coloring of the accompaniment and the far-sounding flourishes on the trumpets during the intervals in the singing, can well be imagined from what we know of the musical service in the ancient Holy City. But it was not only the splendor and dynamic impressiveness of Temple music that made the ancient civilizations admire the achievements of Jerusalem; its inner force and its ethical elevation proved their powerful impact in many centuries to come. Other Oriental civilizations had poetry and music as emphatic and lyrical as that of Israel, but Israel turned from primitive sensualism to re-

---

[3] *The History of Musical Instruments,* pp. 124–127. While Dr. Sachs's general theses are enlightening and fully acceptable in the light of more recent research, there are some errors in the transcriptions and translations from Hebrew.

ligious pathos, from an unrestrained reign of emotion to the fanatical search for truth of expression—a characteristic trait of many a later Jewish composer of art music. In this light we can appreciate why Clement of Alexandria, the Church Father at the threshold of the third century A.D., admonished the Christians to abandon "chromatic" harmonies and modulations and turbulent melodies and to return to the temperate modal art of the psalms of David.

In the Jerusalem of the first millennium—the Holy City of Israel's kings and the spiritual and cultural center of the post-Babylonian Jews—music had the functions it fulfilled in seventeenth-century Europe, and it was most probably felt by contemporaries and by posterity to be as magnificently "baroque" as seventeenth-century music has been considered by contemporary and later generations. Music served three different spheres—the Temple, the Court, and the country—and it accordingly developed three different styles. The organized Temple liturgy, the music at the feast and celebration in the nobleman's house, and the pastoral music of the people differed in their function, their form, their executants, their instruments, and their very character; yet a permanent mutual influence can only have been natural. But while instrumental music completely disappeared in time and only some of the primitive forms of popular music have been preserved, the liturgical song has retained its essential character throughout the two millennia of Jewish dispersion. The musical tradition was preserved in southern Arabia, where the Yemenite Jews lived in seclusion for more than thirteen hundred years; in Babylonia, where the Jewish community has never ceased to exist since the days of the exile; in Persia, the Jewish community of which is as old as the Babylonian center; in Syria; in North Africa; on the Italian peninsula. It also lived on

with the Sephardim—descendants of the Jews expelled from
Spain in 1492—and in some of the oldest eastern and central
European Jewish centers.

The ancient Hebrew melodies and modes were not preserved
as music by the various communities. They were passed on in
the same way that the religious and ethical heritage was kept
alive. When the Jews lost their own statehood, they replaced
their national life with a life in God; the perpetuation of their
belief and their laws helped them to endure the difficult and
often miserable years of dispersion and oppression. In the short
Babylonian exile they had already begun to interpret their once
rural and national festivals as religious holy days when they
could not celebrate them on the land. In the many hundreds of
years of the Diaspora following the second, fatal, destruction
of the Temple, the interpretation and meaning of the Jewish
ritual was subjected to a far-reaching change; music changed its
function with it. Instrumental music, little favored even in the
last centuries of the Second Temple, was no longer cultivated;
pastoral poetry and folk songs were imbued with new, religious,
significance for use in the houses of worship.

The concentration of all thought and speculation upon the
Kingdom of God and the resurrection of the Holy City and its
glorious Temple gave the Jews of two millennia a purpose in life;
it provided them with the moral power to resist assimilation
and cultural surrender and preserved the character of the Jewish people. The ancient Orient yielded its power to Greece and
Rome, and the mighty conquerors built their states and their
civilizations on the remainders of its erstwhile glory. Greece and
Rome in their turn disappeared from the platform of power, and
vacated their places to newly rising nations; their own cultural
heritage now helped to form new civilizations. The Jews saved
their legacy as other nations crumbled and fell. They lost their

nationhood and their country but perpetuated their law and ethics. Israel's strong sense of tradition not only preserved Judaism as such, but handed down to countless generations a poetry and music regarded by all civilized nations of the ancient and the medieval world as heights of achievement. This estimate was not altered, in fact, till the evolution of completely differing ideals denied to the Occident a thorough appreciation of Oriental culture, much as it has haunted the minds of men throughout history. The legendary splendor of the Holy Temple and its music continued to attract the imaginations of poets, artists, and musicians. They may have known less than we do of the shape and real character of Temple music, but indirectly it became responsible for many creations of later music. It is thus that histories of music invariably open with a chapter devoted to the music of the ancient Hebrews and that King David, the founder of the Temple and the organizer of its music, is regarded as the patron of music wherever the art of singing and playing is practiced.

74

Women's Songs

Ex. 1. Song of Yemenite women (Jewish), transcribed by E. Gerson-Kiwi. The song is sung by two women who accompany their singing with frame drum and cymbal. A small, pentachordic motif is repeated many times. The rhythmical period in four-part time is clear. The drum figure is more or less independent of the rhythm of the melody.

Ex. 2. Song of Algerian women (Arabic), transcribed by R. Lachmann. This melody is melodically similar to the Jewish women's song of Ex. 1. There is, however, no instrumental accompaniment; the women clap their hands in regular rhythms instead.

Jewish and Arabic Song Types

Ex. 3. Hymn of Moroccan Jews, transcribed by E. Gerson-Kiwi.

Ex. 4. Ramadan song of Palestinian Arabs, transcribed by E. Gerson-Kiwi. A comparison of the two hymns shows that the melodies are quite similar in scale composition and melodic turns. But their purpose is quite divergent, and so is their rhythmical texture. The Moroccan hymn, which is purely vocal, proceeds in different meters; the Ramadan Palestinian song, which is for soloists, chorus, and orchestra, has a strict rhythmical frame.

Oriental Scale Technique

Ex. 5. Hymn of Moroccan Jews, transcribed by E. Gerson-Kiwi, which is a typical example of Oriental scale technique (which is fundamentally the same as the modern twelve-tone technique): the first phrase contains the exposition of the whole "series"; the "variations" and modifications of the "theme" bring an intensification and contraction of the original series. (Examples by courtesy of Dr. E. Gerson-Kiwi, from her book *Music of the Orient—Ancient and Modern*, Tel-Aviv, 1949.)

Chapter
THREE

Hellas and Rome

D*URING THE TWO CENTURIES* of Persian rule in Asia
Minor the Jewish state was allowed to develop its national and
religious existence in peace and prosperity; the historical and
sacred writings got their final redaction, religious canon and
civil law were unified, and Israel became a community united
both by belief and by the form and rules of life. But in the second half of the fourth century B.C. the Oriental world was shaken
by an event of far-reaching sway: the first collision between
Orient and Occident. Hellas was first in establishing Occidental
rule over the eastern Mediterranean countries, and Rome wrung
the reign from it later; but not for a long time was the West able
to crush the Oriental world and establish cultural centers that
could vie with those of the ancient Orient.

Hellas conquered the Middle East in the third decade of the
fourth century B.C. Alexander the Great was about to material-
ize his dream of a vast empire that would comprise Europe,

Africa, and Asia and be subjected to Greek political and cultural domination. His troops crushed Persian rule in the Orient
and then turned south to Egypt; Judea they conquered on their
way. The Jews did not at once realize the significance of the
change in supremacy; it did not matter much to them that they
had once again come under the rule of another power. But the
importance of the new development was brought home to them
when Alexander's successors divided the empire, for the partition entailed a complete separation of the southern, Egyptian,
Diaspora from Judea. Alexandria, Alexander the Great's own
foundation (331), became the cultural center of the Hellenistic
world, and the Jews there were subjected to the influence of
Greek life, morals, and culture, just as were the Egyptians among
whom they lived. Judea, on the other hand, was able to preserve
its cultural independence for quite a long period.

For the history of Hebrew music the Hellenistic epoch is of
little importance during the time that the Temple still stood in
Jerusalem. There were few points of inner contact between
Greek and Jewish culture and thought. The Jews saw the ideal
state in a Kingdom of God; the Greeks, with their many deities
modeled on human types and imbued with human character,
did not search for the harmonious unity between creed and life
as the Jews did, but attempted an ideal worldly life regulated
by human reason and dominated by the harmony of physical
training, language, movement, and form. The spiritual achievement of the Jews had been the creation of monotheism—the ab-
straction of religion—by doing away with the myths of nature
and magic. But they had remained Orientals by refusing the
last step in rationalization: life remained for them within the
compass of their belief, and they fervently rejected rational science as well as art, which is the visualization of things irrational.
The Greeks, however, were Occidentals in their mode of life;

reason and logic shaped their life and creed, and their music mirrors their spiritual ideas as much as do their philosophy and their art.

Though a few Greek melodies have been discovered and deciphered, our knowledge of them is limited. We hardly need their confirmation, however, to prove that the music of Greece and that of the ancient Orient were direct opposites in their very theory. In Hebrew Temple music a spiritual character was ascribed to the modes, and to each portion of the Holy Scriptures was assigned an appropriate tune; the Greek modes, on the other hand, were associated with ethics and morals and were given their place in the general system of rational physical and spiritual education. In Greece music became a worldly power and served worldly ends. While Hebrew theory was guided by the search for eternal truth, the Greeks searched for the good and the beautiful in life.

There can be no doubt that mutual influence modified the life and culture of the two great civilizations, though in the Hebrew sphere—particularly in Palestine—this influence made itself felt on a larger scale only with the decline of Jewish national power and with the destruction of statehood and the Temple. The influence of Oriental thought as well as its poetic and musical expression is evident in Hellenistic art. A number of musical instruments—and surely the kind of music associated with them—were brought to Greece from the Oriental countries: Greek poets and historians often alluded to the foreign origin of Greek music, which rose to its highest level of perfection only after its encounter with the Orient. Hebrew music, on the other hand, hardly changed its character, though a certain influx of Greek tunes is proved by the fact that some later-day rabbis demanded that they be excluded from the Jewish house and synagogue. Greek influence became especially strong in the last two centuries before the Common Era, at the time when the Greeks intensified the Hellenization of the Orient and when the Greek language replaced Aramaic as the main tongue of Asia Minor.

While religious cult and spiritual music retained its traditional character, yet the influence of the emotionalism, the many-coloredness, and the beauty of Greek life made itself felt in daily life, particularly in that of the wealthier classes. It seems almost sure that Hebrew secular music witnessed a great development under the impact of Greek musical art, but—naturally—neither direct literary evidence nor actual music has confirmed this to posterity. But before we examine the sources regarding the religious practice and the secular music of the period, we must complete our historical survey down to the times in which the Jews had to replace their central Temple by places of learning scattered throughout their world and erect the edifice of their law perpetuating the Biblical tradition.

The Hellenistic epoch came to an end politically with the Maccabean victory and the rededication of the Holy Temple in 165 B.C. Direct contact between Hellas and Judea now ceased, while the Egyptian Jewish center remained under Greek supremacy and influence. But about a hundred years after Judea's victorious repulse of Hellas, the Orient had to surrender to the mighty thrust of another Occidental power. In 63 B.C. the Romans entered Jerusalem under Pompey and subjected the Jews to their rule. Judea never gained independence again after this fatal defeat: the civil war between the successors of the Hasmonean kings was exploited by the Romans, with the result that Judea was made a Roman province, and the dispute about Jesus the Nazarene and his teachings, the opposition to him, and his persecution and eventual crucifixion (ca. 29 A.D.) proved of paramount significance in the history of the Jewish people. In

70 A.D. Jerusalem and her proud Temple were destroyed by Titus, and the Jews set out on their wanderings through the world.

While the remnants of the Jewish people, the survivors of almost a century of civil strife and of war against Rome, were forced to look for new abodes in the Oriental and Occidental world, there were two groups of Jews whose fate proved decisive for Jewish as well as for general history. Both of them had left Jerusalem before the Romans captured and destroyed the erstwhile capital. One was composed of the disciples and followers of Jesus, who renounced Judaism and went out to propagate a new religion in the world; the other founded a new center of Jewish worship and learning at Yavneh in southern Palestine and there perpetuated its tradition. It was the academy of Yavneh which laid the foundations for the scholastic system and for the doctrines and comments later collected in the *Mishna* and the *Talmud*. Centers like these became characteristic of Jewish history throughout the ages of the Diaspora, and as they had no political or governmental power they could change their place whenever this was necessitated by the flow of events. Neither the suppression of Bar-Cochba's heroic revolt nor the Christian attempts at extermination, neither Inquisition nor pogroms have been able to destroy the spiritual power of Judaism, for the Jews preserved their law and mode of life in clandestine spiritual centers if they had to fear oppression in the open.

An outline of Israel's political and spiritual history is necessary for an appreciation of its musical history, for music was part of the ancient Hebrew cultural heritage and retained its former role in the religious service and in communal life—a reflection of its erstwhile glory. The Mishnaic and Talmudic sources abound in references to singing and musical instruments and thus show that music was still regarded as an indispensable branch of learning. The Jewish communities continued to cultivate their ancient forms of worship and singing in the Palestinian, Babylonian, and Egyptian centers and rejected all outside influences. Though Hellenistic civilization and art had temporarily had a strong hold over Hebrew thought and music, Roman culture held no attraction for the Jews, for Rome had no mature and elevated art of its own; pagan Roman music was of a purely showy virtuoso character, while the beginnings of Christian Roman music were based—many centuries after Rome's conquest of Jerusalem—on the foundations of Hebrew Temple music.

The centuries in which the spiritual heritage of Judaism was gathered, put down, and annotated by the Tannaim and Amoraim, who organized the Mishna and Talmud, also saw the development of the synagogue, the service of which was modeled after ancient Temple practice. The synagogues served small communities only, and an imitation of the scope and magnificence of the Temple sacrifices and ceremonies could not very well be attempted. Though the musical service thus lost most of its *raison d'être,* music did not lose its importance in any way; the scholars' detailed discussion of ancient Temple music and their remarks about singing in the places of worship as well as in their homes demonstrate their great interest in the musical side of the Jewish cult.

We learn from the sources that the Levites kept their traditional office as musical leaders and teachers. Singing in the house of worship remained their privilege, and it is told that they did not disclose the professional secrets of their art to anyone. The traditional forms of singing—antiphony of all kinds—were retained; they had in the meantime been cultivated by the Greeks, too, and were taken over by the Christians for the church service. But two important changes shaped the development of Hebrew music in the first centuries of the Christian Era: the style of singing assumed a different character, and a sharp dividing line was protectively drawn by the rabbinical teachers between the music of the religious service and secular music.

For primitive peoples and for the Oriental civilizations singing serves no artistic ends: man raises his voice in song because of his fear that ordinary speech cannot be heard by the supernatural powers shaping his life and deciding his fate. Even in the highly developed musical system of the Hebrew Temple, music was always dominated by the nature of the service: instrumental music only accompanied the ceremonies, and the singing closely followed the words of the texts. The choice of mode was dictated by the occasion or by the portion of the Scriptures to be chanted; the actual "composition"—which we have discussed in detail in Chapter Two—subordinated the melody to the rhythm and content of the words. But the possession of a fine voice and an artful chant became the most desirable features of a precentor in the synagogue (the Greek notions of beauty and artistry had taken hold in the world) and the melodies were embellished and were impressively performed. The chanted recitation of the scriptural texts—which was taken over from the Temple into Christian music, too—is characteristically termed "psalmody" in the Occidental languages, as psalm-singing especially became an important part of the Christian church service.

The study of the Mishna was also accompanied by a chanting of its chapters; a famous remark of Rabbi Jochanan (recorded in the Babylonian Talmud, Megilla fol. 32 a) was: "He who reads the Scriptures without melody and the Mishna without song, of him it can be said as is written: the laws I did give them are not good." The linking of study and singing served as valuable means of memorizing as well as of interpreting the law. The Mishna texts were noted down with the signs and accents used for the Biblical books, and the mode of recitation was thus indicated to the student. It has not been possible yet to establish the exact age of the accents; but scholars recently incline to believe that they were added in the period between the completion of the Talmud (ca. 500) and the time of the first Ge'onim (eighth century). Their interpretation was attempted in the previous chapter, but we must add here the interesting testimony of a rabbinical scholar, which proves that in the Talmudic epoch the accents still had a cheironomical character in addition to their mnemotechnical and musical functions: Rabbi Nahman bar-Yizhaq says that the right hand used to indicate the signs (Berahot fol. 62 a), and Rashi commented that the hand was moved in accordance with the musical accents. We also know that the interpolation of the "cadenza" between the separate parts of the daily song was developed into a great art and that this was one of the secrets with which the Levites were not willing to part. The end of a Biblical passage was also marked by certain closing cadences in the melody (Megilla 3 a).

The ways of singing and of performing music in both Temple and synagogue became a decisive factor in the development of Occidental music; for the earliest Christian precentors were brought up in the Jewish houses of worship and only adapted ancient Hebrew custom to a new purpose when converted to

Christianity.[1] It is thus that the Christian Church took over the responsorial singing, the modal melody, and many other Oriental features. The hand-signs and the accents were also adopted, and from these signs—called by the Church *neuma*, a Greek word meaning "nod" or "sign" and closely related etymologically to the Hebrew word *ne'ima* = "song, melody" —there developed in the beginning of the second millennium of the Common Era the first musical notation that indicated the exact pitches and durations prescribed by the composer. But in early Occidental music, just as in the Temple and in the synagogues of the first Christian centuries, the signs added to the liturgical texts indicated not a single note but the modal formula —a series of related notes—the rhythms of which had to be created in accordance with the word rhythms; the vague character of the signs was the reason for their being differently interpreted in the various Christian communities just as the ancient Biblical cantillation signs were differently interpreted in the various centers of the Jewish Diaspora. The earliest known Christian neumes date from the same period in which the final organization of the Hebrew system must have taken place. Where the neumes developed into a more complex and definite notation, the Hebrew accents did not depart from their ninth-century character.[2] Another similarity between Hebrew and Christian musical practice is the use in Christian liturgi-

[1] To the purely musical evidence new documentary proof has been added by the discovery of two fifth-century Roman epitaphs praising the art of Christian cantors who had been born Jews. See Eric Werner, "The Conflict between Hellenism and Judaism in the Music of the Early Christian Church," *Hebrew Union College Annual*, Vol. XX, 1947, p. 432.

[2] The oldest notated Jewish music manuscript that has actually come down to us is preserved in the Jewish Theological Seminary, New York (MS Elkan Adler 4096) and is described in the Elkan Adler Catalogue. The manuscript dates from the end of the thirteenth century and has been transcribed by various scholars. See Eric Werner, "The Oldest Sources of Synagogal Chant," *Proceedings of the American Academy for Jewish Research*, Vol. XVI, 1947.

a

b

c

The development of musical notation: (a) Hebrew Bible accents, from a 10th-century manuscript. (b) Early Christian neumes, 11th century. (c) Medieval Arabic notation, 14th century.

cal music of specific cadences to mark the different parts of the recitation. External features were also retained by the Church —among them the placing of the singers on the steps leading to the altar: this practice most probably led to certain psalms being called "Schir-ha-ma'aloth" (Song of Degrees) in Hebrew and "graduale" (from *gradus* = "step") in Latin liturgy. The Hebrew practice is confirmed by Nehemiah, who says (9:4), "Then stood up upon the stairs, of the Levites, Jeshua, and Bani, Kadmiel, Shebaniah, Bunni, Sherebiah, Bani, and Chenani, and cried with a loud voice unto the Lord their God," and the Mishna Sukkah (5:4) tells that on the Feast of Libation the playing Levites stood with their instruments on the fifteen steps that led from Israel's Temple to the women's section—against the fifteen Songs of Degrees of the Psalms.

At the time the precentors of the early Christian communities took over the melodies of the ancient Temple service and developed them in their own way—in connection with the new meaning they took on with the new, Latin, texts—some new trends can also be found in the way the Talmudic scholars discuss music. It has already been noted that it was probably the Greek influence that made the Jewish rabbis discover that singing had not only purely functional sides but could also be beautiful. They soon began to choose for precentors men endowed with a particularly fine voice, and a passage in the Proverbs of Solomon (3:9), "Honour thy Lord with thy substance," was interpreted to mean that every possessor of a beautiful voice was obliged to lead in prayer; the Mishna goes so far as to say that the word *hon,* "substance" or "wealth," should read *garon* "throat" (which in Hebrew script is a change of one consonant only). A story from the time of the last Mishna scholars (late second century) relates how a certain Chija bar-Ada, nephew of Bar-Cappara, was found to have a good voice and was at once compelled by his uncle to officiate as precentor.

It was only a natural development when the office of precentor was gradually transferred from the priests to those chosen on account of their voice and musical abilities; theirs became an honorary post, which could, however, be filled only by men of high moral reputation. A description of the ideal precentor is given in the second century by Rabbi Judah ben-Illai (B. Taanith fol. 16 a): he should be a learned man who has music in himself and is endowed with an agreeable voice, who is humble, has a pleasant appearance, is recognized by and popular with the community, is conversant with the Scriptures, able to preach a sermon, and well-versed in law and folklore, and who knows all the prayers by heart. He should also be poor and needy, for then his prayer will come out of his heart. At a later stage the precentor was given two assistants, called *tom'chim* or *mesayim* (supporters); they had also to remind him of the prayers and their tunes, as the writing down of prayers was not permitted till the seventh century. The two assistants have been retained in the synagogue service down to our own days. They stand by the precentor in many communities, especially on the Day of Atonement.

In the decades following the completion of the Talmud the Jews suffered under Christian oppression in Palestine and from the fanatic Magi caste in Babylonia. Many of their cultural centers were destroyed, and for a time the schools had to close their doors. The hardship of the times brought about great difficulties in the organization of worship and learning, and as it proved impossible to find honorary precentors, the institution of a professional *shaliach tzibur* (envoy of the community) became necessary. He was later called *hazan,* a term that had formerly described a secular official, an "overseer" (the most plausible among the many etymological derivations explains the word *hazan* as related to *hazoh* = "to see"); after the destruction of the Second Temple it simply meant a beadle. As the beadle was always present at the synagogue service, it had been logical to introduce him to the office of precentor. With the times he acquired professional knowledge and skill; names of outstanding hazanim have come down to us from the earliest centuries of the post-Talmudic period. The obstacles of the times are mirrored in the ruling of some eighth- and ninth-century scholars that youths of seventeen or eighteen, and in case of emergency even boys of thirteen, were eligible for the office of hazan.

The service was generally divided between two precentors, one sitting with the congregation and the other standing before the pulpit facing in the direction of Jerusalem. The first precentor used to recite the "Hearken Israel" (*Sh'ma Israel*) and the benedictions, while the second followed him with the prayer proper; on the Sabbath and the holy days the morning prayer was recited by the first and the additional prayer by the second precentor—a custom that has survived down to our own days. As the second precentor recited the more elaborate portions of the service and those reserved for the Festival prayers, his office was considered superior to that of the first. The musical elaboration and embellishment of the synagogue chant is due to the efforts of these hazanim.

The mutual influence characterizing the development of synagogue and church in the early Christian centuries is shown by the foundation of Christian music schools modeled on those of the Temple and the synagogue and by the institution in the church of a lector (reader) and cantor (singer) alternating in prayer and chant. The forms of responsorial antiphony and the liturgical chant retained their character for many centuries, but the difference between the worlds of the Orient and the Occident was soon apparent. The Occident had no understanding of the word-born, emotional, and flexible melody of Oriental singers. The Christians disdained sensuality and ecstasy, as they saw in the earthly life nothing but a preliminary existence and a preparation for Heaven; they thus had as little use for the worldly ethics of art preached by the Greek philosophers as for the notions of the beautiful that had crept into synagogue music. The Church Fathers feared, on the contrary, that a fine voice and artful elaboration of the liturgical chant might divert the worshipers' attention from the content and purpose of the prayers.

The fundamental problems of all religious music, as well as the gulf dividing Occidental from Oriental thought, are evident from a passage contained in the *Confessions* of St. Augustine, written about 400 A.D.:

So often as I call to mind the tears I shed at the hearing of Thy church songs, in the beginning of my recovered faith, yea, and at this very time, whenas I am moved not with the singing, but with the thing sung (when namely they are set off with a clear voice and suitable modulation), I then acknowledge the great good use of this institution. Thus float I between peril and pleasure, and an approved profitable custom: inclined the more (though herein I pronounce no irrevocable opinion) to allow of the old usage of singing in the Church; that so by the delight taken in at the ears, the weaker minds be roused up into some feeling of devotion. And yet again, so oft as it befalls me to be moved with the voice rather than with the ditty, I confess myself to have grievously offended: at which time I wish rather not to have heard the music.

The early Christian church tended to cut down the part of music in the service to a minimum, as it was a constant reminder of pagan customs and of the ancient faith. But it was impossible to dispense with music altogether, for its sacred associations were declared not only by the ancient Bible—holy to the Christians—but also by the New Testament Scriptures. Instrumental music and the use of popular tunes became, of course, intolerable in the eyes of the Christian Fathers; but their very antagonism toward them suggests the extent to which folk music and instrumental playing must actually have flourished. The belief in the magical power of prayer and incantation, which the Jews had apparently overcome to a great extent, still haunted people's minds in the early Christian centuries; the widely used exclamation *Kyrie eleison* ("Lord, have mercy") has come down from pagan sun rites via the Jewish Temple to Christian liturgy and still begins the Mass as well as its musical settings. Some of the church ceremonies were accompanied by musical instruments down to the sixth century, and some Eastern churches—the Copts of Ethiopia, for instance—use them to this very day. The organ, the principal musical instrument found in the Western church today, gained a permanent place in the church only at the beginning of the second millennium; the Jews, who had most probably had a similar instrument in the Second Temple, then argued that it was a "Christian instrument" and thus inadmissible in Jewish service.

The Roman church based its liturgy and its music on two direct sources: on the music of the Temple perpetuated by

Christianized Jewish cantors and on Byzantine music. Byzantine music, too, had the closest affinities with ancient Temple music; the Byzantine authors themselves said that their psalms and their musical system and modes as well as their forms of singing were derived from the art of King David and King Solomon. In stark contrast to Rome, which had developed no culture of its own, Byzantium had reached a very high stage of cultural evolution—in which ancient Hebrew and later Hellenistic influences were the foremost shaping forces. The Byzantine influence on the western church proved strong till the final separation of Byzantium from Rome in 1050; but then the western world had already begun to develop decisive traits of its own.

Eastern art and music became a dominant factor in the cultural development of the East of Europe, while the history of western music proper begins with the diffusion of the liturgical chant named after Pope Gregory the Great (who was pontiff from 590 to 604). The Oriental influences began to recede gradually; the new features shaping church song seem characteristically Occidental. The embellishment of certain syllables or words, necessitated by the adaptation of the modes to various texts and then exploited by the professional precentors for virtuosic ends, seemed excessively emotional to the Church Fathers: this can be noted especially in the development of the singing of the "Hallelujah." The ending syllable "jah" had been adorned with melisms and developed into an artful cadence by the Jewish precentors; the church cantors took over the complete melody but later separated the "Hallelujah" from the main text, singing new words to the notes of the cadence.[3] The texts specially written to fit the Hallelujah melisms constitute the first original sacred poetry of the Occident; a much later step is

[3] Eric Werner, "The Doxology in Synagogue and Church, A Liturgico-Musical Study," *Hebrew Union College Annual*, 1945–46.

their independent setting to music and thus their final and complete detachment from the Oriental origin. When in the early Middle Ages the practice of many-voiced singing and—still later —of harmonization was applied to liturgical melodies, western music finally achieved musical independence. The Oriental origin of the liturgical chant—which can be demonstrated by a comparison of the basic melodies with those of the ancient Jewish communities—was still to be divined; nevertheless, medieval history drew a clear dividing line between synagogue music, which became static and archaic, and church music, which developed forms of art that were to prepare the ground for the great art music of the western world.

The antagonism of the Christian Church Fathers toward secular and instrumental music finds an echo in the Oriental world, but there it is based on different reasoning. The church frankly admitted that music, if cultivated as an art, distracted from the religious service, and the Islamic authorities (followed by some of the later rabbinical writers) expressed similar opinions. But the Talmudic scholars prohibited the use of secular and instrumental music as unfit for a people that had lost its Temple and with it its religious and national center. They admonished their fellow-Jews to sing religious hymns at the festivals; Greek tunes were described by them as harmful to the mind, and the use of secular melodies for the reading of the Holy Scriptures was said to be against the spirit of the law, as Moses himself had heard the traditional sacred tunes on Mount Sinai and imparted them to the people of Israel. The preference of the Hebrews for vocal music, in contrast to the instrumental-minded Greeks, seems to be proved by the fact that the Hebrew language abounds in terms for melody, vocal forms, vocal range, and sound, while Greek has a larger vocabulary for instrumental music and the instruments proper.[4] The rabbis of the Hellenistic period went so far in their condemnation of instrumental music that they even scorned the use of those instruments actually used in the Jerusalem Temple of old: "They (the faithful) do not pour blood of sacrifices upon the altar; no tympanon is sounded, nor cymbals, nor the aulos with its many holes, instruments full of frenzied tones, not the whistling of a pan's pipe is heard, imitating the serpent, nor the trumpet calling to war in wild tones," says a famous Hellenistic-Judaic source.[5] It is important to know that the instruments mentioned were largely associated with Greek pagan worship and also partly with the secular orgies so abhorred by the Jewish authorities.

The cultivation of the traditional vocal music was thus considered of foremost importance, and singers with fine voices who declined to serve the synagogue were severely castigated and punished. Drastic measures were also taken, or at least contemplated, against indulgence in secular music: a rabbi of the third century demands that ears listening to such music should be cut off, and a little later a house in which music is cultivated is said to be marked for destruction. One third-century Babylonian rabbi prohibited all secular music in his community. Thereupon all festivities and social affairs were suspended, for nobody cared for social life without music; this led to a complete standstill in social intercourse and commercial life and brought about such a crisis in the market that another rabbinical authority had to relax his colleague's ruling. The prohibition of instruments on weekdays as well as on the Sabbath and at festivals

[4] Eric Werner, "The Conflict between Hellenism and Judaism in the Music of the Early Christian Church," *Hebrew Union College Annual*, 1947.

[5] Oracula Sibyllina 8, 113. See Eric Werner, "The Conflict between Hellenism and Judaism in the Music of the Early Christian Church," *Hebrew Union College Annual*, Vol. XX, 1947, pp. 415 ff.

soon became general, and exceptions were made only for weddings and mourning ceremonies. The authorities did all in their power to stop the people's natural merrymaking associated with gay and popular music; the breaking of a dish in front of a bride and groom at their wedding seems to have come from the wish to remind them in the midst of their merriment of the destruction of Jerusalem. It is also related that when the gaiety at a wedding was becoming extravagant some prominent sages would suddenly break the most costly dishes of the house in order to shock the guests and thus tone down the joy, so that they would not start irreverently singing serious religious music.

The fact that the depreciation of secular and instrumental music on the part of the religious authorities was common to all the centers of the eastern and western Mediterranean at approximately the same time makes a priority difficult to determine; it can be guessed, however, that the exuberance and lasciviousness of life under Roman influence were the common ground on which there grew an aversion to all matters secular. The Jewish rabbis gave vent to their indignation by reminding Israel of its national sorrow, the Church Fathers exhorted the Christians to imitate neither pagan worship nor the obscene theater, and the Islamic theologians followed suit in their condemnation of all those listening to profane music. Psychological and national considerations were additional reasons underlying the sharp words of the clerical authorities against the use of instruments and the singing of popular songs. It must be surmised that the music performed at Jewish weddings and other festivities was not of Hebrew origin, for a real musical tradition had so far been cultivated only in the religious field. Popular songs and instrumental music had largely been influenced by Greek music or had actually been taken over from Hellenistic sources, and the rabbis must have had every cause to keep these influences away from their flock. A similar motive may be assumed in the case of the Islamic authorities, for Arabic secular music had also been subjected to foreign influences to a large degree. The case is somewhat different in the Christian church: in its own sphere secular music meant the music at the luxurious ceremonies of the Roman Emperor's court and at the extravagant circus or theater. The theologians of the three great religious communities were thus one in their condemnation of foreign influence endangering—so it seemed to them—the preservation of their religious tradition, and in their concentration upon the essential values of music in divine service.

The continuous exhortations of Church Fathers, Arab theologians, and rabbinical scholars make it sufficiently clear that their campaigns against secular music did not meet with the success desired. The Jewish sources confirm that no weddings or feasts were celebrated without singing and playing, and the rabbis were forced to cancel some of their prohibitions. One scholar even dared to argue that the Greek language was best fitted for songs. The working songs of the boatmen and plowmen were expressly permitted, but those of the weavers were prohibited as obscene; the professional wailing-women continued to sing their threnodies accompanied by pipes (two at the least); and music retained its dominant role at processions and celebrations, at which even aged rabbis could often be seen rising from an opulent meal, clapping their hands, and joining in a dance to the strains of merry music.

The sparse evidence we could quote here for the first centuries of Jewish history after the destruction of the Temple amply proves that music did not cease to fulfill important functions both in the cult and in the daily life of the Jewish communities. Throughout the insecure period of wanderings and oppression characterizing the early Christian centuries, tradition and law

Ex.6 Tropos Spondeiakos (Greek)

Ex.7 Gloria in Excelsis (Roman)

Ex.8 Moroccan Psalmody (Jewish)

Ex.9 Babylonian Chant (Jewish)

Ex.10 Syrian Psalmody

Ex.11 Byzantine Hymn

Ex.12 Skolion of Seikilos

Ex.13 Roman Antiphon

Ex.14 Spanish Hebrew FolkSong

Ex.15 13th Century Troubadour

Ex.16 Hebrew Hymn

Ex.17 Spanish Cantiga

A Mode Used by Different Jewish Communities and by the Early Church.[6]

Ex. 6. The model framework of the Tropos Spondeiakos, which is a modification of the Dorian scale. Clement of Alexandria (*Paedagogus*, II, Ch. 4.) says that the Greek drinking songs were sung in this mode "after the manner of Hebrew psalms."

Ex. 7. Gloria of the mass in Festis Simplicibus (Liber usualis, p. 55)

Ex. 8. Psalmody of the Moroccan Jews (after Idelsohn)

Ex. 9. Chant of the Babylonian Jews on the high holy days (after Idelsohn)

Ex. 10. Syrian Psalmody (after Parisot)

Ex. 11. Byzantine hymn of the 11th–12th century (after Tillyard)

A Melodic Style Common to Greek, Roman Christian, Spanish Hebrew, and Early European Secular Song.

Ex. 12. The Skolion of Seikilos, of Tralles in Asia Minor (1st–2nd century of the Common Era.)

Ex. 13. Roman antiphon "Hosanna filio David," of the Roman Church (after Gastoue, *Les Origines du chant romain,* Paris, 1907, p. 40)

Ex. 14. Spanish Hebrew folk song, "Rachelina" (sung by the Sephardic Jews of Salonika, quoted after Lazare Saminsky, *Music of the Ghetto and the Bible,* New York, 1934, p. 151)

Ex. 15. Thirteenth-century troubadour song (after Angles; see Davidson and Apel's *Historical Anthology of Music,* Cambridge, Mass., 1947, p. 15, No. 18 c.)

Ex. 16. Hebrew hymn, composed to a text by the eleventh-century poet Ahi Gaon ("Sh'ma koli") and probably introduced from Spain into the various countries in which the Jews took refuge after their expulsion (after D. A. de Sola-Aguilar *The Ancient Melodies of the Liturgy of the Spanish and Portuguese Jews,* London, 1857)

Ex. 17. A Spanish cantiga of the Villancico type, thirteenth century (quoted after Ribera from Davidson and Apel's *Historical Anthology of Music,* Cambridge, Mass., 1947, p. 20, No. 22 c.)

[6] After E. Werner: "The Doxology in Synagogue and Church, A Liturgical-Musical Story," *Hebrew Union College Annual,* Vol. XIX, 1946, pp. 333–35, where all sources for transcriptions used are also given.

were steadfastly adhered to; the remembrance of Temple music and the wish to perpetuate its essential features went a long way toward shaping the synagogue song of two hundred centuries of dispersion, while at the same time it provided the fundamentals for western art music. The secular music of Israel, on the other hand, could begin developing a characteristic style of its own only when the Jews were given another period of rest and prosperity; not until they lived free from suppression and fear could they truly cultivate poetry and art. And such an era dawned upon them when they followed the Islamic conquerors to southwestern Europe, where the Jews were destined to enjoy a golden age of their own in the cultural centers of medieval Spain.

Chapter
FOUR

The Settlement of the West

THE TALMUD, AN ECHO of Israel's splendor and great-ness of old, was the last spiritual creation of the Jews on the soil of the ancient Orient. The centuries following its completion mark a large-scale migration to the West, whose political and cultural hegemony now became firmly established. The Jews began to settle throughout the countries bordering the Medi-terranean as well as in central, western, and eastern Europe and to play their own part in the erection of the great edifice of civilization and culture rising on European soil. They were instrumental in the laying of the foundations, then receded into the background for some centuries when they neither derived great benefit from the younger civilizations nor con-tributed to their development. Finally in modern times they again took an active part in the cultural activities of nations which had meanwhile soared high above the Jews but whose achievements were soon turned to good account by their Jewish citizens. Some Jews distinguished themselves and rose to fame as inventors, craftsmen, thinkers, or artists of great individuality. Many of these renounced their link with the people from which they had originally sprung, and the products of their minds belong to the culture of the people among whom they lived.

The Jewish migration which set in soon after the destruction of the First Temple led to the foundation of the Babylonian community, of the Egyptian Diaspora (which later became the center of the Jewish-Hellenistic culture), and of various settlements in the Mediterranean world; after the Romans' fatal blow against Jerusalem the Jews settled throughout the Roman Empire. But the large-scale migration to the countries of the West and the rise of the first western Jewish communal and cultural centers date from the period in which the youngest Oriental power, Islam, pushed forward into the West and established a strong foothold in Spain.

Islam had originally been the creation of certain Semitic tribes, among whom there also lived a great number of Arabic Jews; but after the death of its prophet, Mohammed, it became a powerful national-religious movement. Islam set out to wring Syria, Palestine, Egypt, and the North African coast from the Byzantine and Roman Empire and on its way also brought most of the Jewish Diaspora under Arab supremacy. The conquests were soon extended to Europe, and everywhere Jewish communities became part of the realm. As trade and commerce flourished in the new Islamic centers, Jewish merchants also followed the routes of the conquerors; Jews prospered in southern Italy and in Spain and also moved northward into Franconia, eastern Europe, and the central European countries. By dint of their connections with the Oriental world they became important agents in the trade between West and East and established their centers in the cities of Europe. After a long period of stagnation the Jewish world had been set moving again; it played its part in the attempt of Islam to subdue the Occident after the century-long supremacy of Hellas and Rome over the Orient. Islam succeeded in maintaining its rule and influence over Spain for seven centuries, and the Jews flourished in its commercial and cultural centers. A lively spiritual exchange between Jews and Arabs on the one hand and between the Oriental and Occidental civilizations on the other characterizes cultural development in the course of these centuries; the Jews again played their role as mediators. History shows that their talent for assimilating what was best in the ways of both Orient and Occident enabled them to remain in Europe and play their part in its cultural life when Islam was forced to give up the positions it had held for so long and returned to the countries of the Orient.

The reasons for the victorious advance of Islam in Europe were not only its fanatical desire for power and conquest and the driving force of its armies but also the inner dynamics and spirit of its achievements. Islam had united the heritage of the ancient Oriental civilizations in a grandiose synthesis. As a cultural force it was greatly superior to the cultures of the West, which were still in the formative stage. Islam's emphatic belief in the beauty of the earthly world, the magnificence of its buildings, the many-coloredness of its stories, and the vivid rhythm of its life proved irresistibly attractive to the countries ruled by the dogma of a church that denounced earthly pleasure and kept a wary eye on art; Islamic culture radiated its light from Spain throughout the Occidental world. While in the sphere of church life and art the Oriental heritage was disclaimed in an ever-increasing degree, the impact of Oriental culture was instrumental in creating western secular art. The young poetry of southwestern Europe, the rise of the troubadour song, and the cultivation of instrumental playing—on instruments mostly imported from the Orient—owed their origin in large measure to the Oriental poets, singers, and musicians at the courts of Islamic Spain. The great inner power of the culture of Islam can well be imagined if we compare the towering influence of the Oriental forces on medieval Europe with the negligible impression made by the Occidental crusaders on the Oriental world.

The Arabs had conquered Spain in the year 711; in 750 this most western outpost of the Arab Empire became an independent political and cultural province. There had been Jewish settlements in the country before, but the Jews had been hated and oppressed by the Spanish Christians. The Arabs did away with the restrictions under which the Jews had had to suffer and let them participate in their economic and cultural life, for they found their character and modes of life more congenial with and related to their own Oriental ways than those of the Spaniards, who were hostile toward the Islamic conquerors and represented a creed and life foreign to them. The Jewish communities thus began to thrive and attracted new settlers from other parts of the world; and the Spanish Diaspora soon prospered to such a degree that it took over the place of Babylon as the cultural center of Israel.

During the existence of the Jewish commonwealth and until the destruction of the Temple, music had been recognized only in its liturgical functions, and in the Diaspora under Greek and Roman rule the will for self-preservation had expressed itself in rigid laws on the use of music. Now the Jews entered upon a new phase. Hebrew music and Jewish musicians had hitherto found their place within their own community only, and their

work had been prescribed by liturgical needs; Jewish popular
music had largely been shaped by foreign influences and had
not been permitted to develop freely. In the Islamic period the
Jews found themselves for the first time in modern history
partaking in a flourishing civilization and enjoying its privileges
as free citizens. They lived and traded unhindered by restrictions; they held important positions in various branches of the
political, economic, and cultural life; and their own development derived great benefit from the impact of a civilization
which in its origins was not far remote from their own and whose
language they had adopted in the Oriental world as well as in
the new European settlements. With the establishment of the
Arab rule in Spain there ended for the Jews the period of mere
colonization; they could turn to organization and creation in
all spheres of life. As so often in history, at this point we can
once more witness the characteristic trend in Jewish culture:
again the Jews based the foundations of their life and art on
those of another civilization but adapted and remolded old
forms in a spirit of their own.

The worldly spirit of the Arab philosophy of life was mirrored
in an ever-growing emphasis on the emotional in Jewish thought.
The laws of the Talmud are found to be too rigid, too much the
product of cold reasoning, and devoid of an understanding of
the demands of heart and soul; it is significant that the most
popular religious book of the eleventh century should have been
called *Duties of the Heart*. Life and cult without beauty no
longer satisfy the community, and the traditional synagogue
service is embellished by products of sensitive minds and hearts
—by poetry. The creation of synagogal poetry (*piyut*) was due
to a good many factors at once: the popularity of church hymns
throughout the western world, the secular poetry of the Arabs,
and the wish on the part of the precentors to find vehicles for

their artistry. In the Christian church the hymns were created in a desire to add purely Christian poetry to the traditional liturgical texts of Oriental origin; the Jewish hazanim based their religious hymns on free elaborations of scriptural texts.

An early example of a Jewish poet and singer may be found toward the end of the fifth century: a converted Jew (according to Eric Werner) born in Syria and active in Constantinople wrote hymns modeled on Oriental patterns for the Greek Church. This poet, who called himself Romanos, was regarded in his own time as the greatest Byzantine hymn-writer and was called *Melodos* ("Maker of Songs") by his contemporaries; about a thousand poems—mainly based on Biblical passages— and their melodies were attributed to him. The work of Romanos became of importance to eastern Christendom and seems to have influenced later Hebrew poets as well; but it was only under the influence of the Arab lyrical poems that there developed a Jewish religious poetry of characteristic imprint. The earliest Hebrew poems known are based on Arabic meters, and this implies that they were most probably sung to Arabic melodies. That Arabic tunes were still popular with the Jews in the golden age of Hebrew poetry and song is shown by the fact that leading eleventh-century scholars and poets—such as Hai (Chiya) b. Sherira ha-Gaon, Isaac Alfasi, and Yehuda of Barcelona—found it necessary to express their opposition to the excessive use of poetry and Arabic tunes in the synagogue. Maimonides permitted the introduction of poetry into the service under certain conditions only and demanded that it should not interrupt the prayers and benedictions; he stressed the inadmissibility of popular and instrumental music. Yehuda Hadassi argued that the worshipers paid better attention when a hazan endowed with a beautiful voice intoned a fine melody and that his song could purify and ennoble their minds. An admirable definition of the purpose of singing is contained in the *Book of the Pious* of Yehuda he-Hassid (died 1217): "If you cannot concentrate in prayer, search for melodies, and if you pray choose a tune you like. Then your heart will feel what your tongue speaks; for it is the song that makes your heart respond." The same rabbi forbade the Jews both to teach Hebrew melodies to the Christians, and to learn tunes from them. Religious songs, he also taught, should never be used for secular purposes, not even for lulling a baby to sleep.

The general attitude of the religious authorities toward music is well summarized in the writings of Maimonides, who saw in all activities of man a means of creating and maintaining "a perfect condition of the instrument of the soul," and in the argument of a twelfth-century Arab writer (Al-Ghazālī) that there can be opposition to music only if one listens to it "for its own sake and not for recreation." The necessity of adorning religious as well as secular life was admitted in this golden age of poetry and art, and the debates fought by the thinkers of the period only symbolize that greater dispute of the time on the preponderance of reason or heart in the regulation of life and worship—a dispute characterizing the entire spiritual development of Judaism in European civilization and forming the dual basis of many Jewish minds, with Spinoza's philosophy as the towering example.

The medieval debates on the place of poetry and music in the synagogue have furnished posterity with a wealth of information regarding the musical practice and the philosophy and aesthetics of music in the Spanish period. We learn that the theory and science of music formed part of the curriculum in higher studies from the beginning of the tenth century; this branch of learning was generally described as "science of music" or "science of composition," while the practical side of instruction was simply called "singing" (*zimrah*). Just as in the Arabic schools, the study of music in Hebrew science was divided into two separate branches: theoretical and practical. Yizhaq ibn Sulaiman (Isaac Israeli), the first prominent Jewish philosopher of the Middle Ages (ca. 842–932), saw in music the last but the best of the disciplines that had to be studied; and the leading thinkers of the following centuries testified to the fact that mastery in the theory of music was counted among the accomplishments regarded by Jewish scholars as highly desirable.

Yet in spite of the abundance of testimony regarding the teaching of music and its part in Jewish cult and education, it is difficult to separate Jewish original thought from Greek and Arabic aesthetics and from a philosophy common to the entire Orient. It has been proved that the basic philosophy and aesthetics of music originated in Asia Minor and Mesopotamia, certainly earlier than 1500 B.C.[1] Greek philosophers transformed and systematized the ancient Oriental ideas and carried them back to Asia Minor, where they were absorbed by early Christianity and Hellenistic Judaism. Syrians and Jews were the mediators between Hellenistic philosophy and Islamic thought, and the medieval world drew its science from the Latin writers, who based their ideas on those of the ancient Greeks, and from the Spanish cultural centers.

This long line of development explains the fact that many old Oriental trends are still found in medieval philosophy. The magical origins of customs and prayers still haunted the mind; the belief in the magic power of music—predominant in medieval writings—was justified by a reference to the famous healing of Saul's mind by the music of David: ". . . and it came to pass, when the evil spirit from God was upon Saul, that David took a lyre, and played with his hand: so Saul was refreshed,

[1] Werner, *op. cit.*, p. 469.

and was well, and the evil spirit departed from him" (I Sam. 16:23). Isaiah had castigated the magicians of Babylonia (47:9 ff.) in scornful language, yet Jewish belief in magic was in no way less strong than that of the other Oriental peoples; it has been noted (in Chapter One) that the shofar symbolizes magic spells to this very day. In the medieval sources—both Arab and Jewish—it is often related how musicians were called to relieve the pains of the sick in the hospital, and an ancient Hebrew manuscript (described in Dr. H. G. Farmer's book on Sa'adyah ha-Gaon, p. 6) contains a picture in which a lutenist is seen sitting in a physician's anteroom, probably called upon to cleanse the mind of the possessed or to perform his part in the healing of the sick.

But side by side with the ancient Oriental ideas of magic and incantation the influence of classical Greece and its ethics is not denied in medieval musical aesthetics and science. The ethos of certain melodic scales, of defined rhythms, and of the different musical instruments, as well as their influence on the soul and character of man, recurs in the medieval writings; and the idea of a harmony of spheres took firm root in the minds of both the Greeks and the later Jewish philosophers, who could quote in support a passage in the Book of Job (38:7): ". . . the morning stars sang together, and all the sons of God shouted for joy." [2] Greek and Arab authors said that only Pythagoras had been able to hear the celestial harmonies, but a Jewish source (Philo Judaeus 2:299) ascribed the same capacity to Moses—who, as was said in Chapter One, was regarded as the patron of musicians in the Islamic Orient.

Astrological considerations fill a prominent place in both the Arabic and the Hebrew writings of the Middle Ages (they are

[2] Eric Werner and Isaiah Sonne, "The Philosophy and Theory of Music in Judeo-Arabic Literature," *Hebrew Union College Annual*, 1941.

a most ancient heritage from the Chaldeans and Babylonians),
and the relations of the strings and tones to the planets and sea-
sons and the influence of sounds, melodies, and rhythms on the
humors of the body are discussed at length by the scholars of
the period.

New trends in Hebrew music are indirectly attested in the
writings of the first Jewish scholar who devoted to music a complete chapter of his philosophical system—Sa'adyah ha-Gaon,
who was born in Fayyum, Egypt, in 892 and died in Sura, Mesopotamia, in 942. The tenth chapter of his *Book of Doctrines and
Beliefs* (933), a book famous among both Jews and Arabs, contains an important paragraph on music; and as Sa'adyah's teachings exerted a great influence on all centers of Jewish learning,
it must be surmised that his musical aesthetics was as widely
discussed as his religious philosophy. An interesting feature is
the absence in Sa'adyah's writings of a discussion of the problem
that very much occupied the minds of scholars in Spain—the ad-
missibility of music in the cult; it has been deduced that in contrast to other Jewish centers, that in Babylonia, by far the oldest
community in the Jewish Diaspora, had raised no objection to
music. Sa'adya's paragraph on music deals with the influence of
music on the mind and is part of a general discussion of the
effects of sensual impressions—seeing, hearing, smelling—on the
human soul. In the sphere of seeing and smelling Sa'adyah expresses the opinion (in the footsteps of Al-Kindi, the great Arab
philosopher before him) that single colors or aromas cannot
produce a beneficial effect on the soul, whereas a combination
of colors or perfumes pleases the senses and stimulates the soul.
The same argument is applied with regard to music, where also

only the mixture of colors can exert a beneficial influence on soul and character.

Sa'adyah's paragraph on music has long puzzled scholars, as it has come down to us in a number of divergent copies and translations. But a thorough investigation of the different versions has led Dr. Farmer to demonstrate that Sa'adyah's interest centers round the rhythmic and not the melodic modes, as was hitherto thought, and that he spoke, therefore, in favor of a mixture of "rhythmic colors." This is most important for the history of musical theory, as in ancient Oriental music the rhythmical—like the melodic—practice had not been theoretically systematized. The prominence of rhythmical questions is due to the rise of poetry built on metrical verses—a conception foreign to ancient Hebrew poetry—and it is only natural that the philosophy of music as well as the theory of rhythm should have been taken over by the Jews from the Arabs, whose poetry had actually inspired their own hymns and songs. Not only Sa'adyah, who is much indebted to Al-Kindi, but all the scholars who then flourished in the Spanish centers based their theory on Arab writings and actually recommended Greek and Arab texts to their disciples and readers for study—and theory, of course, is but a mirror of factual practice. Yussuf ibn 'Aknin (died 1226) copied for his teachings on music almost half of the theoretical writings of the greatest Arab theoretician, Al-Farabi, and the echoes of Arabic theory resound in all textbooks of the Jewish world. But with the continuous increase in the circulation of Hebrew writings, the Spanish Jews preferred to base their speculations on Jewish authors—even if those had originally derived their knowledge from Arab sources; among the best-known writers on music, apart from those already mentioned, were Abraham bar-Chiyah (died ca. 1136), Yehuda ben Shmuel

ibn 'Abbas, and Shem Tow ben Yosef ben Palakera (both
thirteenth century), Immanuel ben Shlomoh, the Italian-Jewish
poet of the fourteenth century, and the cabalist Abraham ben
Yizhaq of Granada (fourteenth century). The Hebrew theory
of music remained dependent on Arab models much longer than
other branches of science, in which original traits can be found
at a comparatively earlier time; the Greek influence is also strong
and can be explained both by direct contact and by the Greek
elements in Arab philosophy.

In addition to the musico-theoretical writings in Arabic or
Hebrew, there was one important Jewish contribution to musical
theory which was written in Latin; this is the *De numeris harmo-
nicis* (1343) of Magister Leo Hebraeus or Gersonides, whose
real name was Levi ben Gershon (died 1344). The treatise was
written at the suggestion of Philip de Vitry, one of the most outstanding European poets, composers, and theoreticians of the
time, the pioneer of the *ars nova* movement in France. It is significant that rhythmic changes should be among the dominating
elements of the new music superseding the "old art." [3] The last
contribution of medieval Jewish scholars to musical theory dates
from the end of the fourteenth or the beginning of the fifteenth
century. It is contained in a fragment found at Genizah near
Cairo, written in Hebrew characters but in Arabic language;
it most probably constitutes a copy from an Arab compendium
of science and the arts. The story of musical theory shows the
Jews in the Middle Ages as active in the field of science and
philosophy as they were destined to become in more modern
times; while enjoying the blessings of a flourishing civilization
in medieval Spain, they slowly prepared the ground for independent thinking. In the degree to which they developed their
thought and philosophy they must surely also have shown traits

[3] Eric Werner and Isaiah Sonne, *op. cit.*, 2nd part, 1942–43.

of their own in the field of living music proper; but here again
—just as in the most ancient history of Israel—no actual notation and description have come down to us, and we must rely
on comparisons and speculation if we want to get an idea of the
music sung and played by the Jewish musicians at the Spanish
courts and by the singers and instrumentalists interpreting the
poems of the time.

In order to appreciate the changes brought about in Hebrew
music by the impact of the Islamic world, we have only to look
at the development in the precentor's position. Not only had the
hazan meanwhile gained the status of an accomplished master
of his craft whose name was handed down to posterity and
whose achievements were marveled at both by his own community and by people in remote places, but he had also assumed
other than purely liturgical functions. The hazan of the Middle
Ages was poet, singer, and composer, and in the course of the centuries he was also given the task of entertaining the community
on the Sabbath when no work was being done. The many-
sidedness of his office and his cultivation of many talents put him
in the same rank with the Arab singer (*shu'ar*), the French
troubadour, and the later German minnesinger; the art of all
these poet-singer-player-composers was indeed nursed by one
common source—the (Arab, Greek, and Jewish) Orient. When
in our own days we can note an astounding similarity in melodies sung in Eastern communities, in certain Balkan regions, and
in districts of southern France, as well as those noted down in
medieval troubadour manuscripts, we can imagine how great
was the effect of the Oriental lyric song on the Occidental world;
moreover, we can divine the character of the melodies composed
by the medieval Jewish *paytanim*.

There is evidence that Jewish singers based their songs on
melodies borrowed or adapted from foreign sources; it is ex-

pressly stated in some Judeo-Spanish prayers that they are to be sung "to an Arabic tune," and in other cases Spanish popular songs are indicated as tunes for synagogal hymns. But the pay-tanim also composed melodies of their own, many of which have remained in favor down to our own day; we are not quite sure, however, whether the tunes that have come down to us were en-tirely their own creation, and it is also difficult to determine to what extent these were adapted and changed by later genera-tions. An important figure among the early precentors and hazanim is Rabbi Yehudai Ga'on, who lived in the eighth century and who seems to have codified Jewish musical tradition as well as introduced new hymns into the synagogue service; [4] the intro-duction of the "Kol Nidre" prayer for the Day of Atonement is ascribed to this sage; the tune familiarized through the ar-rangements by nineteenth-century composers is a compilation —containing only a few archaic elements—of a much later, Ashkenazic origin, while in Sephardic synagogues an ancient— perhaps medieval—version is still employed. Famous examples of later piyutim are *Ata Hu Eloheinu* and *Ein Kamocha,* by Meshullam ben Kalonymos (ca. 1100), *Adon Olam,* by Salo-mon ibn Gabirol (eleventh century), *Yigdal,* by Daniel ben Yuda (thirteenth century). The *Selichot* (prayers of penitence) were also created by paytanim; they go back to the sixth cen-tury, but no names of their poets and composers have come down to us.

The art of the paytanim, among whom was included the gen-ius Ychuda ha-Levi, flourished down to the fifteenth century, though the conditions of life had in the meantime changed for the Jews once again. These created the Sabbath songs (*Zemirot*), the songs for the *Seder* service on the eve of Passover (with the

---

[4] Eric Werner, "The Doxology in Synagogue and Church, A Liturgico-Musical Study," *Hebrew Union College Annual,* 1945–46.

exception of the ancient and traditional *Hallel*), and later those for the Hanukkah- and Purim-feast, for the ceremonies of circumcision and wedding, and the like—most of them being in use down to our own days. The last poet-singers whose melodies were popular and well known throughout the Jewish world were three Palestinians of the sixteenth century: Solomon Alkabetz, author of the popular Sabbath hymn "L'cha dodi"; Isaac Luria, who wrote cabalist songs—in the Aramaic language—which achieved great popularity in the Hassidic movement; and Israel Najara, who published in 1587, in Safed, the first songbook ever printed in the Orient ("Zemirot Israel"). Najara's song collection—reprinted later in Venice—is arranged after the pattern of an Arabic "Divan": the songs are grouped according to the tunes used for them. The origin of many of his melodies is Arabic, Greek, Turkish, and Spanish; but the collection of foreign tunes—to which Najara added many of his own creations —shows the Jewish spirit at work, for even the songs most popular in character were adapted to suit the style of synagogal hymns. Israel Najara was the last poet, hazan, and composer in the direct succession of the paytanim, who created their religious-lyrical songs in Hebrew for use in the houses of worship and introduced poetry, beauty, and lively rhythm into a service that had become stilted and was lacking in creative force.[5]

In the golden age of Jewish poetry and music in the Spanish centers we also find a number of Jewish musicians at the Islamic and Christian courts, where they seem to have undergone the same process of emancipation that became typical for western European Jewry in the nineteenth century. As early as about 800 the name of an eminent Jewish musician at a Spanish court is mentioned in the annals of history: he was Al-Mansur, esteemed court musician of Sultan Al-Chakam I (796–822), a

[5] A. Z. Idelsohn, *Thesaurus of Hebrew Oriental Melodies,* Vol. IV.

generous patron of science and the arts who did much to foster the cultivation of music in Arabic Spain. When one of the most famous of Arab musicians was summoned from Baghdad to the Sultan's court, Al-Mansur was chosen to prepare his festive reception at the port of Cordova. The next Jewish musician whose name has come down to us is the virtuoso Yizhaq ibn Sim'an; he lived in Cordova in the eleventh century. From that time on the names of important musicians are legion, but special mention is due to Ibrahim ibn al-Fahhâr, an eleventh-century Jewish musician at the court of the Christian King Alfonso VI in Toledo and a special envoy and confidant of the King.

The frequent travels of the musicians who were in a king's or a sultan's service and the fact that some well-educated Jewish slaves also traveled freely in the Spanish realm and abroad offer sufficient explanation of the spread of Islamic culture to many European countries, where a lyrical poetry also sprang into being under the impact of Oriental poems and songs. The Jews once again were trade agents and mediators of civilization in one and carried the Spanish-Oriental culture to remote places on their missions. The knightly singers and musicians derived inspiration from the flowery language and the lyrical-metrical music of their Oriental prototypes; just as the metrical verses of the Arab hymns had helped the Jewish paytanim to enliven the service in the houses of worship and to introduce new elements into the traditional cult, thus there now rose in the Christian countries of Europe a new popular art that was to exert a far-reaching influence on liturgical practice. For the "new art," the aims of which were served by the treatise of Gersonides, the Jewish theoretician mentioned earlier in this chapter, received its main impulse from the popular rhythmical song; it was only as a consequence of its reforms that European art began its soaring flight into sublime heights. It achieved the supreme synthesis between the spiritual and the purely artistic and popular—the synthesis denied to the Jews, who soon had to suffer the destruction of yet another center of their cultural activities.

In order to follow the succession of paytanim down to their last representative in the medieval world we have far transgressed the boundaries of place and time set for this chapter. For in the fifteenth century great changes again occurred in the political power spheres of the East as well as of the West, and the Jews—victims of other nations' political fate from the destruction of the Temple till modern times—were greatly affected by them. In the East Constantinople fell to the Turks in 1453, and in the West the Arabs were finally driven from Spain in 1492 —the year Columbus discovered the New World. The Turkish conquest put an end to the Eastern-Roman or Byzantine Empire once and for all and thus expelled western influence from the lands of the Orient; the expulsion of the Arabs from Spain dispossessed the Orient of its powerful stronghold in the Occident. The Jews were driven from Spain—together with their Arab brethren—and sought havens in the countries of western, central, and southern Europe; their prospering cultural centers were destroyed, and once again they could save only their spiritual possessions. The "Sephardim"—descendants of the Spanish Jews who were able to escape the massacres of Spain—established their communities and continued to cultivate their old traditions in new European centers; large numbers also followed the Arabs back to the Orient and settled in the countries from which their forefathers had once set out with Islam to conquer Europe. In the Turkish Empire Jewish tradition was continued by the Oriental as well as the newly migrated Sephardic communities—a mixture that was to produce characteristic features of its own.

A subject that still awaits scholarly investigation is the musical practice of the Marranos—the Jews that pretended to have been converted to Christianity but had never really embraced it. It has often been stated that the Marranos had no liturgy of their own before the Jewish expulsion from Spain, but a number of manuscripts have recently come to light to show that the secret Spanish Jews had actually developed their own liturgical practice. Eric Werner has made accessible one such manuscript out of a dozen which are known to exist but which have not been published so far; [6] this is a three-part motet for cantus, tenor, and contratenor written about 1450 in northern Spanish notation. The text of this motet contains words in different languages—Hebrew, Spanish, Arabic, and a number of unidentified, probably corrupted words—and this has been taken to show that the text is written in a semisecret code of the Marrano Jews, to camouflage Hebrew liturgical texts before the dreaded Inquisition. The music is composed of three different tunes: the cantus sings the ancient Ashkenazic tune of the preamble of the Kedusha for the High Holidays; the tenor seems to imitate the shofar signals; the contratenor has the tune of the Gregorian hymn "Alma redemptoris mater." The skill of the composer in combining this material is remarkable; if the remaining manuscripts are of a similar character we could well presume a high standard of composition among the Spanish Jewish musicians. Whether the piece was actually written in northern Spain—which might have meant death for the scribe—or belongs to a slightly later

---

[6] See Eric Werner, "The Oldest Sources of Synagogal Chant," *Proceedings of the American Academy for Jewish Research,* Vol. XVI, 1947, pp. 228 ff. See also illustration facing p. 64.

period in a north Italian center (a theory advanced by Rabbi D. A. Jessurun Cardozo [7]) this curious piece represents an early example of an art later developed by the Mantua school of Jewish musicians headed by Leone da Modena and Salomone Rossi; the Marranos doubtless carried with them the tradition of their liturgical practice.

One blow had set an end to a magnificent chapter in Jewish civilization—a chapter that never found a real continuation. The history of the Jewish people and of their culture, art, and music characteristically never continues in one place for more than a certain period of time; but while one flourishing center is cut off and destroyed, another has already risen into importance and developed interesting traits. The history of the music of Israel continues in another Mediterranean country about a century after the expulsion of the Jews from Spain; it is there that Jewish composers created the first art music that became of importance for their own—spiritual—sphere as well as for the general development of musical art. But before turning to the music of the Renaissance in Italy we shall have to survey the state of music in the Jewish settlements of medieval Europe.

[7] See Werner, *op. cit.*

Chapter
FIVE

Medieval Europe:
Music of the Ghetto

IN THE SPANISH CENTER under Islamic rule conditions were most favorable for a prospering Jewish community and culture, as the Jews could take part in the economic and cultural life of the ruling nation. In the central European countries, however, they were completely cut off from such participation. This was not a matter of persecution: the Jews enjoyed freedom of movement and trade—especially in southern France and in Germany—with only temporary violations of their peace through persecution of individuals or communities. Even the Crusades, which resulted periodically in horrible oppression and massacre of the Jews, were over by the end of the thirteenth century, and the Jews were again able to enjoy a life of comparative peace. But the Catholic Church, which had completed the first phase of its cultural development toward the end of the first millennium, was the spiritual center of all Europe in the Middle Ages. As a result the Jews were excluded from all phases of life that centered in the church. They lived together within the sphere of their own community and took no part in the life of the Christians and in their economic, social, political, cultural, and artistic activities, which were all directed by the omnipotent Church of Rome.

The conditions of Jewish life in the central European countries offered no foundations for a cultural development and for the creation of poetry and music such as the Jews were able to contribute in the Spanish sphere. At the same time European musical art reached its first great synthesis. In the eleventh and twelfth centuries France was the great musical center, and the masters of Notre Dame de Paris created musical forms equaling the Gothic architectural design and style in purpose and character. The liturgical chant was enriched by the addition of a second, a third, and a fourth polyphonic voice—invented and constructed with much care by the composer and not improvised on the spur of the moment; the liturgical melodies thus lost their real inner connection with the ancient Hebrew chant. In the fourteenth century there arose a "new music," full of individualistic traits and taking over the emphasis of rhythm from popular art and Oriental dance songs; with this "new music" art emancipated itself from the realm of the Church, but since it became the art of the higher strata of society, it was as inaccessible to the Jews as was the clerical art. In the fifteenth century the musical hegemony passed from Paris to Burgundy and to the Netherlands, where grandiose religious musical works were created by masters who are among the greatest in musical history. Secular music—though cultivated in an always increasing measure by the composers who now stepped out of anonymity and were widely acclaimed—did not as yet achieve complete independence from clerical forms; the final emancipation was reserved to Renaissance Italy. Almost the only representatives of profane singing and playing throughout the history of medieval music remained the—mostly anonymous—successors of the wandering minstrel, troubadour, and minnesinger, whose kinship with the Oriental musicians we have already discussed.

As long as great music could grow only in the realm of the Church or was cultivated by composers who were men of the cloth, the Jews had no place in the development of this art; it seems that the only Jewish personality who stepped into the sphere of nobility met with eventual failure. Characteristically it was a minnesinger who achieved temporary fame outside his own community; his picture can be found in the illuminated manuscript prepared about 1300 and kept in the Heidelberg Library as a most important source for the German minnesong. The picture shows a Jew with a long beard and a broad-brimmed hat, standing beside a nobleman and a clergyman; his name is given as "Süsskind, the Jew of Trimberg." [1] Of the twelve poems attributed to him six have been proved to be genuine; of his life very little is known, and his poems—and this must also be true of his melodies, none of which have come down to us—seem at first sight to differ very little from the songs of other poets of the time. A more thorough study of the poems shows, however, that many of the verses derive from phrases or lines of the Bible or Talmud and that some passages were even taken from Jewish prayers; and this minnesinger sings in praise of the perfect wife, where as the German poet would have sung of a noble lady or of the Virgin Mary.

This Jewish minnesinger seems to have been a solitary exception in the medieval world, but another example of Jewish activity in the non-Jewish sphere might well be mentioned: The

[1] See illustration facing p. 65.

scribe of the larger part of the *Lochheim Song-Book,* which was compiled ca. 1450 and which contains the earliest German secular polyphonic songs, was a Jew—Woelflin von Lochheim. The manuscript of this collection, which is an important source for German musical history, bears a dedication by the Jewish scribe to his Barbara, written in Hebrew characters.[2]

As the Jews were given no chance to partake actively in the literature, art, and music of medieval Europe, they concentrated on developing their own religious and home life. Though not always enclosed by the walls of a ghetto, they lived a life of seclusion within their own communities and disdained all foreign influence on their mode of living and their customs. In periods of persecution especially they always escaped into their own domain: the study of Bible and Talmud, which recalled in their minds the echo of Israel's magnificent past and inspired them with hope for a brighter future. The dilemma between reason and heart—which figured so prominently in the theological discussions on Spanish soil—was before the Jews here as everywhere: it was decided in favor of the heart when in the thirteenth century the cabala was created in southern France and in Germany out of a desire to give free rein to emotional religious experience without the reasoning control of the Talmudic laws. Oriental mysticism and an unbridled emotional expression characterize the world of the cabala, which later became instrumental in forming the thoughts and emotions of the Hassidim and found expression in the prayers, in literature, and in music alike.

The spiritual centers of Jewry during the period just discussed were the settlements in southern France and in southern Germany—provinces where Jewish communities are known to have

2 See illustration facing p. 128.

been in existence in the earliest centuries of the Common Era. In Provence and in the Rhenish cities the Jewish settlements prospered, and with the expulsion of the Jews from England (1290), Spain (1492), and Portugal (1497) a new influx swelled the French and German communities. It is thus that the Ashkenazim (as the western, especially German, Jews had been called since the early Middle Ages—with reference to a passage in Gen. 10:3: "Ashkenaz, son of Gomer") rose to a prominent position with the destruction of the Sephardic center; with the later migration eastward and the resettlement in central Europe, Ashkenazic Jewry amounted to more than 90 per cent of the total number of Jews, and its language—derived from middle high German and spiced with words and phrases from Hebrew —became the universal language of the Diaspora Jews. It is comprehensible that customs and manners as well as the forms of worship, the regulation of life, and the singing of the Ashkenazic Jews in the synagogue and in the home should have become universal in the medieval Jewish world.

Life in the Jewish communities at that time must have been many-colored, for it seemed greatly attractive to the Gentiles. The fact that from the earliest centuries of Jewish settlement in the European countries kings and bishops vied with each other in forbidding the Christians to celebrate the Sabbath together with Jews, to adopt Jewish songs, and to waste time in studying the Hebrew language and writings, certainly suggests that this was exactly what the Christians liked to do. The Jews, on the other hand, prohibited the use of Christian music, which, owing to the highly developed and distinctive forms and styles, threatened to overwhelm synagogal chant. The Jewish authorities in medieval Europe were confronted with the same situation as that which had characterized the Hellenistic period; they had to isolate Jewish communal life in order to preserve the fundamental character of Judaism and thus were forced to prohibit the influx of foreign tunes which could pollute the traditional chant. But the authorities could arrest the course of events as little as their forefathers had been able to do at the time of Greek political and cultural supremacy; the songs of worship and prayer of medieval Europe exerted their influence on Jewish musical custom, and the Jews could not escape the impact of popular song which they heard everywhere in the streets. Many folk songs of Provence and of German origin crept into the synagogue, but there they gradually lost their popular character and were adapted and transformed to suit the spirit of the occasion.

But the influx of folk music into the synagogue song—paralleled by an increasing influence of popular song on the church service—is only one aspect of music in the Ashkenazic sphere; the Ashkenazic song developed other traits that gave it a specific character of its own and distinguished it from music in the Sephardic and Oriental spheres. European music had in the meantime departed from the practice of absolute polyphony based on the ancient ecclesiastic scales, drawing nearer to the modern conception of harmony. The changes in the character of European music were mirrored, of course, in the development of the synagogue chant; the traditional chant preserved by the Jews from Oriental times gradually adapted its melodic lines under the impact of European song and, much later, also introduced polyphony and harmony. Another peculiarity of the Ashkenazic song was the custom of rabbis and hazanim to choose for each holy day in the Jewish year specific tunes believed to be especially suited to the occasion in mood and character; thus one and the same prayer was sung to different melodies in accordance with the day on which it was chanted. This custom has been preserved to this very day, though the tunes chosen are different in the various Ashkenazic communities.

The influence of Gentile music on Jewish singing was felt in the house as much as in the synagogue, all the more since no basic difference existed between synagogue and popular song. The synagogue was both house of worship and community center; and just as popular tunes were adapted for the synagogue service, so the most popular hymns were sung in the Jewish homes and on the occasion of feasts and celebrations. It goes without saying that the German folk song entered the Jewish sphere by way of the home and only from there found its way into the synagogue.

The more the Jews had to suffer under oppression and restriction, the more they were wont to cultivate their own spiritual possessions and the less they could be expected to have inspiration for creative efforts. Not even the hazan, whose importance in office could have led him to raise the standard of singing and composing, was given leisure to develop creative talents; for the dwindling of a community here and the rise of another there, the expulsion of Jews from one place and the establishment of new centers elsewhere made the hazan lead an unsettled life. He often changed his place of employment, and in order to be able to compete with singers who wanted to serve the more prosperous communities he concentrated on the artistic, virtuoso qualities of his singing rather than on the musical and creative side. Brilliant coloratura and great emphasis on the emotional attributes of prayer were his main concern, and the traditional chant suffered no little from his exhibitory and ill-suited performance; his mannerisms became worse still with the triumphant rise of Italian opera in the seventeenth century.

The music of the Ashkenazic communities was adopted by the Jewry of the greater part of Europe when the persecution of the Jews in Germany necessitated a new migration. The Ashkenazic Jews found in the countries of eastern Europe a Jewish community that differed greatly from their own in many respects. The early settlements of the East had considerably grown in the medieval epoch, when the Turkish Empire had received large numbers of Jews expelled from southern European countries; the Osmanic rule permitted them to prosper in Asia Minor as well as in eastern Europe. In the latter province the communities were largely made up of Oriental Jews; these communities grew to such an extent that as early as the thirteenth century the Poles granted them privilege and independent administrative facilities. Eastern Jewry was so strictly organized that it had very little contact with the outside world, and the influence of eastern European life on the Jews was therefore negligible. But the influx of the Ashkenazic Jews which set in during the fourteenth century brought about considerable changes in the life of the eastern communities, which suddenly met with a Europeanized Jewish culture superior to theirs; the Slavonic dialects spoken by the eastern Jews gave way to the German-Jewish language, and the Oriental character of the synagogue service and of the melodies used for its prayers was greatly modified under the impact of Ashkenazic custom and song.

But the meeting of western and eastern Jewry by no means produced a one-sided picture only. The Ashkenazic rite and song changed, too, and the art of the hazan especially was influenced by Oriental custom. The freely improvised melodic elaboration of the liturgical chant and a highly emotional style of singing characterized the Oriental as well as the Ashkenazic practice, but the eastern communities had retained the modal style and free recitation to a larger extent than the Ashkenazic precentors, whose song had taken over so much from German popular music. The eastern hazan had also preserved the many-sidedness of his office since the earliest times of the hazanut and particularly

since the period of the paytanim; he was the main bearer of
the musical tradition and enriched the spiritual life of his congregation by his own hymns, poems, and musical settings. The
mutual influence exerted by the western and eastern hazanim
and their music led to extensive debates in rabbinical literature,
a study of which is most rewarding but transgresses the purpose
of our survey; the Biblical passages on music and the Talmudic
comments were subjected to a new interpretation in the light
of contemporary practice, and the merits of important or famous
poets and hazanim were discussed in great detail. Where the
art of the Ashkenazic hazanim had developed great virtuosity
for its own sake, the character of eastern synagogue music had
retained one important and fundamental feature of ancient Hebrew music: the shaping of the music and its performance in
agreement with the content of the words sung. In order to give
vent to their emotions, the eastern rabbis and hazanim revived
a good many poems and hymns from the golden age of Hebrew
poetry and song—many of which were unknown in the western
sphere—while most German singers had been particularly concerned with variety in the brilliant musical interpretation of a
popular hymn they especially favored. The synagogue of later
times shows a synthesis of the diverging elements which was
arrived at before the remigration of large numbers of Ashkenazic
Jews into the western European countries.

We must close our survey of Jewish music in medieval Europe by a short account of popular music in the ghetto, in which
Jewish life was concentrated down to the age of assimilation in
the eighteenth century. The Purim feast and the wedding were,
just as they had been since time immemorial, the main occasions for general rejoicing and for extensive musical perform-

ances, but in some districts the rabbis enforced the Talmudic prohibition of instrumental playing with such rigor that Christian musicians had to be employed to provide the music at the Jewish festivals. On the Sabbath, too, non-Jews came to play in the ghetto, but it was forbidden to invite them expressly to perform. Many centuries passed before the Jews began to take up instrumental playing themselves: in the sixteenth and seventeenth centuries there were founded Jewish music-guilds, the existence of which is reliably proved in Frankfurt on the Main and in Prague.

The Jewish musicians were originally called "lezim" or "lezanim," a term found in the Talmud with reference to secular music ("the fiddle played by the lezim"): later they were also described as "badchanim," and this word is still used by eastern European Jews in the same sense. The repertoire of these popular musicians consisted of Judeo-Spanish, Judeo-Provençal, and Judeo-German melodies; their character as wandering minstrels—and the very word used to describe them (meaning jesters)—reminds us of the singing instrumentalists, the minstrels and jugglers of the earlier Middle Ages in Europe. The rabbis had no friendly word for them, but it cannot be denied that they played their own modest part in the preservation of Jewish tradition and created a typical Jewish folklore.

Though originally Jewish popular music had been derived from the folklore of the people among whom the Jews had been living, it was nevertheless considered strangely different by the Gentiles; this proves that the Jewish musicians changed the original melodies considerably in order to make them suit Jewish taste. As the lezim or badchanim played their music not only at the Jewish festivals but also at popular celebrations outside the ghetto, we find notices about it in different sources; in addition there have come down to us the descriptions and actual melodies of "Jews' Dances," in which non-Jews tried to imitate the manners and forms of Jewish dancing or to caricature the Jewish melodies that sounded so strange to Gentile ears. The "Jews' Dances," preserved in manuscripts in France, Germany, and elsewhere, are the first examples in a long series of musical parodies by non-Jews, such as are later found in an Augsburg song book of the eighteenth century, in the piece "Samuel Goldenberg and Schmuyle" contained in Mussorgsky's *Pictures at an Exhibition,* in Richard Strauss's opera *Salome,* and in other great musical works.

Our survey of Jewish music in the countries of western and eastern Europe outlines a development of many centuries and brings our story down to the seventeenth and eighteenth centuries—the period in which the "Jewish Middle Ages" came to an end, more than two hundred years after the European peoples had overcome medieval life and thought. The beginning of a new time for Europe was marked in the fifteenth century by liberation from the rigid rule of clerical authority—the foundation for a free development of science and art—while the discovery of new continents enlarged the outlook of trade and intercourse with the world; in that period the Jews had nothing but their spiritual mission and their religious life to seek refuge in while being chased from one domicile to another. Only in the course of the eighteenth century did conditions in Europe favor emancipation of the Jews and development of their spiritual and artistic qualities; but then it appeared that a specific Jewish culture could not grow without a national or spiritual center to guide them, as the creations of great Jews became possessions of the entire civilized world.

The Hassidic movement, taking its spiritual roots from the

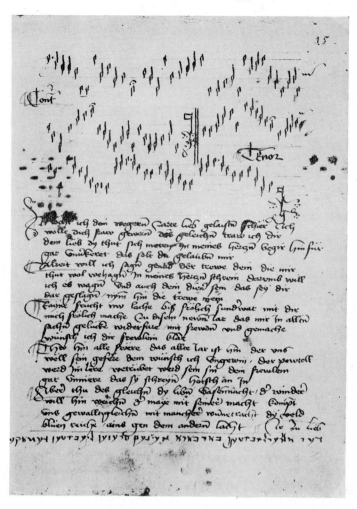

A page from the Lochheim Songbook, written by Wölflin von Lochheim ca. 1450, with the dedication in Hebrew characters in the last line.

The Gonzaga Castle at Mantua, where Salomone Rossi was in charge of the music.
(*Musical Courier*)

mystic and sensuous world of the cabala, is the last creation of the Jewish Middle Ages; many of the "Zadikkim," the successors of its original founder, Israel Baal-Shem-Tov, granted singing and music a prominent place at their "courts." The depth of emotion and the pronounced sentimentality characterizing the Hassidic world are mirrored in the song of the Hassidim; not only the folk song but also the hazan's prayer tunes were greatly influenced by these elements, and their seemingly exotic coloring inspired many a Jewish and non-Jewish composer to serious musical works.

The Hassidim prospered at a time when western Jewry had just begun to seek entrance into the general culture of the period and to put an end to the secluded life the Jews had for so long been forced to lead. The period of enlightenment and reason that dawned upon the western world favored Jewish emancipation to a degree the Jews had not before experienced—or had experienced only for a short stretch of time in seventeenth-century Italy, a period that forms an important chapter in the history of general music as well as in that of the music of Israel.

Chapter
SIX

Jewish Musicians in
Seventeenth-Century Italy

THE CONDITIONS OF JEWISH LIFE in the Middle Ages sufficiently explain why the Jews had not been able to take part in the cultural activities of the people with whom they lived, and why they do not figure in the history of medieval music. The music of medieval Europe was firmly rooted in the religious sphere, in the creed and belief uniting all Christian people and nations. The purpose, language, and style of the great religious music—composed on Latin liturgical and non-liturgical texts by all the masters—spread beyond the boundaries of states and nations, and it was understood by the entire Christian world.

While the great church music of the Middle Ages rose to the sublimest heights of perfection in the works of the Flemish masters—followed, in the Renaissance, by the Latin and Germanic nations—secular music only slowly developed a style of its own. The art of the troubadour, of the minstrels, and of the minnesingers—who, as we have seen, derived their popular style from Oriental models—served as a basis for the different forms of song and dance that gained prominence toward the end of the Middle Ages. The people began to demand their due, and with a general rise in the standard of education and knowledge they took possession of the art forms as well. Highly skilled performers—"composers" in the original sense of the word—were able to elaborate dance tunes in the style of church polyphony and to accompany a melodious song.

Music became popular both with the nobility and with the masses: minstrels performed gay music at all festivities, and the feasts resounded with their playing. Foreign visitors to a town were greeted at the gates and accompanied into the town by musicians, and tournaments and chases as well as performances of plays were other occasions for the sounding of instrumental music. Instruction in music and dancing gradually became part of the general education of a nobleman, and the music cultivated in earlier days by roaming minstrels only was raised to a higher level. The musical instruments—most of which had been introduced by Oriental musicians—were perfected, and new instruments were designed to fill the needs of the players. The secular art lagged behind church music in passing the stage of mere improvisation and molding its forms and style of performance, and till well into the baroque era there was no distinction between vocal and instrumental music; all pieces could be sung or played, or sung and played by a variety of (unspecified) instruments at will.

The slow rise of secular music can be witnessed almost simultaneously in various countries, but the first creation of truly independent instrumental forms and original types of secular songs must be ascribed to Renaissance Italy. Italy had not taken part in the great development of polyphonic music that had flourished in France and the Netherlands; it had only enjoyed its last fruits and supreme synthesis in the works of Palestrina. The Roman Church had not favored the musical embellishment of the service to the same extent as the northwestern European centers; on the other hand, there had developed in Italy much earlier than in other countries a highly colored social life: the country's position in trade and commerce had led to a great economic and social prosperity of the towns, and it is urban life that leads to the organization of musical activities and the growth of specific forms of musical expression. Italy was the country of a nature-loving society enjoying common singing, playing, and dancing; many Italian pictures represented musical scenes, and the stories of the Renaissance—particularly its most characteristic book, Boccaccio's *Decameron*—as well as its poems prove how greatly Italian society craved music and the dance. Secular choral singing reached its greatest heights in the madrigals of the sixteenth and seventeenth centuries—songs for mixed voices composed on lyrical poems and in colorful polyphony—while the perfection of the stringed instruments and of the keyboard instruments for continuo purposes stimulated (about 1600) the development of a new type of social instrumental music: chamber music.

Italian society was first in diminishing the domination of the Church, for it enjoyed art as such and acknowledged no spiritual or stylistic bonds with the clerical sphere. Singing and chamber music were cultivated for the sake of social and artistic pleasure only, and no view of a higher spiritual purpose guided their forms. The Church soon could not afford to deny the worshipers the pleasures they so greatly looked for at the court, the theater, and social festivities; without magnificent choral singing and instrumental music the churches would soon have become empty. So in the church, too, music gradually ceased to be a servant to a higher purpose only but took on an aspect of artistic embellishment and attraction; it was no longer the privileged possession of pious communities but became an art practiced by skilled individual musicians for the sake of society. Individual expression and magnificent coloring had come to characterize music as much as the paintings of the Italian masters. The strict polyphonic style—symbolizing the spirit of community and unity of purpose—gave way to a style in which one individual melody dominated the vocal or instrumental voices of an entire piece; and the performing virtuoso wanted to attract the attention and gain the applause of society as much as the original creator of the music—composer and performer being in most cases united in one person in the sphere of instrumental music. With this development the clear distinction between clerical and secular art—the revolutionary innovation of this period—was established once and for all.

The historical and sociological development of music in Italy enabled the Jews to contribute for the first time to European musical art; though several Jewish communities in Italy were in ghettos where living conditions were dreadful, the spiritual position of the Jews was raised by the fact that they represented a valuable heritage of the ancient world which the Renaissance tried so hard to revive in all spheres of philosophy and art. Italy had had much contact with the Orient throughout the centuries; Emperor Frederick II (1194–1252), who had crowned himself Emperor in Jerusalem, drew to his pompous court of Palermo a great number of Arabic and Jewish scholars and attempted in Italy an imitation of Oriental court life and art. Oriental studies were pursued at the Italian academies throughout the Middle Ages, and the growing commerce of the Italian cities greatly fa-

vored relations with the Oriental world. The Oriental and classical spirit gave Renaissance style its specific stamp, and the Jewish world—particularly that of the mystic cabala—proved an
especially attractive part of the Orient. Life in fifteenth-century
Italy, with its emphasis on the social instead of on the spiritual
elements, stimulated the Jews, too; and in the works of Leone
Ebreo, son of Don Isaac ben Yuda (Abravanel) of Portugal,
a Jew succeeded in blending Oriental-Jewish thought and
Renaissance spirit.

Jewish history in medieval and Renaissance Italy is as much
a story of the rise and fall of communities and of tolerance and
persecution in turn as that of other European centers; but the
spirit of the times favored in Italy—in stark contrast to central
Europe—the cultural development of the Jews. With the migration to Italy of Sephardic Jews expelled from Spain and Portugal and of Ashkenazic elements from northern European countries and with the steady influx of Oriental Jewish traders, the
Jewish communities in Italy soon became the most universal
of all Jewish centers. This made itself felt in music as much as
in other spheres: it is known that just as singers from all civilized
countries came to Italy to perfect their technique and instrumentalists sought the instruction of the great Italian virtuosos,
so hazanim were sent to Italy to study the art of song in the synagogues. The most famous of these were Abraham Sagri and
Jacob Finzi, Ashkenazic singers and probably composers at
Casale Monferrato in the last quarter of the sixteenth century.

The first field in which Jews excelled outside their own community and partook in the cultural activities of the Renaissance
period was the dance, and it seems that in this sphere the Jews
could boast of a long tradition. The name has been preserved
of one famous Jewish dancing master active in Spain in the
fourteenth century, Rabbi Hacén ben Salomo, who was called

to teach Christians a dance in a Spanish church in the year 1313. In Renaissance Italy Jews were famous for their art of dancing, and in 1575 a special license was granted by the Pope to two Jews from Ancona for the teaching of dancing and singing. At the same time the Jews Ambrosio and Guglielmo Ebreo—said by contemporaries to have danced "above all human measure" —taught dancing at the court of Urbino, and Guglielmo's disciple Giuseppe continued in his master's tradition.[1] It is interesting to note that the Jewish dancing masters were instrumental in gaining an honored place in society for professional dancing in general; dancers had stood in low regard in the Middle Ages, but in Renaissance Italy they could become confidants of dukes and princes. On the other hand, the high perfection reached by the Jews in the art of the dance—and at the same time in music —also improved their own position with the secular and clerical authorities.

In the second half of the sixteenth century a considerable number of Jewish musicians distinguished themselves at the Italian courts, the Papal Court included. Venice and Mantua, however, were the places of their outstanding activities—the former the state with the most developed Oriental connections and thus dependent in some degree on Jewish good will, the latter ruled by dukes who did not prove much love for their Jews in general but who were great patrons of all artistic activities.

The court of the Gonzagas at Mantua was served by many especially privileged Jewish musicians. There have come down to us the names of the harpists Abramo dall' Arpa Ebreo and his nephew (or grandson?) Abramino, of the composers Davit da Civita and Allegro Porto (whose name "Allegro" is said to have

---

[1] Eduard Birnbaum, *Jüdische Musiker am Hofe von Mantua von 1542–1628.*

been the translation of his Hebrew name *Simcha* = "gaiety"), and the lutenist, singer, dancer, and ballet-master Isacchino Massarano. These musicians belonged to the court band, which was organized and led by one of the greatest violinists and composers of early instrumental history, Salomone Rossi.[2] It is possible that the entire band consisted of Jewish musicians, as a letter written to the court and preserved in the archives contained a request that "Solomon the Hebrew be sent together with his party" to entertain at the festivities of another court: a parallel is offered by the dramatic society led by the Jew Leone de Sommi Portaleone, who himself was a playwright and also wrote the *Dialoghi sull' Arte Rappresentativa*—the first extant work on the art of the stage. Rossi's own sister was a stage singer famous in the world of early opera; she was commonly called "Madama Europa" and is known to have taken part in the first performance—staged at Mantua in 1608—of the opera *Arianna*, the work of the first great master of opera, Claudio Monteverdi. Monteverdi himself was attached to the Mantuan court from 1590 to 1612 and must have been in constant contact with Salomone Rossi and his musicians; his *Arianna* was actually performed on the occasion of the wedding festivities at the court, in which Rossi was also represented by a composition: one of the intermezzi for the drama *L'Idropica* was from his pen.

Salomone Rossi, who always added "Ebreo" to his name, stemmed from an illustrious family which claimed to have come to Rome with the earliest settlers after the destruction of Jerusalem as captives of Emperor Titus. The name of Asarja dei Rossi (died in Mantua in 1578) had become famous through his religious philosophy, which united elements of Jewish-Hellenistic thought and Talmudic-rabbinical tradition. But Salomone Rossi, his descendant, who was probably born in the early 1570's, be-

---

[2] Rossi dedicated one of his ballets for orchestra to Massarano.

came as well known as the learned and much-disputed rabbi; his instruction in violin playing and the services of his orchestra were much sought after, his printed works bear dedications to some of the most prominent noblemen of the time, and the various editions of his madrigals and instrumental music reached the courts of all European countries (where down to our days they may be found in the libraries). The King of Portugal's library, which was unfortunately burned in 1755, contained the entire works of the composer, as is confirmed by the extant catalogue.

We know little of Rossi's life, but his activities at the Mantuan court from about 1589 to 1628 are established by the works published in this period. He was highly esteemed by the Gonzagas and by the court nobility, and in 1606 he got permission to walk about without the yellow badge prescribed for the Jews—an exception only rarely made from the rule established by the Lateran Council in 1215 (originally the yellow badge had been introduced by a Moslem ruler for "unbelievers" of all creeds), but which Rossi shared with the actor and dramatist Leone de Sommi.

In general music history Rossi has his place as a composer who was among the first to apply to instrumental music the principles of monodic song (in which one dominant melody is accompanied by secondary, accompanying parts—in contrast to the polyphonic style, in which all melodic parts are equal in importance); the monodic style had so far been cultivated mainly in opera. Just as in opera the monodic aria served virtuoso singers as a vehicle for an exhibition of their vocal brilliancy (Monteverdi was then almost alone in endowing the aria with a profoundly emotional content), so in instrumental music there developed a virtuoso art for entertaining the society present at court or in the theater. The novel monodic and virtuoso instrumental music of the late sixteenth and early seventeenth centuries marked the first steps in the evolution of musical forms designed to attract an audience; only in the second half of the eighteenth century—that is, with the rise of the public concert and the symphonic form created for its sake—did the seventeenth-century reforms attain their goal. In Mantua there also rose, under Salomone Rossi's leadership, the first great school of violinists; this marked the beginning of a magnificent line of instrumentalists who spread Italy's fame throughout the seventeenth- and eighteenth-century world.

In his madrigals and in his instrumental chamber music Rossi shows a specific melodic talent, characteristic of many Jewish composers. Harmony, the typical Occidental musical feature, held no attraction for him; this makes his music strikingly different from that of his great contemporaries, who made dramatic use of bold and colorful harmonic combinations. Rossi is among the very first composers to develop the form and technique of variation; he has written variations on Italian popular melodies, many of which were later sung in the synagogues, and he seems also to have used for his variations tunes that were already popular in the synagogue or the ghetto.

In the field of the synagogue Rossi was the first composer to attempt complete reforms in the style of traditional liturgical music. His collection of religious songs which appeared in Venice in 1622, printed by Pietro and Lorenzo Bragadini, under the title *Ha-Shirim Asher Li'Shlomo* (in allusion to the Biblical Song of Solomon) contains thirty-three musical versions of the ancient liturgical texts; the music is conceived in the style of the madrigal period, apparently without the composer's ever using ancient Hebrew motives of chants. Rossi had undertaken the composition of the psalms and prayers "to glorify and embellish the songs of King David according to the rules of musical art" (as stated in his Hebrew dedication), and they were set for three, four, five, six, seven, and eight voices, for chorus and solos. The music was printed—the parts only—in the customary way; but the texts were added below in the Hebrew characters running from right to left in complete lines (not as Hebrew songs are printed today: with one Hebrew syllable printed below the note to which it is to be sung). Rossi's synagogal songs contain veritable gems of choral music, but they preserved next to nothing of the original character of synagogue music; the Italian composer's reform thus meant the first step in the process of assimilation which Hebrew religious music underwent in the European countries—with Sulzer, Lewandowsky, Naumbourg, and others completing this musical assimilation in the nineteenth century.

There was a strong—and natural—opposition on the part of the rabbis to such musical reforms, which endangered the preservation of the ancient tradition, and Rossi had a difficult stand against the rabbinical authorities. His compositions were regarded as a precedent, but though they were indeed the first to appear in print, he had had a forerunner in his attempts to introduce new elements into the synagogue service. In 1605 one of the most versatile Jewish scholars of the Italian Renaissance, Yehuda Arieh (called Leone) da Modena, a skilled musician and singer himself, had conducted a choir of six to eight voices in the Ferrara synagogue and led them "according to the relation of voices to each other, based on that science," which means in the harmonic style of the period. The innovation had met with strong opposition but was upheld after the rabbinical assembly had expressed its approval. This progressive scholar and musician, the outstanding figure in Renaissance Judaism, now stepped to the defense of Salomone Rossi against the antagonistic authorities and introduced the printed edition of the com-

poser's songs with a lengthy foreword. This is a most characteristic document: it is spiced with quotations from the Bible (especially from the Psalms and the books of the Prophets) and the
Talmud and abounds in skilled and learned puns, and the ad-
monitions addressed to the opponents of reform in synagogue
song throw a most interesting light on the debates of the time.
As no accurate modern translation of this foreword is available,
we here present a new version—with only minor omissions of
passages that have no direct bearing on our subject: [3]

Yehuda Arieh of Modena, the eldest son of Rabbi Isaac,
addressing all ears that can understand the truth.

"The lip of truth shall be established for ever" [4]—the
poet is right when he lets music speak to the non-Jews: [5]
"Indeed I was stolen away out of the land of the Hebrews." [6] For the scholars have grown like grass and have
spread all sciences of Israel and have mounted up to great
heights like eagles with wings, and all peoples have admired and feared them. Like other sciences, music was also
adopted from the Hebrews by other people. Who could
forget King David, who taught music to the sons of Asaph,

[3] The French version contained in Naumbourg's modern edition of Rossi's
music (Paris, 1877) and the German translation given by Paul Nettl in "Alte
Jüdische Spielleute und Musiker" (Prague, 1923) and reproduced several times
later are highly inaccurate; our interpretation is based on the thorough study
made of the original by Mr. Ephraim Trochae and contained in the Hebrew
book on the music of Israel published by this author in 1945 (pp. 79–86). The
text abounds in Biblical quotations and allusions, and the author makes frequent
use of Hebrew word-plays and puns; we have used Biblical phrases in most cases
in which the original did so, but it is not always possible to reproduce the original style, especially where the author plays with Hebrew words and their different meanings. We have annotated only such passages as demand an explanation; interpretative additions of our own are marked in the text by brackets.
[4] Prov. 12:19.
[5] The poet: Emanuel ha-Romi Manuello, the Italian-Hebrew poet, a friend
of Dante.
[6] Gen. 40:15.

Heiman, and Yeduthun—as is told in the Chronicles—and
made them understand singing and the playing of instruments, and who sang and played as long as the House of
the Lord stood in its place, the first and second [Temple],
and preserved its tradition ever after. But our dwelling
in foreign lands, our dispersion all over the world, and our
troubles and persecution have made them [the people of
Israel] forget all knowledge and lose all understanding.
The wrath of God was kindled against the people, and he
fenced them and gathered them out and cast them into a
pit empty of all knowing.[7] And when they lived in lands
that did not belong to them, the wisdom of their wise men
perished, and they had later to borrow what had been left
of it with their neighbors. Let us praise the name of the
Lord, for Solomon alone is excellent [8] in this science in our
days and wiser than any man, not only of our own people:
for they liken and equal him to many famous men of the
earth, because of which he was taken into the service of
the Dukes of Mantua, having served the late Duke and
now being with the present Duke. May he rise and prosper
in his majesty, Amen. May his music printed in foreign
language [9] meet with just appreciation, as it was liked
by non-Jews—and they hanged their lyres upon the willows
in the midst thereof and said: The Lord openeth the eyes
of the blind.[10]

[7] Passages from Isa. 5:2, and Gen. 37:24.

[8] This is an adaptation of verse 13 from Psalm 148, in which the word *shmo*
= "his name" has been changed to *shlomo* = Solomon; the wisdom of the composer is, of course, likened to that of his Biblical namesake, King Solomon.

[9] This can mean the Italian songs—set in a language foreign to the Jews—or
the Hebrew synagogal songs proper—composed in a language foreign to the
Duke, Rossi's patron.

[10] The scholar may have intended a pun here, as the Hebrew word for "the
blind," *iw'rim*, has the same pronunciation—though a different spelling—as the
word for "the Hebrews."

Frontispiece from Salomone Rossi's song collection, *Ha-Shirim Asher Li'Schlomo*, Venice, 1622.

A page of music from the Salomone Rossi songbook.

His power is unto his God, and he actively served the profane and the sacred to honor the Lord with all his talent. He tried to perfect the work that had made him famous in spite of the opposition of his brethren and constantly added psalms, prayers, hymns, and songs of praise till he could collect them in one volume. And as the people sang them and were pleased by their excellence and the listeners shone—and whosoever ear was delighted by them desired to hear more—he was urged by the nobles of the community, and first among them that generous and noble rabbi Moses Sullam (May God guard him from above!), to have them printed, so as to give him a name lasting longer than children (for he begins and will not be surpassed, and such music has not existed in Israel) and for the good of his friends, so that they may sing it and that the rabbis may embellish the service and feasts. I, who have been one of his admirers from the beginning, have also very greatly urged and requested him, till at last, thanks to the Almighty, he came to bring forth and agreed to the printing as he had promised. . . . And he asked me to watch that nothing untoward should happen to his composition, to prepare it for printing, and to read the proofs carefully. And though my lyre has turned to mourning and I am sad about the heart of the fallen—my beloved son Zebulun, aged twenty-one, musically gifted, endowed with a sweet voice and a comely countenance, was murdered six months ago . . .—I did not want to refrain from fulfilling the demand, and I thought the Lord would reward me by having mercy in his soul and it would be brightness and joy to all Jews. And so I stand here to watch the work done and say that it is not easy as it has never been done before—and so I must be forgiven for errors. The reader will see that the author preferred that the words be read backward [This means that the Hebrew words follow each other from right to left.] contrary to our Hebrew custom . . . to changing the music notation.[11] He also omitted the writing of the vowel signs, for our expert singers know the texts by heart and read correctly without the signs—which is to their great honor.

And now, my brethren, you are blessed, because we were able to start, the great man [the composer] having taken his pen and the songs of praise having been written and engraved. Praise the Lord with these songs in His house of worship on the holy days! Teach them to your children to instruct them in the science of music, and the teacher to the pupil—as is said of the Levites—for I am sure that from the day of their publication the students of music in Israel will grow in number to praise our Lord with these and similar songs.

There will certainly be found among us some people who fight against all that is new and against all knowledge— which is beyond their understanding—and will unreasonably ban them; and so I have thought fit to refer to the answer I wrote with regard to this question eighteen years ago, when I was rabbi of the community at Ferrara, in order to silence a confused antagonist, and all great contemporary scholars of Venice agreed with me.[12] . . . Many who have so far shunned the science [of music], even though they desired to sing and play, should learn and perform it—till the Lord has mercy on us and builds again

[11] Hebrew script is read from right to left, but in setting Hebrew words to music, the syllables are usually printed below the note (or notes) to which they belong, and thus run from left to right with the music.

[12] The response is actually added to the Preface of Leone da Modena—see below.

His holy House and commands the Levites and their families and classes to perform their music at their times, and all singing in the House of the Lord and in all Israel will be happy and joyous again—not like to-day, when each of us sings with a heavy heart and in anguish of spirit and heavy bondage for the pain of our dispersion, and while he sings his heart is sick: for then there will be no song in Israel without joy; they will have their silver and gold with them, their fields and vineyards, and their God shall be their everlasting light, and they will lift up their voices together: for they shall see eye to eye when the Lord shall bring Zion again quickly. Amen.

Leone da Modena's preface to the printed edition of Rossi's songs is followed by his reprint of the answer given in the rabbinical dispute at Ferrara and alluded to in the foreword. The learned scholar seeks to prove in this "judgment" (as he himself calls it) that both the Bible and the Talmud permit singing and the use of musical instruments in the house of worship provided it is *in accordance with the custom of the times.* Five Venetian authorities signed his declaration.

Salomone Rossi dedicated his sacred songs to Moses Sullam, a member of one of the most esteemed Jewish families in Renaissance Italy and a prominent and wealthy citizen of Mantua; his parents had already supported Rossi in his youth, and he himself was an ardent patron of the arts; his daughter-in-law, who lived in Venice, was the poetess Sarah Copia-Sullam, who is said also to have been musically gifted. It is of interest to quote some passages from Rossi's dedication to Sullam; it is written in the same style as Leone da Modena's preface and similarly abounds in quotations from Biblical and Talmudic passages and allusions to traditional phrases:

For a long time now the Lord has endowed me with a talent for music and for the science of singing . . . and this inspired me to praise the Lord with my song as best as I could. And God helped me and put new songs in my mouth, which I had composed according to the laws of art for the occasions of joy and the holy days. . . . I always attempted to glorify and embellish the psalms of David King of Israel according to the rules of musical art so that they might be more pleasant to the ear. And after the Lord had permitted me to finish my work, I saw that it would be worth letting the people enjoy it by printing a selection of my songs; and I did this not for my own sake but in honor of my Father in Heaven Who has given me this life and Whom I shall always praise. . . . And as I thought in my heart: to which noble man could I dedicate this token of thanks? I saw I could offer it to no better than to you, esteemed and great man in Israel; for the entire community knows your merits and virtues. . . . And thus I felt it my duty to dedicate my songs to you. And more: for you have often supported me and I have endeavored to create my songs and to return to you what you have given to me . . .[13]

The dedication is dated:

Mantua, Rosh-Hodesh Heshwan 5383 [Winter, 1622]

and signed:

Shlomo Mi-ha-Adumin the Younger [Rossi, like other members of his family, used to translate his Italian name into Hebrew].[14]

[13] The passages left out by us are either further praise of the Lord or an enumeration of all the virtues of the dedicatee, about whom we have spoken above.

[14] I can offer no explanation for the fact that the composer describes himself as "the Younger," for though this must certainly mean that his father was well

But with Rossi's dedicatory preface we do not reach the end of the forewords preceding the music of the songs; the printed edition contains yet another document of great historical interest: a notice signed by four rabbis, Leone da Modena among them, in which the reprint or sale of an "unauthorized version" of Rossi's music is prohibited in the strongest possible terms; this is of particular importance because an *author's* right in his creations is commonly supposed to have been recognized for the first time in the Statute of Anne (Queen of England) in 1710, though copyright provisions for *printers* had been confirmed in Venice in 1491. The notice contained in Rossi's collection of songs—though a quite indisputable interpretation seems impossible—doubtless concerned the rights of the author, and they are reserved in forcible language indeed: [15]

> We are [herewith] complying with the justified request of the Right Honorable Salomone Rossi of Mantua, may God bless him, who has labored much and was the first ever to print Hebrew music.[16] He has [however] issued a deficient [17] edition, and he ought not to come to harm by anybody's [? re-] printing them [i.e. copies of this edition] or by their being purchased from any [other?] person. Therefore, having been granted permission from the dis-

known to his patron and readers, we know of no musician that could be meant. But would the epithet make sense otherwise? The only Rossis known that may have been relatives of our composer are: Matteo Rossi, who appears in a pay list of the Mantua Court in 1621 as a bassist; Anselmo Rossi, a composer who printed a three-part motet in Mantua in 1618; and the writer Bastiano de Rossi.

[15] This translation and its interpretation are also based on the studies of Mr. Ephraim Trochae, contained on pp. 91 and 92 of the above-mentioned book. Additions and explanations are again added in brackets.

[16] This is the first instance known of the term "Hebrew music" being used in a Hebrew document.

[17] The meaning of the Hebrew word used here (*bilti-m'suderet*) is dubious. Literally it means "not in order." This may be interpreted as "containing errors" (on the part of the composer or the printer), as "incorrect," or as "not arranged" with regard to the printer's or author's rights.

tinguished Court authorities, we, the signatories to this
document, herewith issue a strict prohibition, by the decree
of the watchers and the word of the Holy Ones, and by
the bite of the serpent,[18] that no Jew, wherever he may be,
may print under any circumstances within fifteen years
from this day the above-mentioned work, the music, or
part thereof, without the consent of its author or his heirs,
nor may any Jew, according to this decree, buy from any
person, whether Jewish or not, copies of any of these compositions, without the composer's having authorized their
sale by a special mark on them. And every son of Israel
shall hear [the words of this edict] and take care not to
be entangled in the net of this curse—and the obedient
shall dwell in peace and abide under the shadow of the
Almighty.[19]

With the blessing of Amen,

> Izhaq Gershon
> Moses Cohen Port
> Yehuda Arieh of Modena
> Simha Luzzato
> Venice, Heshwan 5383 [Winter, 1622].

The edition of *Ha-Shirim Asher Li'Shlomo* has come down
to us in a small number of the printed parts only, and no variants
have been discovered so far in the copies extant. It seems that
the "deficient" version has not been preserved in manuscript or
print, to the satisfaction of the signatories and the composer

---

[18] The words here used for the ban or curse are condensed from passages from
Dan. 4:17: "By the decrees of the watchers, and the demand by the word of
the Holy Ones" (according to rabbinical interpretation, "watchers"—literally
"angels" or "guardians"—and "Holy Ones" stand for "Jewish scholars") and
from Eccles. 10:8: "And whoso breaketh an hedge, a serpent shall bite him."
The condensed phrase became the official formula for decrees of this kind.

[19] The concluding formula is taken from Psalm 91:1.

in whose favor the rabbis issued their decree, but to the utter dissatisfaction of the modern scholar, who would certainly be glad to know what kind of "deficiency" was deplored by one of the foremost masters of the early Italian Baroque and by one of the outstanding Jewish composers of all time.

In 1630 the last of the Gonzagas died, and his town, Mantua, was stormed by Austrian troops. The Jewish population, which since 1610 had been enclosed in a ghetto, were called upon with all other citizens to man the fortifications and to build new walls; not even on the Sabbath were they permitted to rest. The Jewish inhabitants fought in the actual battle, but the city could not withstand the armed hordes and fell after a seven months' siege. The ghetto was ravaged, and some 1,800 Jews fled the town; Emperor Ferdinand, approached by a Jewish delegation at Regensburg, ordered the Governor of Mantua to permit the resettlement of the banished Jews and to return to them their homes and possessions; but migration and death had decimated their number, and only a few came back to the devastated city. No trace is found of Salomone Rossi and his musicians after that catastrophe, and the short but magnificent intermezzo in the story of the music of Israel thus came to a sudden and tragic end.

Rossi's music, too, was destined to temporary oblivion. As an instrumental composer he suffered the fate of many pioneers: the splendid works of a long line of ingenious successors made him seem a mere forerunner of greater masters to come. His first *Sonata a Tre*, with its variations on a popular dance tune, was one of the earliest trio sonatas, if not actually the very first, and the sonata called by Rossi himself *La moderna* (published 1613) offers the earliest example of the four-movement type of sonata which was four decades later called *sonata da chiesa,* church sonata, in contrast to the *sonata da camera.* This four-movement sonata consisted of a slow movement in polyphonic style and in quadruple time, a quick fugal movement in triple time, a slow and homophonic-melodic movement in quadruple time, and a quick homophonic finale in triple rhythm. Masters like Legrenzi, Vitali, Bassani, and Corelli perfected the form created by this early master of instrumental chamber music; and the great later virtuosos that made Italy famous throughout the world caused their contemporaries to forget the founder of the splendid Mantua school. Rossi's secular vocal compositions—from his canzonets of 1589 down to the last known publication from his pen, twenty-five *madrigaletti* for two sopranos or two tenors, Opus 13, published 1628—were charming contributions to popular "utility music" but could not hold their own beside the great creations of Luca Marenzio and Claudio Monteverdi. A pioneer in instrumental music, Rossi seems to have been a composer of a delightful yet common brand of songs.

The fate of his synagogal music was sealed by historic events: the Austrian conquest put an end to the flourishing culture of north Italian Jewry, and all desire for artistic reform was buried with it. The rabbinical authorities watched the keeping of the tradition with increased zeal, and it is doubtful indeed whether seventeenth-century Jews knew of Rossi's reform, let alone heard or sang his songs; for when, more than a hundred years after Leone da Modena's attempt to introduce new music into the synagogue service of Ferrara, a citizen of that town, Nehemia Cohen, dared to introduce a new musical version of the priestly benediction, he was excommunicated by the rabbinate.

It is a certain irony of history that a hundred years after a Jew—Salomone Rossi—had turned away from the traditional synagogue song and provided the Hebrew psalms and prayers with new music, a Gentile musician should have been attracted by the ancient Hebrew melodies and based a fine collection of psalm settings on the traditional Jewish chant. He was Benedetto Marcello (1686–1739), who published his psalms in

Musicians in Purim procession, woodcut, Amsterdam, 1723.

Venice in 1724–1727. This eight-volume work contains fifty settings for one to four voices with occasional solos for violin and violoncello and with figured basses added, under the title *Estro poetico-armonico*. The inspiration for these psalm settings seems to have come to Marcello from the singing in the Venetian synagogue, which was famous at the time and which attracted many a Christian musician and listener to attend the service. Venetian Jewry had a rich musical tradition, and its chain had not been broken so cruelly as that of Mantua. At the time the Jewish musicians flourished in Mantua there must have existed a magnificent musical practice in Venice. Names of outstanding composers or performers have not come down to us, it is true, but it is known that the Jewish music teachers enjoyed such a reputation that many Christian noblemen asked them to instruct their children—a custom against which the clerical authorities issued a decree. But musical performances in the ghetto of Venice went on, and many Christians came to listen to them there. It may be mentioned here that Venice had actually been the first city to relegate Jews to a ghetto and that the very word "ghetto" is of Venetian origin: in 1516 the Jews were given a domicile in a district in which since 1306 there had existed a "ghetto"—a cannon foundry.[20]

The Jewish actress and singer Rachel achieved great fame with the Venetian nobility and was often invited to appear at court (in the first decade of the seventeenth century), and Sarah Copia-Sullam—whom we mentioned in connection with the dedication of Rossi's psalm book—was also famous in Venice. When in the ghetto a musical comedy was performed in 1607 with the participation of the entire Jewish community, a large audience enjoyed the show, and many Christians made it a rule to attend the festivals of the Jews. Instrumental music was permitted in the Venetian synagogue; a complete orchestra officiated in the Sephardic synagogue, while in another house of worship

[20] Eric Werner, "Die hebräischen Intonationen in B. Marcellos *Estro poetico-armonico*," *Monatsschrift fuer Geschichte und Wissenschaft des Judentums,* November 1937.

orchestral playing was replaced by an "imitation of the movements of musicians." When, on the occasion of the Rejoicing of
the Law (*Simhat-Torah*), an organ was brought to the Sephardic
synagogue to augment the orchestra, there came such a crowd
of both Christian and Jewish listeners that the police had to be
called to prevent disorder at the doors. The organ was then
removed, and the experiment was never repeated; but the orchestra was permitted to remain. In 1629 an *academy* of music
was founded in the Venetian ghetto, and twice a week concerts
were arranged there by the Jewish musicians: it is most probable
that this academy was a foundation of musicians that had fled
from Mantua (who knows whether Rossi himself had been
among them?). Leone da Modena became the leader and conductor of the society, which adopted the name *B'sochrenu et
Zion* ("Remembering Zion") in quotation of Psalm 137, which
also formed part of Salomone Rossi's liturgical work.[21]

The activities of the musical society in the ghetto were greatly
hindered and undoubtedly curtailed by the epidemic of plague
in 1630; we know no more about the academy than that it existed for about ten years. But we may be sure that the tradition
was fostered in the Venetian ghetto throughout the seventeenth
century—for how else could the musical life of the Jews have
so greatly prospered a hundred years later! Marcello was not
the only musician to testify to the high standard of Jewish music in Venice, but he has erected a lasting monument to his
fellow-musicians of the Jewish ghetto.

Marcello achieved universal fame by this very work, the fifty
psalms; he was ever after regarded as a "prince of music" in
Rome and Bologna, and the songs themselves were widely per-

---

[21] See Eric Werner, "Manuscripts of Jewish Music in the Eduard Birnbaum
Collection," *Hebrew Union College Annual*, 1943–44, where original sources
are given.

formed in Italy as well as in Germany, France, and England, where they were translated into the vernacular. The original settings were composed on Italian texts prepared by Girolamo Giustiniani and constituted free poetic versions of the original psalms. Each of the eight volumes of the printed collection is preceded by a lengthy preface in which the composer discusses ancient Greek and Hebrew music—according to the knowledge of his time—and also informs us of his reasons for incorporating original Hebrew material in his music: he wanted to approach in his settings the spirit as well as the ancient musical style of the psalms. He used the original melodies for his polyphonic settings in the same way that Catholic liturgical melodies were elaborated or used as foundation in an artistic composition, and he also concedes that he somewhat adapted the ancient tunes— that is, he Europeanized what had remained in them of their ancient Oriental character. Not all of his psalms contain traditional melodies; but where they are lacking his own melodic invention shows their influence. He had noted down from memory eleven actual Jewish chants, and it is most interesting to see that he carefully distinguished between Spaniolic (Sephardic) and Ashkenazic melodies. The Sephardic chant contains a good many Arabic traits, while the Ashkenazic melodies show a great affinity with Gregorian music; the former tend to dance forms and to songlike recitation in turn, while the latter is often given a marchlike character. Coloratura melisms are frequent in Marcello's compositions, and though archaic Italian elements mix freely with the Jewish traits, the composer carefully avoided falling into the mannerisms and stylistic expression of his own time.[22]

[22] Eric Werner, "Die hebräischen Intonationen in B. Marcellos *Estro poetico-armonico,*" *Monatsschrift fuer Geschichte und Wissenschaft des Judentums,* November 1937.

For the purely Jewish sphere Marcello's music has as little importance as Rossi's synagogal songs: only indirectly did both prove their influence when new attempts at a reform of synagogal music in the contemporary style were made in nineteenth-century Germany. But Marcello's book stimulated new interest in Hebrew music, which had in former periods so much occupied both the Jewish and non-Jewish scholars. The great humanist Reuchlin had published his treatise on the Hebrew accents in 1518 and was followed in his investigations by other scholars of his century; among Jewish scholars there must be singled out the rabbi Yehuda Moscato, who devoted his first sermon to music; Abraham Portaleone, the learned author of *Shiltei ha-Gibborim* (Mantua, 1612), who devoted some chapters to Temple music, which he pictured in a true Renaissance spirit; and Yehuda ben Yizhaq, whose fragment of Hebrew musical theory was based on the work of the fourteenth-century Italian author Marchettus of Padua.[23]

With the decline of the Jewish communities in the Italian cities the Jews again disappeared from the annals of musical history. They took no further active part in the cultural life of the nations with whom they lived till there dawned a new cosmopolitan era—the period of enlightenment and reason of the eighteenth century, which did away with the barriers that had so long separated the Jews from the society of Gentiles. It is only then that Jewish participation in general culture again produced distinctive works of art, but then the desire for emancipation became so strong that the creators and artists left Judaism

[23] Eric Werner and Isaiah Sonne, "The Philosophy and Theory of Music in Judeo-Arabic Literature," *Hebrew Union College Annual,* 1941.

far behind them and felt no obligation to serve their own people.

Leone da Modena and Salomone Rossi—two ingenious men, progressive and daring in spirit and creative will—turned against tradition in their own way; but their reform aimed at an enrichment of their own, the Jewish, sphere. Rossi remained the "Ebreo," the Hebrew, in title as well as in feeling and purpose throughout his life, even though the majority of Jews did not recognize his artistic reforms in his lifetime and posterity was quick to forget them. Thus he belongs in Jewish musical history to a much greater degree—in spite of his creations being Italian music of late Renaissance and early baroque character—than the emancipated Jewish composers of nineteenth-century Europe.

Chapter
SEVEN

From Mendelssohn to Schoenberg–
A Century of Emancipation

THOUGH THE STORY OF musical activity in the synagogue and the Jewish home goes on without a break through the
centuries of Jewish settlement in Europe, there is a conspicuous
hiatus in the field of art music between the period of the first
great Jewish master of European music, Salomone Rossi Ebreo,
and the composer who opens the next chapter in our historical
survey, Felix Mendelssohn-Bartholdy. Considering the fact that
Jewish artists have so often played important roles in periods
of transition, it is somewhat puzzling that they had no part at
all in the great stylistic changes that occurred in eighteenth-
century music, when creative artists broke loose from the bonds
of patronage and began to serve a middle-class public rather
than a prince of the church or the court.

The history of the place of the Jews in seventeenth- and

eighteenth-century European society is responsible for the absence of Jewish musicians in the history of music after that short and magnificent intermezzo at the court of Mantua; only nineteenth-century liberalism opened the doors for Jewish participation in the cultural activities pursued in the European countries. For the "Middle Ages" of Jewish history in Europe ended with the victory of the slogan of the French Revolution: Liberty, Equality, Fraternity. The call to forget national barriers and to recognize the universality of mankind and of philosophy, science, and the arts was addressed to all civilized men, Jews included. And who could indeed so eagerly grasp the idea as the Jews, whose life had been made miserable by the very lack of tolerance and liberal thought? For centuries they had been stamped as foreigners and had been forbidden to practice any but the lowest trades; with the French Revolution various western European countries allowed them to become citizens. As such they could take part in the political and economic life of the countries to which they belonged, and it was only natural that they should always side with the liberal and progressive forces in all spheres of political, social, and cultural life.

But the Jew's progress in nineteenth-century society occasioned tragic conflicts: on the one hand, he was not always accepted by society as enthusiastically as he himself plunged into it for sheer joy over the doors being opened to him; on the other hand he placed himself in opposition to his own tradition-bound community, which watched the process of emancipation with suspicion and foreboding. Since time immemorial it had been the strength as well as the weakness of Judaism that its laws combined the religious code with the foundations of ethics, morals, politics, and science; though this had made the development of independent thinking and scientific progress impossible, yet it had given the spiritual achievements of the Jews a singular unity. With participation in liberal politics and their occupation in all branches of progressive science, the Jews left the world of the ghetto and the synagogue far behind them. The enlightened Jews who continued to keep the traditional laws and observe the prayers and holy days did so to placate their conscience; they also held some sentimental affection for the ancient ceremonies and perpetuated in them the memory of their parents and ancestors. But liberal science and religious tradition were irreconcilable in Judaism, and with his emancipation the nineteenth-century Jew entered a historical phase that opened the gates of the world to him but also put him in a spiritual vacuum—for Gentile society continued to think of him as a member of his own community, to which he no longer wholeheartedly belonged.

With the emancipation there began an epoch that witnessed great achievements by Jews in all branches of science and art, but most of them have little or nothing to do with the Jewishness of their authors. The Jew was quick to learn what had been denied to him for many centuries, and the development of European culture away from the ecclesiastical and feudal order to a middle-class rule favored his entrance into European society. Moreover, as the Jews had always been excluded from agriculture and thus been forced to turn to urban occupations, they were able to play a conspicuous role with the rapid rise of the towns in the nineteenth century and with their ever-increasing commercial and social life. It is thus that Jews quickly appeared in all urban free professions: their thorough training in the legal subtleties of Talmudic literature made them eager students of the law, a century-long interest in medicine had created a unique medical tradition, their preoccupation with the world's most ancient Book of Books had developed their literary and philosophical talents, and their traditional affection for music now also found new outlets. Faculties that had before been subdued in the desperate fight for existence could now be devoted to creative activity and applied to an almost unlimited range of subjects.

The period of assimilation and emancipation brought about a complete estrangement between the Jewish centers in eastern and western Europe. The West had hitherto drawn much of its cultural strength from the East, but when the western Jews plunged deep into a civilization remote from the ideals of Judaism and renounced many of their own spiritual possessions, there ensued a sharp separation. The liberation from Jewish seclusion was a comparatively slight step for the western communities, in which the tradition had become somewhat cramped and had little bearing on everyday life; but in the East the living contact with the tradition and the moral forces of Judaism had just been rekindled by the Hassidic movement. The eastern Jews continued to live their Judaism with all their emotional and spiritual might and condemned all occupation with the liberal arts and sciences—as practiced by their western brethren —as heretical; they preserved the religious and social code of Jewry, and the East could thus become the birthplace of the Jewish national renaissance at a time when the Jews of the West had lost almost all their contact with Jewish life and ideas.

Against the spiritual background of Jewish emancipation was written another chapter in the history of music in Israel; yet this is no longer the story of Jewish music but the story of music by Jewish masters. Just as in politics and economy, in philosophy and science, the Jews could play their own part in the development of the arts; Jewish musicians and composers abound in the history of European music. Some of them were active in the Jewish as well as the general sphere, while others renounced their bonds with Judaism; none of the greater nineteenth-century composers have created works that had a decisive bearing on the history of Hebrew music—as did Salomone Rossi in seventeenth-century Italy.

The approximately one hundred and fifty years of Jewish emancipation in European music are bounded by two ingenious composers, both conspicuous figures in general music history: The period opened with Felix Mendelssohn-Bartholdy, a musician who stemmed from a family famous in the Jewish world but gradually abandoned all bonds with Jewish tradition till his interest centered solely in Christian ideas and German music; it closed with the spiritual development of Arnold Schoenberg, who came from completely assimilated circles but was irresistibly drawn toward the values of Judaism and at last was inspired to a number of important works by the greatest creation of the Hebrew spirit—the Bible.

The sudden breaking of the Jews into western culture and music was not the immediate consequence of the impact of the French Revolution only. Music itself had undergone a far-reaching evolution, the very foundations of which enabled the Jews to play a part in its cultivation. The stylistic transition of the mid-eighteenth century was based on the same ideas as the movement that led to the French Revolution: it marked the change from the feudal order to the rule of middle-class society. In feudal Europe the Church had been the center of musical science and practice, and the Jews had for this reason been denied an active participation in European musical art; in seventeenth- and eighteenth-century Europe another center of music making had been created—that is, the aristocratic court—

but this, too, was inaccessible to the central European Jews. Individualistic traits began to show in the musical works and their performance, but there still reigned in them the community spirit, expressed in the polyphonic style, which gave all singers and players an equally important share in the performance of the music. The creative as well as the performing artist —generally united in one person—was in the service of a clerical or worldly lord; only at the Italian courts had Jews temporarily been able to penetrate beyond the feudal barrier.

Johann Sebastian Bach was the last great master of this epoch, and his compositions are the final examples of an art created almost exclusively in fulfillment of the demands of service and loyalty. But already in his lifetime there began to develop the public concert, an institution which enabled the middle classes for the first time to enjoy the luxuries hitherto reserved to nobility and to purchase the pleasure of a musical evening like any other commodity. In Bach's time were found the first signs of the stylistic transition which was to lead to the symphonies and the chamber music of masters like Haydn and Mozart and which was—sociologically as well as musically—crowned by the symphonic work of Ludwig van Beethoven. Haydn was still the servant of a noble prince and derived his income from service, but his music breathed the spirit of the new times and conquered the young concert halls of the world; Mozart's tragedy was the social descent from pet child prodigy to struggling and unappreciated master which paralleled his development from an obliging composer and performer of entertainment music into an individual artist whose works of sublimest perfection were created in complete indifference to the tastes of superficial society; Beethoven, finally, was able to establish the demands of genius and liberated the artist from the bonds of service once and forever.

While the Jews can often be found in the first row of inno-
vators or pioneers—Salomone Rossi may serve as an early example, and in modern times there are many instances of this
fact—they took no early part in the period of transition and
the creation of the symphonic style in the eighteenth century.
It is interesting to inquire into the cause of their late appearance
in the general history of music: the creation of the public concert (in England at the end of the seventeenth century, and
in France early in the eighteenth century) was the work of
a privileged middle class at a time when the Jews had not yet
been admitted into Gentile society; and the first musicians
searching for new ways of expression and eventually paving
the ground for forms and style suiting the new public came
from Italy, Austria, southern Germany, and Bohemia—Catholic
countries in which the Jesuits educated the youth in their
schools, colleges, and universities. The social background of
the public concert and the spiritual education given to its first
composers were thus unfavorable to Jewish participation in the
early history of classical music, and only with the eventual
victory of the middle-class order do Jews appear in the annals
of musical history.

Among Mozart's friends and supporters we find a number of
prominent Jewish personalities. Members of the wealthy financial circles of Vienna were among the subscribers to his printed
compositions, and the Jewish Baron Wetzlar was his temporary
landlord and godfather of one of his children; Mozart's associa-
tion with the Italian poet of Jewish parentage, Lorenzo da
Ponte, was responsible for his greatest operatic works. Beethoven's connections with Jewry came principally through his
making the acquaintance, at the Bohemian resort of Teplitz, of
Rahel Varnhagen, the Berlin Jewess whose salon was the meeting place of the spiritual elite, and her circle. In 1825 he was re-

quested by Viennese Jewish dignitaries to compose a cantata for the dedication of a new synagogue. This task, like many others proposed, he did not carry out, but he seems to have seriously contemplated its execution for some time.

Shortly before Beethoven's death a seventeen-year-old Jewish musician surprised the world with two enchanting compositions —an octet for strings, which was a perfect romantic work in a medium that had never been used before, and a truly fairy-land overture to Shakespeare's *Midsummer Night's Dream* fantasy. He was Felix Mendelssohn-Bartholdy, grandson of Moses Mendelssohn, the profound Jewish scholar and one of the leading figures in the period of the enlightenment in Germany. Moses Mendelssohn (died 1786) had come from a narrow ghetto milieu, where his father kept a Hebrew day school, and had risen to be one of the best-known thinkers of his age. His lifework was mediation between the Jews and their surroundings: he wanted to get the Gentiles to understand the Jews and to accept them in their society, while he desired the Jews to study the language and the cultural achievements of the Germans. An encyclopedic knowledge and a lofty character secured Moses Mendelssohn a prominent place in the high society of Berlin, where his second son, Abraham, was born in 1776. Abraham Mendelssohn took to banking and greatly succeeded in business, and he made many friends by the straightforwardness of his character and by his wide sympathies and high cultural standard. In 1804 he married Leah Salomon, a wealthy banker's daughter and a remarkable woman of many talents, especially for languages, drawing, and music—talents all four children inherited from their mother. Abraham Mendelssohn had lost contact with the Jewish world after the death of his father, though his wife came from a religious Jewish family too; when his children were born he decided to follow the trend of the times and educate them as Protestants. In order to distinguish their family from the branch that did not renounce Judaism, the Christian Mendelssohns added to their original name that of Bartholdy —the name taken on by Abraham's brother-in-law after he had become a Christian.

The house of the Mendelssohn-Bartholdys was a model home, and the education of the children was exemplary in its many-sidedness. Abraham himself was a connoisseur of the arts and exerted great influence on the spiritual development and artistic views of his children. Young Felix (born 1809), the second of Abraham and Leah's four children (Fanny was born four years before him) grew up in an artistic atmosphere: among his parents' friends were some of the brightest luminaries of the time, and the parties and Sunday morning concerts at their house were famous throughout Berlin. The prominent visitors included the politician and philosopher Wilhelm von Humboldt, the diplomat and writer Varnhagen von Ense and his wife Rahel, Goethe's music friend Karl Friedrich Zelter, who was conductor of the Berlin Singakademie, Adolf Bernhard Marx, the Jewish theoretician and editor of a leading musical journal, and the piano virtuoso Ignaz Moscheles. After 1822, when the musicales were instituted for Felix's sake, the house was crammed full on Sunday mornings.

At the age of seven the talented boy had already been to Paris and had taken piano lessons there after initial instruction from his mother; when he was thirteen he went to Switzerland, and at eighteen to Paris again. He could then boast of having met and played to the best-known musicians of the time—among them Weber, Spohr, Hiller, Moscheles, Cherubini, Meyerbeer, Rossini, and Halévy—and having de-

lighted the aged poet Goethe by playing to him the music of
Haydn, Mozart, Beethoven, and Johann Sebastian Bach. He had
enjoyed a thorough general education and musical training, and
in 1829—in his twentieth year—embarked on extensive travels
which led him to England, Wales, and Scotland, to Italy (where
he met Berlioz), to Switzerland, and to France (where he met
Liszt and Chopin). He played the piano, conducted, sketched
landscapes, and composed, and he never knew repose. "The
habit of constant occupation instilled by his mother made rest
intolerable to him," said his friend Eduard Devrient. "To spend
any time in mere talk caused him to look frequently at his watch,
by which he often gave offence; his impatience was only paci-
fied when something was being done, such as music, reading,
chess, etc." His must have been a singularly attractive personality: "You had only to be in his presence for a few moments to
feel how completely his appearance and manner represented
the genius he possessed . . . ," wrote John C. Horsley, one of
Mendelssohn's English friends, in a letter to Sir George Grove
when the latter prepared his *Dictionary of Music and Musicians*,
"he had a lithe figure, was very active and had a great deal of
what may be termed sinuous movement in his action, and
which was inimitably in harmony with his feeling of the moment. . . . It would need a pencil of fire to catch the brightness of Mendelssohn's countenance and wonderful animation
of manner." [1]

The restlessness and continuous activities soon told on Mendelssohn's health, and in 1837 he confided to his friend Hiller
that "two months of constant conducting takes more out of me
than two years of composing all day long. . . . I often think I
should like to retire completely, never conduct any more, and

[1] The quotations are taken from Jack Werner's article on Felix and Fanny
Mendelssohn in "Music and Letters," Vol. XXVIII, 1947, pp. 303–337.

only write; but then again there is a certain charm in a musical organization, and in having the direction of it. . . ." He found haven and happiness in the exemplary family life of his parents' home and always followed the advice of his father—to the extent of giving up the composing of small forms and turning to the composition of large-scale religious works.

His father's death in 1835 was a severe blow for him, and only his marriage a year and a half later could bring happiness into his life again. He had meanwhile met Schumann and Wagner, become conductor of the Leipzig Gewandhaus concerts (in 1843 he opened the Conservatory in that city), and had made history by conducting the first revival of J. S. Bach's *St. Matthew Passion* at the Berlin Singakademie. As a conductor he was much sought after, and the list of his compositions began to swell. In 1834 he published the first of his eight volumes of *Songs without Words,* the most popular piano pieces ever composed and a definite departure from the piano music current at the time. And though his restless traveling and creating also necessarily produced works of minor inspiration, Mendelssohn's immortality is firmly based on his "Italian" and "Scotch" symphonies, the violin concerto, the delicate chamber works, the fine lyrical songs, the psalms and oratorios, and the *Midsummer Night's Dream* music. Mendelssohn's death at the premature age of thirty-eight was mourned by musicians great and small the world over, and even though uninspired imitations of his music have brought some undeserved discredit to his own compositions, his creative genius never needed assertion or vindication.

Friedrich Nietzsche called Felix Mendelssohn "the beautiful incident of German music"; but it did not take long for anti-Jewish circles to start agitating against the unreserved acceptance of a "Jewish composer." Mendelssohn himself, though endowed with many Jewish traits and apparently Jewish in appearance, is known to have alluded to his descent only once in his life—on the occasion of his conducting Bach's *St. Matthew Passion.* "To think," Mendelssohn is reported to have said to his friend Eduard Devrient, the singer and actor, in a triumphant voice, "that it should be an actor and a Jew that give back to the people the greatest of Christian works." Zelter, Goethe's musical friend, had still described the composer as "son of a Jew but no Jew," but during the barbarous intermezzo in German history a century later Mendelssohn was labeled "a Jew who falsified the sacred treasures of German culture" and "whose true intentions are obvious in the oratorios, the heroes of which are a Hebrew prophet (Elias) and Paul the apostle who implanted Jewish thinking into young Christianity."

Though such libelous criticism—springing from a general antisemitic attitude and not from factual analysis—cannot really be considered seriously, it remains an astonishing fact that no Jewish genius—not even the one who believed himself most remote from Judaism and most perfectly assimilated—ever found unreserved acceptance in Gentile society: if he himself had completely forgotten his descent, there was always the other side there to remember, maybe to remind him as well. Few were the occasions in the era of emancipation when Jewish writers and artists actually encountered outspoken antisemitism, but a large number of critics—both Jewish and non-Jewish—have attempted to prove Jewish traits in the poetry of Heine as well as in the music of Mendelssohn, Meyerbeer, Offenbach, Mahler, Schoenberg, and others; and whenever personal dislike, bitterness, or competition entered the relations of Gentile and Jew, the latter was reminded of his foreignness. A famous example of a composer campaigning against Jewish musicians in a period of physical and mental exasperation is Richard Wagner's scurrilous pamphlet, *Judaism in Music* (1850). The question must be asked whether there do exist any common traits linking Jewish musicians together in the same way that the great masters of Bohemian music or the composers of France can be identified by certain common national characteristics throughout the ages.

The search for Jewish traits uniting works as far apart in time and spirit as, say, Mendelssohn's *Midsummer Night's Dream* music and Offenbach's naughty satirical operettas or as Rossi's Italian madrigals and Schoenberg's string quartets seems ridiculous and farfetched at the outset. It is difficult enough to explain in the unbroken chain of a national history such phenomena as the completely different styles of "Russianism" in Mussorgsky's and Prokofiev's music or the fact that the Austrian spirit could produce in one period such widely diverging musical characters as Anton Bruckner and Johann Strauss; nevertheless the existence of some typical national traits cannot be denied in the case of the great musical nations. The works of Jewish composers living in their midst might be expected to be more characteristic of the musical tradition of the people who gave them their background and education than of the Jewish culture which they had left behind them. But even the most complete assimilation into another culture has seldom destroyed all traces of the emotional and spiritual heritage of the Jews. It might be expected, then, that such emotional and spiritual traits would find expression in their creative work.

"The older the culture of a people, the more does intellect predominate over instinct," says the great Jewish sociologist Arthur Ruppin. Indeed, the conditions of living had forced the Jews to concentrate on the intellectual professions; their meticulous study and interpretation of Bible and Talmud pursued through the centuries had sharpened their wit, and their role as economic and cultural mediators between countries and con-

tinents had broadened their outlook. As they had been excluded
from the land and become early town dwellers, they had developed the white-collar professions in an ever-increasing degree: in 1933 a quarter of the Jewry of the entire world was concentrated in nine capital cities—New York, Budapest, Buenos
Aires, Kiev, London, Moscow, Paris, Vienna, and Warsaw—and
a large percentage was active in the intellectual world. The exigencies of life had always demanded from the Jew intellectual
agility and a knack for quick decision and action, and this again
had developed in him a singular talent for adaptation and adjust-
ment. Considering the Jewish composers of the different periods,
we can in fact discern the prevalence of intellect over impulse;
this is particularly striking in the romantic era, where music
served artists as a vehicle for an unrestrained effusion of emotion
and feeling. The Jews, intellectually awake on the one hand and
warned to restrain their instincts on the other, did not bring
forth a composer as demoniacally profound as Mozart or as
spiritually transcendental as Beethoven; nor have they produced
musical masters as free in lyricism and romantic sensitiveness
as Schubert and Schumann, and the sublime synthesis of classical
form and romantic spirit achieved by Johannes Brahms had
been denied to Mendelssohn. The Jewish composers are characterized by a highly developed sense of formal design, by a
skillful utilization of musical and technical means, and by their
universality.

This should not be understood to mean that the Jews are in-
capable of experiencing or of giving artistic expression to their
inner life. But in Jewish art there seems to be a deeper gulf between art and nature than is commonly found elsewhere.
"Genius learns from nature—from his own nature—while talents
learn from art," Arnold Schoenberg once said, and this remark
may serve to explain the opinion—frequently, and not quite un-

justly, expressed—that the Jews can boast of a great number of talents but are lacking in men of genius. Living among other people whose hostility he had always to fear, the Jew was compelled to mask his feelings and restrain his natural impulse; his nature seemed distorted and his inner life buried under the demands of his intellect. He suppressed his nature and checked his emotion, but he easily mastered the rules of art found in the sublime creations of other composers. It is thus that in the works of Jewish musicians mastery of craftsmanship is met side by side with lack of emotional depth and playful artistry often replaces meditation. Where the great romanticists are passionate and expansive, exaltation and contemplation characterize the compositions of the masters of Jewish descent, many of whom seem possessed by a vehement yearning for another being and a different world.

In Mendelssohn's music we can feel an ardent longing for the serenity of classical antiquity and for the past splendors of German music, and there is in it a characteristic cosmopolitanism and universality of talent and style; his supreme command of form is shown particularly in his pianistically perfect *Songs without Words,* in which he adapted vocal forms to instrumental purposes in an original way. Meyerbeer was a virtuoso master of the opera technique of three countries—Germany, Italy, and France—without being able to penetrate to a grasp of real life and drama. Mahler's dilemma was his ardent desire to mediate between his Jewish-spiritual heritage and the Catholic spirit, and between the mysticism of his belief and artistic being and the simplicity of the German folk song. Each of these three great figures in nineteenth-century musical history was a split personality in his own way and a foreign element in all spheres of activity. In the works of Offenbach, the ingenious critic of French society, there appeared still another trait characteristically Jewish: sarcasm, satire, and irony, which the Jews had developed as weapons of the weak and helpless against the powers of oppression. We can often find Jews as masters of caricature and satire—in literature, painting, and music—and the grotesque has always attracted them.

It is of little avail to search for suggestions of synagogal or popular Jewish melodies in the works of the assimilated composers of Jewish descent. Reminiscences or affinities of the kind can be proved in a good many cases, but they are inconclusive; for not a conscious or unconscious use of certain melodic phrases but only the composer's personality and the spiritual background of his creative activity can give us clues to the understanding of his works and his art.

Though it is interesting to inquire into the characteristics that distinguish Jewish composers from their Gentile fellow-artists, we should avoid the danger of ascribing all personal traits in their work to their Jewishness. We must remember that romanticism, the main stream in nineteenth-century music, generally fostered the development of a highly individualized personality, and that the isolation of the artist from his surroundings and from the reality of life had created a deep gulf between artist and public as between a privileged and an ordinary man. An analysis of the individual achievements of great Jewish composers can thus never intend to claim their works for Jewish musical history, though the Jewishness of these masters does offer an explanation for *some* characteristics of their life, their artistic growth, and their aesthetics.

When we describe Felix Mendelssohn as the first of the long line of Jewish composers who rose to extraordinary fame and created immortal works of music, we are apt to forget that a long tradition had developed the Jewish talent for music, though it had been able to express itself only in the popular, and not the artistic, sphere. The Mendelssohn family itself had cultivated music for many generations. Felix's grandfather, the philosopher, is known to have been greatly interested in music; it was not only mathematical interest that led him to the study of piano tuning and equal temperament, a science about which he actually published a treatise. Moses Mendelssohn counted among his friends in Berlin a number of outstanding theoreticians and musicians and himself took piano lessons; he also wrote on the aesthetics of music. His son Abraham, Felix's father, was musically gifted and interested, too, and his tastes and opinions exercised a decisive influence on his son. From his mother Felix had also inherited musical talent, and his sister Fanny, who married the painter Wilhelm Hensel in 1829, was a fine pianist and composer in her own right. The composer's bonds with her were so strong that her premature death in 1847 accelerated his own physical decline: he died six months after his beloved sister.

The youth and spiritual background of Jacob Meyerbeer—by eighteen years Mendelssohn's senior but acknowledged as a composer much later in life than he—were similar to those of the early romanticist. He, too, grew up in a well-to-do banker's house in Berlin (his father was Herz Beer) and showed musical talent at an early age: he was an accomplished pianist at the age of nine. His father's house, like that of the Mendelssohns, was a social center visited by Prussian courtiers, by nobility, and by spiritual luminaries, and the young musician was denied no means in his general and musical education. When he succeeded to the legacy of a rich relative named Meyer, he added his name to his own and thereafter became known in the musical world as

Meyerbeer. His name Jacob he later Italianized into Giacomo.

Meyerbeer's star rose more slowly on the musical firmament than that of Felix Mendelssohn. His first large-scale work he completed at the age of twenty, in 1811; this was an oratorio, *Gott und die Natur*. It was followed two years later by his first opera, *The Vow of Jephthah*. His first compositions were taken from the religious sphere; with his second operatic work, a comic opera, *Abimelek, or The Two Caliphs* (1813), he turned to the Oriental world. Though Meyerbeer never completed a large-scale religious or Biblical work again, he once considered writing a "Judith" opera and also composed some psalms and a Biblical romance *Rahel to Naphtali*. Between the first operas and his next attempts in this form there is an interval of five years in which Meyerbeer traveled extensively till he found himself in Italy, where he had immediate success with some skillful works in the style of the time. For ten years he failed to produce anything but occasional works till his visit to Paris in 1826 proved to be the experience decisive for his future life; he made Paris his second home and wrote most of his future compositions for the Paris Opera. The death of his father and the loss of the two children born in the early years of his marriage kept the composer away from public activity for a considerable period, but he devoted much time to a thorough study of the principles and theatrical possibilities of opera. When in 1831 his first operatic drama in French—*Robert le Diable*—was produced in Paris, it met with instantaneous success; this opera ushered in his greatly successful French stage works. The combination in his music of Italian songfulness, French pathos, and German romantic spirit created a unique and novel species of opera; his sense of dramatic stage action added to the effectiveness of his works. With his *Huguenots* (Paris, 1836) he made a spectacular impression and put in the shade even the success of Halévy's *La Juive*—the best work of this French Jewish composer, which had been produced in Paris a year before.

Meyerbeer was a true genius of the theater and a master of musical effect, and all operatic composers after him have studied his scores—and the dramatic librettos of Scribe—with profit. This is particularly true of the young Richard Wagner, whom Meyerbeer had supported in his early attempts to gain the stage but who later criticized and abused the older master. Meyerbeer's merits remained remarkable even in comparison with the mighty musical dramas of Wagner; the great German conductor Hans von Bülow was certainly right in maintaining: "Good old Meyerbeer is by no means a vanquished dragon, and the young dilettantes had rather put their noses in his scores than turn them up at him." Meyerbeer's operas are distinguished by rich musical invention, a splendidly colored orchestration, and exciting changes of mood within the dramatic scenes; lack of depth is made up for by musical effects that are at times genuinely stirring. And though we may scorn the musical content of his scores nowadays, his works can still serve as perfect models for sound operatic theater, while his adaptability and intellectual skill may well be marveled at even in the light of the greater achievements of profounder masters. Meyerbeer died in 1864 at the age of seventy-three, having witnessed in his lifetime the rise of the star of Richard Wagner, who was to perfect many of his own theatrical innovations and who put all his predecessors in the shade.

Mendelssohn and Meyerbeer conquered the great world of music and decisively influenced the development of musical history, each in his own way. A distinguished part in the history of German romanticism was also played by Jewish musicians and composers who were only minor masters in comparison with the ingenious romanticists and who have therefore been unable to hold the interest of posterity to the same degree as the men of greater genius. But some had been greatly successful in their own day, and a number of their works are still widely played.

An outstanding figure in romantic Vienna was Carl Goldmark (1830–1915), a composer of Hungarian-Jewish descent who made his home in Vienna and there produced some successful operas, among them *The Queen of Sheba* (1875) and *A Winter's Tale* (1905); in the orchestral field his Orientally colored *Sakuntala* overture and his symphonic suite *The Rustic Wedding* have become famous, violinists still perform one of his two violin concertos, and among his vocal works there is a fine setting of Psalm 93. Goldmark endowed his music with a subtle romantic coloring, and rich and warm melodic invention distinguishes his symphonic and chamber music; in opera the composer was much influenced by the works of Meyerbeer and, later, by the early music of Wagner. Slow and contemplative creation and continuous rewriting and polishing of an almost finished composition characterized Goldmark's work, and though lacking the last touch of genius his music is a remarkable contribution to the treasures of romanticism.

Less successful than Goldmark but an attractive romantic composer in his own right was Friedrich Gernsheim (1839–1916), who was active as a conductor and teacher at Cologne, Rotterdam, and Berlin. His most felicitous medium of expression was chamber music, but he also composed some choral works and four symphonies, the third of which is entitled *Miriam*.

Of Moravian extraction was Ignaz Brüll (1846–1907), who passed most of his life in Vienna and there produced in 1875 his best-known work, *The Golden Cross,* an opera which was widely performed in his time and which remained in the operatic repertoire for a considerable period. Brüll composed nine other operas, a number of symphonic and chamber works, and some Jewish songs. He was a noted teacher and traveled widely as a piano virtuoso, no less successful than other nineteenth-century Jewish virtuosos. Among the latter the prominent figures were Ignaz Moscheles (the friend of Beethoven, Mendelssohn, and Meyerbeer), Sigismond Thalberg, and Henri Herz.

A singular position in nineteenth-century musical history is held by Joseph Joachim (1831–1907), a Jewish violinist of Hungarian extraction. This outstanding musician was the first to perform widely the violin concerto and the chamber music of Beethoven—especially the quartets, which he played with his famous "Joachim-Quartet"—and his friendship with Schumann and Brahms led to these great masters writing concertos specially for him. Joachim also composed a few musical works himself, among them a *Hungarian Concerto;* of his chamber music the "Hebrew Melodies" for viola and piano have become popular. Joachim instructed an imposing line of pupils, many of whom were among the best-known violinists of the twentieth century; their most famous was Bronislaw Hubermann. Nor was the violin the only instrument favored by Jewish artists; a long succession of piano virtuosos opened to the Jews the salons and concert halls of the world.

Two interesting Jewish musicians were active in nineteenth-century England. One was Isaac Nathan (1791–1864), son of a Canterbury cantor, who enjoyed a great vogue as a singer and composer; the other was John Braham (1777–1856), a famous operatic tenor who took part in the first performance of Weber's operas in London and also made a name as a composer. Both men have a noted role in the history of Lord Byron's beautiful "Hebrew Melodies."

Isaac Nathan had in 1813 set to music Byron's *Bride of Abydos —A Turkish Tale* and sent a printed copy of his music to the poet a year later. Shortly after this he wrote a second letter with the following request:

"I have with great trouble selected a considerable number of very beautiful Hebrew Melodies of undoubted antiquity, some of which are proved to have been sung by the Hebrews before the destruction of the Temple of Jerusalem, having been honoured with the immediate Patronage of Her Royal Highness the Princess Charlotte of Wales, the Duchess of York and most of the Names of the Royal Family together with those of a great number of distinguished personages. I am most anxious the Poetry for them should be written by the first Poet of the present age and though I feel and know I am taking a great liberty with your Lordship in even hinting that two songs written by you would give the work great celebrity, yet, I trust your Lordship will pardon and attribute it to what is really the case, the sincere admiration I feel for your extraordinary talents. It would have been my most sanguine wish from the first to have applied to your Lordship had I not been prevented by a knowledge that you wrote only for amusement and the Fame you so justly acquired. I therefore wrote to Walter Scott offering him a share in the publication if he would undertake to write for me, which he declined, not thinking himself adequate to the task, the distance likewise being too great between us, I

could not wait on him owing to my professional engage-
ments in London.

I have since been persuaded by several Ladies of literary
fame and known genius, to apply to your Lordship, even at
the risk of seeming impertinence on my part, rather than
lose the smallest shadow of success from your Lordship
acceding to my humble entreaties. If your Lordship would
permit me to wait on you with the Melodies and allow me
to play them over to you, I feel certain from their great
beauty, you would become interested in them, indeed, I
am convinced no one but my Lord Byron could do them
justice. . . ." [2]

Byron accepted the suggestion of Isaac Nathan—who, by the
way, seems to have tried his own hand at Hebrew melodies before—and assigned to the composer the copyright of his poems.
Poet and composer became close friends, and Nathan annotated
and commented upon the poems of Lord Byron. A curious episode in their relationship is Nathan's sending of Passover cakes
(matzot) to the poet when the latter embarked on a voyage.

When the printed edition of the songs was offered for subscription, John Braham showed great interest in the Hebrew
Melodies and not only subscribed for two copies but offered
to perform them in public and to assist Nathan in the arrangement of the music on condition of his being given an equal share
in the publication. "To this I readily consented," reported Nathan
himself, "under the impression that I should but be paying a
just tribute to the first poet of the age by having his verses sung
by the greatest vocalist of the day, and I accordingly paid Mr.
Braham his moiety arising from the sale of the first edition."
The collection was dedicated to Princess Charlotte of Wales,

[2] Letter of June 30, 1814.

who was Nathan's singing pupil, and signed by Braham as well as Nathan. It is difficult to determine the share of Braham in the actual composition and arrangement, but it cannot have been extensive, as his name was later withdrawn from the publication. Braham—whose original name was Abraham—was probably a blood relation of Nathan's, and the latter called his first-born son after him. "A beast of a man but an angel of a singer"—thus Sir Walter Scott called the celebrated singer who after the decline of his voice sank into obscurity. Nathan, after some involved legal and financial affairs, settled in Australia and there died at the age of seventy-three after a street accident.

A figure of peculiar interest in nineteenth-century music is Jacques Offenbach (1819–1880), son of a hazan at Cologne, whose original name was hitherto believed to have been Eberscht or Levy but was apparently Wiener. The father had published a synagogue songbook and a Passover Hagada with some new melodies, and had composed songs and piano music. The son's musical talent was soon detected, and he began learning to play the violoncello. In 1833 the fourteen-year-old boy was sent to Paris, where he studied at the Conservatoire for four years and earned some money by playing in the orchestra of the Opéra-Comique. He then took to conducting, and in 1849 became conductor at the Théâtre Français. Offenbach had not then discovered his own particular talent for theater music, for he made his first attempt at a work for the stage as late as 1853 —at the age of 34—when he produced his first operetta, *Pepito*. It was only when he took over the Théâtre Comte, which he renamed "Bouffes Parisiens," under his own management in 1855 that there began the long line of delightful stage pieces which Offenbach then turned out in quick succession to create a repertoire for his theater. In the course of twenty-five years he composed no less than ninety operettas. He gave up the management of his "Bouffes Parisiens" in 1861; but he felt unhappy without a stage of his own, and in 1873 he took over the Théâtre de la Gaîté, which he managed till 1875. In the following years he went to America, but finding that France was the only proper soil for his works, he returned to Paris. There he was occupied for many years with the composition of his masterpiece, the lyrical romantic opera *Les Contes d'Hoffmann;* fate did not permit him, however, to complete this crowning achievement of his life: after his death in 1880 the opera was revised and its orchestration completed by Ernest Guiraud.

Offenbach was the sharp and witty critic of the Second Empire and its superficial and decadent society, but though itself mercilessly ridiculed in the operatic satires, the public was delighted by the charm of Offenbach's melodic invention, the sparkling fire of his cancans, the delicate sentimentality of his airs, and the fine orchestral coloring of his scores. Even today the freshness of his enchanting music has not worn off, and Offenbach's operettas are popular in many countries. In his only serious opera, *The Tales of Hoffmann,* he left parody and satire behind and wrote a work full of yearning for an alter ego —a fantastic opera of deep spiritual content.

Offenbach's works, with their biting satire on a decadent world, are typical of the general crisis and decline of romanticism, for even in his own contribution to romantic opera he symbolically shows the dual aspects of the romantic and the fantastic. His turbulent cancans swept away sentimental meditation and dreamy romance just as, at the same time, the polkas and Viennese waltzes of Johann Strauss brought a fresh spirit into a declining world. But the decline of the romantic era, which expressed itself in one way in the rise of the masters of satire and the dance and later in quite another form in impressionism and in the revival of classical ideals, had also serious sociological aspects. A reaction had set in against the liberal and cosmopolitan tendencies of the classical and romantic ages, and late romanticism developed distinctly national trends. Nationalism had already been a latent force in early German romanticism. Weber's "Lyre and Sword," on poems by Koerner, was its earliest example in music. With Richard Wagner's revival, in the frame of his great music dramas, of ancient German legend and lore national consciousness had deeply penetrated into the sphere of art. At the same time there rose in northern and eastern Europe national schools of composers whose works put on the musical map a number of countries that had not played a part in the history of the art of music up to that time. They, too, revived their national legends and folklore and thus also attempted to oppose literary and musical values of their own to the ever-growing influence of German romantic art.

The cosmopolitanism and the tolerance of society in the eighteenth and early nineteenth centuries had enabled the Jews to vie with the luminaries of the nations with whom they lived in all branches of science, literature, and the arts. The national trends in late nineteenth-century romanticism shattered the dream of equality and fraternity and the feeling of security harbored by the Jewish Europeans, and some storm signals disquieted them. But the reaction set in very slowly and was at first heeded only by a few far-sighted men. The actual catastrophe occurred—as far as western and central Europe were concerned—only in the first half of this century. Only then were the processes of emancipation reversed and the assimilated

Jews of Europe taught that their actual place was within their own community.

It is a characteristic sign of the times that in the years 1894–95 there were completed two momentous and stirring works, created in the same city by two men of exactly the same age but of diametrically opposed ideas: Theodor Herzl's bold "fantasy" of a "Jewish State" and Gustav Mahler's Second Symphony, the symphony of the life, death, and resurrection of all that is earthly. Mahler's mighty symphonic work is crowned by a finale originally styled "The Great Call," which contains the composer's own credo: "Prepare to live . . . for you will rise again, my heart." This musical genius, of Bohemian-Jewish descent, was possessed by the mysticism of the Catholic world, and in his symphony pictures the call to Judgment Day, on which the beggars and the rich, the people and the kings will be equal before the Creator; Herzl's visionary "Great Call"—originating from the alarming implications of the Dreyfus Affair, which brought home to him the failure of Jewish emancipation—was addressed to the Jews in dispersion in order to stir them up from their lethargic indifference and to gather them in the upbuilding of a new and independent community. Mahler's mystic creed, part of an unhappy and dual personality tortured by his struggle for artistic truth, stamps the style of his musical works, which in tendency as well as in content and expression mark the end of the romantic period; Herzl's vision points toward a realistic future. The tragedy of the epoch in which the Jews believed that they could be completely absorbed in European society is profoundly mirrored in Mahler's music, which—though we can hardly call it Jewish in any way—has always proved singularly attractive to the Jews, while the German musicians showed a hostile attitude toward his symphonic works under varying pretexts, even before racial discrimination had poisoned their minds.

Gustav Mahler (1860–1911) is an important figure in musical history as one of the last symphonists of the romantic era and as an outstanding precursor of the Vienna modernist school. The Jewish aspects of his personality can be detected in the mental and spiritual background of his creative work. In his symphonies, in which—according to his own words—he built himself a world with all the means of musical technique at his disposal, there is mirrored a probing mind deprived of its roots; his pathos has no deep passion; intellect and spiritual uproar shape his emotion; his ecstasy is that of the Biblical prophets. Mahler loved the German folk songs and employed his own folk-song settings for his large-scale symphonic works. In his music resound the martial rhythms of the regiments whose march he watched in his small native town—but strange melancholy strains transform these melodies and march rhythms to such a degree that they almost resemble the plaintive Jewish songs of eastern Europe. In his final masterpiece, *The Song of the Earth,* his inspiration is guided by far eastern poetry: this exotically colored symphonic song cycle—the style of which imprinted itself on Mahler's last symphony as well as on the works of many a later composer—is a moving portrayal of an artist and a man who lived in a spiritual world of his own and longed for fulfillment in remote, inaccessible spheres.

The great influence exerted by Mahler on the coming generations of composers was due to the novel style of his later works as much as to his high ethical aims, and his inspired and faithful conducting (most of his life Mahler spent as an operatic conductor) likewise served as a supreme ideal to his disciples and followers, of whom Bruno Walter became the most famous.

The tragedy of Gustav Mahler is that of nineteenth-century western Jewry. It represents the failure of the emancipation movement at a moment when the Jews began to realize that the European countries would one day set the clock back and close the doors that an enlightened period had opened wide to Jewish citizens. A few far-seeing Jews were early in their recognition that the century of liberty and equality was drawing to an end, and they took the consequences in various ways: some tried to fight against antisemitism and to defend the Jewish position, while others looked out for the restoration of an independent Jewish religious or national community. But Herzl's prophetic appeal and the activities of a few ardent followers of his "Jewish State" idea made slow headway, and only in our century did the growing Zionist movement of central and western Europe find contact with the national renaissance that had already gained momentum in the eastern European countries.

The Jewish way of Arnold Schoenberg (born 1874), who succeeded to the musical and ethical heritage of Gustav Mahler, is in many respects typical of the development in the western European sphere. It began in the paths of late romanticism, in the assimilated circles of Vienna, but the first World War brought home to Schoenberg the absurdity of Jewish assimilation, and he tried to give his searching ideas literary form. In a prophetic drama of the early twenties, the composition of which he once considered but never actually began, he attempted to make it clear that the Jews could not entrust their fate to other people and would soon learn this on a large scale. In this drama, *The Biblical Way*, Schoenberg points to the possibility of an independent Jewish state on the models of Biblical times; but even before the ideas leading to *The Biblical Way* had taken shape he had sketched the text of another work connected with ancient Hebrew lore. This was a poem, *Die Jakobs-*

leiter (*Jacob's Ladder*), in which Schoenberg gave allegorical expression to his own personal philosophy: the rationalists, the cowards, the skeptics, the cynics, the cunning ones, the journalists, and the unclean ones are all lined up on Jacob's ladder in order to ascend to Heaven; before them and nearest to the goal are the demons, geniuses, stars, gods, and angels. The Angel Gabriel opens the work—which is a sort of oratorio—with words that have often been quoted as typical of Schoenberg's own aesthetic creed:

> "Whether right or left, whether forward or backward— one must always go on without asking what lies before or behind one.
>
> That should be hidden; you ought to—nay, *must*—forget it, in order to fulfill your task."

The text of this interesting work was written in 1915–16 and later published separately. The composition was immediately begun but often interrupted; it was not before 1945 that Schoenberg finally completed the oratorio. The most important of the composer's Biblical works, however, is the opera *Moses and Aaron*—a work also full of philosophical ideas. Schoenberg's main problem in this opera is the clash between principle and politics, between the divine and the masses; for him only the divine idea can be victorious in the struggle. The composer's preoccupation with Jewish subjects found another outlet in 1938, when he composed a "Kol Nidre" for speaker, chorus, and small orchestra; a curious affinity with the traditional Jewish melody strikes the listener in the Largo of Schoenberg's Fourth String Quartet of 1936.[3] In 1947 Schoenberg completed a moving work in cantata form, *A Survivor from Warsaw* (words by the composer), written for narrator, male chorus, and orchestra

[3] See Example 19, p. 246.

to give artistic expression to the strong feelings aroused by the tragedy of Jewish extermination and the Warsaw Ghetto rising in central Europe's ghastly Nazi period. Schoenberg's composition culminates in the singing, by the chorus, of the "Shema Israel" prayer melody.

With the rejection of the emancipation and the Jewish genius's return to the spiritual values of his own people—symbolized also in Schoenberg's return to Judaism from his one-time conversion to Catholicism—the twentieth-century Jew annuls the movement which the Mendelssohn family had started a hundred years before. At the same time there also ended the epoch of which Felix Mendelssohn had been an early representative— romanticism, which had developed to sublimest heights musical poetry, musical painting, and an art to lull the listener into sweetest dreams. With romanticism there also ended a larger epoch of European musical history—the era that had opened with the institution of the bourgeois concert and the creation of a symphonic style suiting the new social form. The symphony had at first been designed to entertain and to please the large middle-class public as well as the fastidious connoisseur; but with the highly individual art of the late classicists and of the romanticists there had come an estrangement between genius and everyday listener, and the pretentious individualization and extravagant exclusiveness of late romanticism had widened the gulf. Romantic music reached its climax in the two largest scores of musical history: Gustav Mahler's Eighth Symphony (called *Symphony of the Thousand*) and Schoenberg's early *Songs of Gurra*. Mahler as well as Schoenberg realized the impossibility of raising the means of musical expression to a still higher level, and both attempted to lead music back to its purer, classical forms: Mahler by following up the grandiose score of his gigantic symphonic-choral work with the chamber-musically scored *Song of the Earth* and the likewise lucidly conceived Ninth Symphony, and Schoenberg by taking up the idea of a "chamber symphony" which had already attracted Max Reger.

Three distinct trends then characterized the ways of music in our century: one following the paths of national renaissance, another reviving the polyphony of the baroque era, and the third concentrating on the purely melodic values which had been drowned in the luxurious harmony of the late romantic works. All these trends attempted to give music a new stimulus and to re-establish active listening in place of the musical revelry of the late nineteenth century. National music stressed the rhythmic forces and the directness and naturalness of musical expression: the early Stravinsky started from an almost barbaric emphasis on the rhythmical impetus; Béla Bartók, the Hungarian master, is the greatest representative of contemporary music which grows on national soil but can still soar to sublime artistic heights. The revival of the polyphonic style symbolizes the composers' desire to make music again the possession of a community united in ideals and purpose; Paul Hindemith is the leading spirit of a movement that was originated, and largely promoted, by musicians siding with progressive youth.

It cannot be incidental that the regeneration of melody was the achievement of a Jewish composer, who on his way smashed the edifice of romantic harmony that was so typical a product of Occidental-German music. Schoenberg put melody high above all other musical elements and based the structure of his music on a unifying melodic idea, which not only produces in his works all the other ideas but also regulates their accompaniments and the chords, the harmonies. He thus disregards the limitations exercised by the seven-tone major or minor scale and returns to the most ancient principles of composition.

He finds his ideal in twelve-tone-scale themes that serve as basic scale as well as melodic foundation for an entire musical work. The twelve-tone scale, making use of all the half-tones included in the octave of the equal-tempered scale, cannot but remind us of the ancient Oriental technique, in which a mode is basic scale and motive in one.

Arnold Schoenberg's art is expressionist, predominantly lyrical —as purely melodic music must necessarily be. The exquisite lyricism of his early compositions has finally led to universal recognition of his genius, though the first listeners to these works —in the beginnings of this century—were utterly bewildered by what seemed to them a complex and incomprehensible style. It later appeared to his critics that the composer had abandoned the lyricism and romanticism of his early works and turned to a "purely mathematical way of composition" and "replaced inspired composing by constructive engineering." The reason for this verdict was the unprecedented degree of concentrated elaboration and emotional content in the later compositions and their renunciation of romantic harmony. The critics overlooked the fact that an almost unequaled wealth of inventive ideas characterizes both the early and the later Schoenberg works and that even when dressed in a cloak of romantic harmonies, as in the first compositions, the richness of variation and elaboration had been beyond the powers of appreciation of many listeners. In fact, as Cecil Gray observed as long ago as in 1924, the early works occasioned only that "negative and obviously insincere admiration of the see-what-he-can-do-when-he-likes order which is always so profusely lavished upon the immature productions of a master by those who most detest and abominate his later works, simply because they sound more like the music to which they are accustomed."

Schoenberg shares this fate with Mozart as well as with Beethoven, Wagner, Mahler, and Richard Strauss; it took him fifty years of unwavering steadiness to achieve the recognition due to his genius: whether he will figure in the musical histories of a coming period as a great stimulator and pioneer, whose work was superseded by a still greater synthesis of styles, or whether his achievements will be viewed as the greatest of his age, only time can tell. That a great affinity exists between the principles of his musical style and the characteristic Oriental way of composing cannot be denied, but that only "decadent Jewish minds" can create and appreciate music of this kind (as not only the outspokenly antisemitic writers have been wont to assert) is clearly refuted by the fact that there is hardly a single twentieth-century composer who has not passed through a stage of joining issue with Schoenberg and his music—no matter whether to the effect of acceptance or rejection—and that an ever-growing number of young composers, the majority of whom are non-Jews, have been developing his aesthetics and theories of musical composition since the formation of his new style.

The years after the first World War witnessed a particularly high activity of Jewish musicians in the countries of the West, and they held a conspicuous place in the universal search for new ideals and new ways of expression in a shattered world. Vienna, Berlin, and Paris were the prominent centers of their activities, and they also took an active part in the newly founded International Society for Contemporary Music and in the international musical research of the time. At the same time the spectacular rise of music in the New World exerted its attraction on Jewish musicians, and they figure largely in the recent music history of the most liberal of countries.[4]

The central figure among young French musicians after the first World War was Darius Milhaud (born 1892), descendant of an ancient Jewish family that claimed to have been among the very first settlers in southern France after the destruction of Jerusalem. Milhaud is a most prolific composer and has written music for every combination and in all fields of composition; traditional prayers of southern French Jewish communities have inspired him to some of his finest religious songs, an ancient legend is the background to his Purim opera *Esther de Carpentras,* Jewish folk songs and Hebrew poems figure in the long list of his lyrical songs, and in America during the second World War Milhaud composed a symphonic work for a ballet on the story of Cain and Abel. Milhaud belonged to a group of composers ("Les Six") who strove to get away from romanticism and to fight for clarity of expression and form. His main interest, like Schoenberg's, lies in the melodic element; while typical French playfulness and easy charm also give his music a characteristic imprint. Milhaud's own contribution to modern musical language is "polytonality"—the simultaneous sounding of melodies in different tonalities—created in the desire to increase the melodic content of a composition.

[4] Research conducted in 1933 threw interesting light on Jewish participation in American music. The percentage of Jewish players in symphony orchestras was found to be 34 per cent in the string section, and 23.9 per cent in the percussion section, but only a little more than 9 per cent in the woodwinds and brass—with an individually higher figure for trumpet and oboe. The total percentage of Jewish musicians in the major orchestras was 25.7 per cent, while the figure for conductors was 45.9 per cent, for violin virtuosos 47.5 per cent, for piano soloists 35.4 per cent, for cellists 14.3 per cent, for composer-artists 23.8 per cent, and for (American) composers 14.5 per cent. Research into the musicality of Jewish children aged 10–11 years showed no basic difference in comparison with non-Jewish children of the same age. (Keith Sward, "Jewish Musicality in America," *Journal of Applied Psychology,* Ohio University, Athens, Ohio, Vol. XVII, pp. 675–712, 1933.)

In his fondness for exotic coloring (apparent in some of his "Brazilian" works and in the operas) Milhaud merely follows earlier French composers: the nineteenth century had shown a new interest in the Orient, and French literature, painting, and music had been highly colored by Oriental or would-be-Oriental elements. The exotic had been a decisive element in impressionistic painting and music, and from Debussy onward French composers craved exotic effects. It is small wonder that Jewish artists were particularly attracted by the Oriental fashion —which also showed its impact in Mahler's "*Song of the Earth*" —while at the same time the study of Eastern music and of the ancient Hebrew chants stimulated interest in their Oriental heritage as well: many non-Jewish composers—foremost among them Mussorgsky in Russia and Ravel in France—have adapted Jewish religious or folk tunes.

It was the charm of the exotic, too, that gained an overwhelming victory in the entire world for a new kind of music that came to Europe from the New World. This was the music of the exotic strains and the powerful rhythmic impulse of jazz, which—just like European music of modern times—was destined to bring new vitality into a world of decline. From modest attempts jazz developed into a powerful and stimulating force in contemporary music, and Jewish composers have been prominent in the field of jazz music as well as in its symphonic application. Irving Berlin (whose original name was Israel Baline) was one of the first writers of popular songs. George Gershwin created in his famous *Rhapsody in Blue* a remarkable concert-jazz symphonic composition and with his Negro folk-opera *Porgy and Bess* one of the greatest stage works in this style. His premature death robbed music of a genuine and versatile talent.

Among the first European composers to grasp the possibilities

of American jazz in serious music was Kurt Weill, pupil of Fer-
ruccio Busoni and a composer of symphonic and operatic music
before he succumbed to the impact of jazz. Weill created in
modern music a new song style; again it can be no pure coin-
cidence that a chant-like declamatory style of singing was introduced into music by a Jewish cantor's son. In various stage
works, which met with an unprecedented success in central
Europe about 1930, Weill practiced his new style and technique,
and the number of his imitators soon became legion. On emi-
grating to the United States, Weill found in his new country
ample opportunity to apply his singular gifts for stage music,
and soon gained a prominent position among composers for the
theater and for the films. In the Franz Werfel–Max Reinhardt
production of a Biblical pageant, *The Eternal Way,* Weill could
turn to a purely Jewish subject.

In Germany, Kurt Weill had been only one in a school of
young composers among whom were many Jewish musicians
who had little interest in the Jewish sphere as such but who
made a name for themselves in the world of new music. The
most prominent of these composers—most of them active in
America or England after the advent of Nazism—were Erich
Wolfgang Korngold, who made a meteoric ascent as a child
prodigy composer but later abandoned serious music for the
theater and films; Hanns Eisler, the author of aggressive prole-
tarian music and of interesting concert music influenced by the
Schoenberg style; Ernst Toch, a modernist of great individuality; Egon Wellesz, composer and musicologist; Hans Gal, a
sensitive musician; Adolf Schreiber, a romantic talent whose
development was cut off by early death; Franz Reizenstein, a
modern composer of the Hindemith school; the Hungarian
Matyas Seiber, an original mind influenced by jazz trends; and

the Pole Josef Koffler and the Czech Erwin Schulhoff, both of whom met a premature death in the Nazi persecutions.

Beside these central European figures worked some other musicians who devoted some of their efforts to the creation of music for the Jewish sphere, as for instance Paul Dessau, composer of a Hagada oratorio written by Max Brod; Karol Rathaus, who wrote the stage music for the Habima Theater's *Uriel Acosta;* Berthold Goldschmidt, Hugo Kauder, and others. Mario Castelnuovo-Tedesco is a prolific composer of Italian descent who showed much interest in Jewish music. In France Manuel Rosenthal, Daniel Lazarus, Marcel Mihalovici, and Tibor Harsanyi are well-known Jewish composers; Sem Dresden is a prominent figure in modern Dutch music; Benjamin Frankel is a rising star of British music; in America Aaron Copland, Frederick Jacoby, Leonard Bernstein, David Diamond, and Lukas Foss have contributed to the treasure of musical works inspired by Jewish themes, while other Jewish composers—like William Schuman, Samuel Barber, Louis Gruenberg, Israel Citkowitz, Marc Blitzstein, Nicolai Berezowsky, Nicolas Slonimsky, Arthur Cohn, Irving Fine, Ellis B. Kohs, Harold Shapero, and others—belong in the general history of modern American music. Prominent Jewish composers in Latin America are Jacobo Ficher of Argentina and Jacobo Kostakowsky of Mexico.

The entire Jewish world—and not only those communities immediately affected—got into motion with the reactionary development of the 1930's. And the large-scale migration from central Europe and the decimation of Jewry from 1933 to the end of the second World War had far-reaching effects on the structure of Jewish society throughout the world. For even those who believed that migration meant no more than a change of domicile could not but feel that one more chapter in Jewish history had been completed—a happy chapter ending in a catastrophe of incomprehensible proportions. The great world became Jew-conscious again—no matter whether people stood for or against the Jews; and the works of art created by Jewish as well as by non-Jewish artists in the time preceding and following the second war are vivid testimony of the stirring experiences of the decade. The utter destruction of the flourishing central European Jewry, the Biblical precedents for events in modern history, and the dramatic story of a people which reads stranger than fiction have been occupying the mind and struggling for artistic expression ever since the storm began; while the basic conception of the assimilated Jewish romanticists was proved fallacious and their works seemed but memories of a period that had passed for ever.

Chapter
EIGHT

The Bible in Music

*T*HE BIBLE IS KNOWN to all civilized nations, and its books have been translated into more than seven hundred different languages. No wonder, then, that the world of the Bible has influenced the spirit of mankind to a greater degree than any other creation of the human mind. The Book of Books has attained its towering position by its unequaled universality: it not only embodies religious creed and ethics, a legal and moral code, and a philosophy of life, but also contains a treasury of legends and stories that are among the most beautiful and the most dramatic of the world. The Bible provided the foundation of all western civilizations; its stories are among the first a mother tells to her children, and its morals form the basis of all education. By translating the books of the Bible into the vernacular great men have created new styles of expression in their own languages, and the poetry of the Psalms, the Lamentations, and the Song of Songs have decisively influenced the poets of all nations. A larger number of pictures, plays, and musical works have been based upon Biblical scenes than on any other source; the historical, philosophical, and religious contents of the Bible as well as the innumerable dramatic incidents described have proved to be the greatest source of inspiration for poets, artists, and musicians alike.

The musical works inspired by the Bible cannot be said to contribute to our knowledge of the music of Israel proper, but a short survey of Biblical compositions is of more than passing interest, for in treating an ancient literary or pictorial theme composers have often tried to recapture the Biblical spirit and have studied the ancient heritage preserved by its creators, the Jews. For the oratorios and operas and the symphonic works based on the world of the Bible, composers have often used traditional Hebrew melodies or have attempted a musical characterization of ancient Jerusalem and Judea and their inhabitants; and though the music of those composers mirrors, of course, the masters' own conception of the Orient and the state of music in their period, it is most fascinating to study not only the various ways in which they have attempted to bring the Biblical subjects to life but also their actual reasons for falling back on the Bible for a European work of art.

We need not enlarge upon the obvious fact that artists could always draw upon the Bible because of their own familiarity with the subjects and because of the popularity they have enjoyed with the public throughout the ages. Painters and sculptors began employing Biblical motives in the earliest Christian centuries, and though the ancient aversion to pictorial representation at first led the Church Fathers to prohibit the creation of such images, they could not prevail. The Orient thought that the eternal and boundless in man would perish on being given external form, while the Occident could only do homage to the visible embodiment of the objects of their worship. The artists were indeed instrumental in popularizing the figures and stories of the Bible, and in their creative work they also satisfied their own religious zeal. While the New Testament provided them with the themes directly concerned with the Christian creed of the Occident, they often chose scenes from the Old Testament for their more colorful and dramatic aspects.

In music the creation of independent works of art began at a later stage of European history than in the pictorial arts and in literature. Earlier composers were almost exclusively concerned with setting Biblical passages to music and elaborating traditional liturgical chants for the clergy and the religious community. The Psalms and the Lamentations were the texts most frequently composed for the Church, and they kept their prominent position throughout the centuries. For the Protestant Church Martin Luther wrote his songs paraphrasing psalms or psalm passages, and the Huguenots got their own Psalter from no less a poet than Clément Marot. The Protestant songs accounted for some of the most beautiful compositions of Heinrich Schütz and Johann Sebastian Bach, while the Huguenot Psalter was composed by Claude Goudimel and exerted its influence on many musical masters—the Dutch organist Sweelinck above all. There are few composers who have not written psalms —from the German and Swiss composers of the Reformation through Lasso and Palestrina to J. S. Bach in the early eighteenth century, and from the classical period down to our own days. Christoph Willibald Gluck and Philipp Emanuel Bach were psalm composers in the early classic era; Felix Mendelssohn gave a new impetus to psalm composition in the romantic age; Dvořák's psalms are sublime examples of religious music in the nineteenth-century national idiom; Liszt wrote psalms at the height of the romantic era, while Max Reger returned to the pure religious spirit of Bach in his psalm compositions; in modern times Igor Stravinsky and Ernest Bloch, the American composers Loeffler and Wilder, the English masters Elgar and Walton, the Swiss Honegger, and a great many Palestinian composers have cultivated the composition of psalm poetry. The delicate lyricism of the Song of Songs and the possibilities it offers for pastoral tone-painting began to attract the composers at a time when naturalness and pastoral atmosphere were favored by a society that had turned away from the rigidity of the medieval Church; its first great setting was that of Palestrina, completed in 1584. A beautiful "Serenata" on the Song of Solomon was composed by William Boyce in eighteenth-century England, and in our own time the outstanding works based on this lyrical book are by Ralph Vaughan Williams (*Flos Campi* for voices, viola solo, and small orchestra, 1925), Arthur Honegger (*Das Hohelied Salomons,* for speaker and small orchestra, 1926), Marc Lavry (*Shir ha-Shirim,* oratorio, 1944), and Lukas Foss (*Song of Songs,* for mezzo-soprano and orchestra, 1946).

The Psalms attracted the composers by their sheer poetical beauty and spiritual greatness; some of them were chosen because of their inherent musical character and for their designation as songs of praise to the accompaniment of musical instruments. The Song of Songs, on the other hand, has proved to inspire especially those musicians with outspoken pastoral and lyrical leanings and at times in which naturalness was the foremost demand of an artist—such as in the Italian Renaissance and in the early eighteenth century or in twentieth-century trends opposed to the exalted romanticism of the preceding age.

But few are the western composers who attempted to give their setting of Biblical poetry an actual Oriental background; an exception is the American composer Carl Hugo Grimm, whose choral "Song of Songs" (1930) contains exotic elements.

But while the poetical sections of the Bible have been set to music without much regard for their original context and their essentially Oriental character, the inspiration of the composers of opera, oratorio, and symphonic works was kindled by the Biblical legends and stories and their characteristic background. They turned to the world of the Bible particularly in periods of an increased interest in the Orient and in the exotic—such as the romantic era—and it is interesting to follow their imaginative trends from the beginnings of dramatic music down to our days.

The oratorio originated in the sixteenth century from sacred services into which elements of the mystery play and Biblical scenes were introduced to attract the worshipers; with the late Renaissance attempts to combine music and drama there was brought into being not only the dramatic musical play for the stage—opera—but also the more contemplative and epic form of the oratorio. The early oratorio composers gave no pictorial background to the music, but simply attempted to bring the sacred stories of the Old Testament closer to the public by glorifying their heroes; these works are written in the operatic style of the period with the emphasis on vocal expression. The earliest Biblical oratorios known are those by Giovanni Francesco Anerio (1567–1620), younger brother of Palestrina's successor at the Papal Chapel; his *Teatro armonico spirituale* (1619) contains settings of the Joseph story, of Abraham's sacrifice, Jacob and Esau, Adam and Eve, and David and Goliath. The most famous of early oratorio composers is Giacomo Carissimi (1604–1674), who increased the part of instrumental music in his vocal works—which made the music much more dramatic

—and also introduced a narrator to link the different scenes; among the heroes of his works are Isaac, David and Goliath, King Solomon, Jephtha, Jonah, Hiskia, Belshazzar, and Job, and he also wrote an oratorio, *The Great Flood.*

While few composers of opera turned their attention to the Bible before 1800, Biblical stories accounted for the greater part of the oratorios written in the seventeenth and eighteenth centuries—among which Giovanni Battista Vitali's *Hagar,* Giovanni Legrenzi's *Esther,* Giovanni Paolo Colonna's *Moses* and *Samson,* Giovanni Bononcini's *Josua,* and Alessandro Scarlatti's *Hagar and Ismael, Judith,* and *Abraham's Sacrifice* are a few outstanding works chosen from a multitude of largely unknown compositions.

The vocal and dramatic style of these compositions closely resembles that of the operas; the only difference between the Italian operas and oratorios of early times is the stageless character of the latter—though many of them were actually presented with action and in costumes, too. In Germany, however, the oratorio took on a purely religious, devotional character, and it is because of this that the composers there more often turned to the New Testament; only in the enlightenment period and in early classicism do we find Old Testament oratorios in Germany, with Carl Philipp Emanuel Bach's *Israelites in the Wilderness* (1775) as an early and outstanding example. The early classics took up the operatic trends of the Italian oratorio but achieved greater instrumental freedom and dramatic expression; a characteristic work is Mozart's *La Betulia liberata* (composed in March and April 1771 on a text by Metastasio), in which the youthful master—fifteen years of age!—accomplished some ingenious dramatic characterization; he also introduced a psalm tune for one of the choruses. The same master's *Davidde penitente* is nothing but a pasticcio made up in 1785 from some movements taken out of the Mass in C minor of 1782–83 and two new arias; the text is probably by Lorenzo da Ponte, the librettist of *Figaro, Cosi fan tutte,* and *Don Giovanni*—a poet of Jewish descent. The classical oratorio reached sublime heights in the works of Haydn. His earliest attempt in the field of Biblical oratorio had been *The Return of Tobias* (completed in 1775); his masterpiece was *The Creation* (1797–98), in which all means of Haydn's great symphonic art are applied to the dramatic setting of the first chapters of Genesis, while no special interest is shown in the Oriental conception proper. An eighteenth-century curiosity is the "Biblical Sonatas" for the keyboard by Johann Kuhnau, J. S. Bach's predecessor at St. Thomas' in Leipzig—early examples of instrumental program music.

The rococo, with its emphasis on emotion and feeling and its love of ornament, had rediscovered the Orient; but in music it so far expressed itself only in the "Turkish" strains introduced in operas dealing with Oriental subjects (such as Mozart's *Entführung aus dem Serail*) or for the sake of special instrumental effects (the "Turkish" Marches of Mozart and Beethoven, the Janissary music in the middle section of the "Ode" in Beethoven's Ninth Symphony, etc.). But with the rise of romanticism the Orient and the world of the Bible were seen by artists in a new light. Symbolism and mysticism had lived on in the Freemasons' temples (Mozart's *Magic Flute* abounds in symbolic allusions of the Masonic kind) and in many other secret societies of a similar character. Journeys to the Orient were a great vogue, and the customs and manners of the Oriental countries were studied. Herder tried to conjure up Oriental moods in his German versions of Eastern poetry and thus gave inspiration to a long line of poets, leading from Goethe's "West-Eastern Divan" to Heine and Rückert. The artists craved the exotic and the mystical in music just as in poetry, and much of the romantic coloring is due to Oriental influence.

The Biblical operas and oratorios of the romantic era are the creations of musicians who did not compose their works for the sake of their church and for the spiritual, religious elevation of their communities; theirs were compositions for the theater stage and the concert hall. Dramatic effect and sharp musical characterization were their main concern, and they found many pretexts to exercise their faculties for colorful music in the Biblical stories. George Frederick Handel—the earliest composer in history to have created music with a view to public appreciation—had already discovered the attracting power of the heroes of ancient Hebrew history when his Italian opera did not flourish in early eighteenth-century England; the new public that streamed to the theater showed little interest in the Italian and Greek heroes that were far removed in time and ideals from their own actuality and were presented to them in a language (Italian) foreign to them. But with his dramatic oratorios based on the Biblical stories with which the English were traditionally more familiar than most other Europeans Handel quickly regained public favor, and it has been said that another reason for his subject choice was the considerable interest shown in his concerts by the Jewish community of the time. Handel used many different Biblical stories for his oratorios: Esther, Deborah, Saul, Israel in Egypt, Samson, Joseph, Belshazzar, Judas Maccabaeus, Joshua, Solomon, and Jephthah are the subjects of the Biblical works composed between 1720 and 1751. His example set a vogue in England that was to last till the end of the nineteenth century, but the later composers found contact with the general romantic trends and often gave their works a striking Oriental background. The Handelian oratorio not only influenced the composers of England and the European continent but also found its way to the New World. An Americanized German musician, Charles Zeuner (1795–1857), performed in Boston his lavish *Feast of Tabernacles* but later destroyed all copies of the work, his own manuscript included; while his younger American contemporary John Hewitt (1801–1890) composed a "Jephthah" oratorio.

It is impossible to list in the frame of this survey all the Biblical operas and oratorios written in the course of the nineteenth and twentieth centuries, but some outstanding works may be named to show how many of the great composers turned to the Bible for inspiration. A study of these works—no matter whether in the field of the oratorio proper or the acted musical drama— reveals a rather obvious development: the works of the romantic age make an ever-increasing use of exotic tone-painting and melismatic would-be Oriental melody, while in late nineteenth-century and contemporary compositions the barbaric aspects of the ancient stories are stressed in particular. There is a world of a difference between the delicate Orientalism in, say, Saint-Saëns's *Samson and Delilah* (which, by the way, could not be performed in Paris for many years after its premiere in Germany—for a Biblical subject could not be staged at the Paris Opera till 1890!) and the clashes of moods and temperaments in Honegger's Biblical works, or between the dramatic exotism in Verdi's early *Nabucco* and the stirring barbarisms in Walton's *Belshazzar's Feast*. The modern composer—opposing the emotional ecstasy of romanticism by the strength of melodic expression and the compelling forces of rhythm—either shows the temperamental Jewish masses in their opposition to their spiritual, prophetic leaders or contrasts the Jews as bearers of an idea to the barbarous peoples that grudged them their power in Judea. In many works by Christian composers the prophetic spirit is taken to symbolize Christianity. Thus in Honegger's dramatic psalm "King David," which—together with Willy Burkhard's "Isaiah," William Walton's "Belshazzar," and Leonard Bernstein's "Jeremiah"—is among the most powerful Biblical works of our time.

Biblical opera began with Johann Theile's *Adam and Eve,* with which the Hamburg Opera was opened in 1678, and with Nicolas Adam Strungk's *Esther,* produced there two years later. The earliest French Biblical opera was Rameau's first operatic work, *Samson* (1732). The form reached a notable stage of development with Méhul's *Joseph in Egypt* (1807) and Saint-Saëns's *Samson and Delilah* (1877); the latter work abounds in scenes that are imbued with Hebraic flavor. The actual Oriental fashion had been introduced in France by Félicien David, who had collected impressions and tunes on his journey to Turkey, Egypt, and Palestine in 1833–35 and himself composed an oratorio, *Moses on Sinai* (1846). In Italy it was Rossini who first turned to Biblical opera; he wrote his *Cyrus in Babylonia* in 1812 and his *Moses in Egypt* in 1818. The oratorios of Mendelssohn (*Elias*), Schubert (*Song of Miriam, Lazarus*), Spohr (*Fall of Babylon*), Neukomm (*David, Mount Sinai*), Costa (*Naaman, Eli*), Sterndale Bennett (*The Woman of Samaria*), Cowen (*Ruth*), Parry (*Judith, Job, King Saul*), and Goldmark's "Queen of Sheba" opera were the most successful romantic contributions in the Biblical field; but Mendelssohn's great work is the only one to have survived the period. Anton Rubinstein's *Lost Paradise, Tower of Babel, Sulamith,* and *Moses*—works that once enjoyed a great vogue—occupy a position between opera and oratorio.

A new trend was brought into Biblical drama by Oscar Wilde's sensual dramatization of the Salome story; this found an ingenious musical setting in Richard Strauss's opera *Salome* (composed 1903). It also inspired an opera by Antoine Mariotte (written before but produced after the Strauss work), a ballet, *La Tragédie de Salome*, by Florent Schmitt (1907), a tone poem by Henry Hadley (1907), and a symphonic "Poem of Passion" by Alexander Krein (1913); a more recent work is Bernard Rogers's "Dance of Salome" (1940). The novelty in Richard Strauss's master opera was the lavish use of Oriental devices; the composer not only tries to recapture the Oriental sensuality of the heroine and the barbaric character of the king but also depicts in music the speech and behavior of the Jews and precedes the dance of the Princess with a short orchestral prelude that conjures up the playing of a group of Oriental musicians. Most composers of Biblical works in modern times have followed Richard Strauss in his conception of the Orient, and particularly in his orchestral effects; with the predeliction of contemporary composers for percussion instruments and their skillful use of their possibilities—demonstrated in modern jazz —the exotic coloring could be further increased. It goes without saying, though, that all these composers see the Orient with their own, Occidental, eyes.

The means used by Arthur Honegger in his Biblical works are much less spectacular than those of Richard Strauss, but their effect is no less striking. His *King David* was originally composed for a band of fifteen musicians only—six woodwinds, four brasses, harmonium, piano, kettledrums, gong and tam-tam, and double bass—and kept its strange coloring even after the composer had rescored the work for a larger orchestra. In his incidental music for André Gide's *Saul* (1922), in his *Song of Songs* (1926), and in his opera *Judith* (1925) he also uses orchestral effects to underline the dynamic contrast between mass movement and idea and between primitive barbarism and divine spirit—the spiritual forces that are also opposed to each other in Arnold Schoenberg's Biblical opera *Moses and Aaron*. William Walton is nearest to Honegger's spirit and conception in his powerful *Belshazzar's Feast* (completed 1931), in which the barbarism of Babylon's king is contrasted in a stirring way with the grief of the exiled Jews in the beginning and their joyous praise of the Lord in the hour of their redemption; Walton employs a narrator who links the scenes in a declamatory-musical style reminiscent of the ancient psalmody of the Jews. Two additional oratorios of great spiritual impact are Lennox Berkeley's *Jonah* (1932) and Willy Burkhard's *Vision of Isaiah* (1935).

A few more outstanding works should be listed to complete the survey of the most important compositions in the field of Biblical music. "Judith" operas were written, apart from Honegger, by George W. Chadwick, Max Ettinger, August Klughardt, Natanael Berg, Eugene Goossens, and Alexander Serov; a tone-poem "Judith" was composed by the American composer Philip James. The story of Joseph inspired Arthur Farwell to a symphonic suite (for a play), while Richard Strauss and Werner Josten have written ballets on the theme; the Palestinian composer Erich-Walter Sternberg's *Joseph and his Brethren* is a suite of variations for string orchestra. Moses is the hero of an oratorio by Ettinger, and the American Negro composer R. Nathaniel Dett has written an impressive choral work, *The Ordering of Moses*. "Cain" operas were composed by Eugen d'Albert and Felix Weingartner and, more recently, by Marc Blitzstein and Rupert Hughes in America; the Exodus forms the subject of a symphonic-choreographic work by the Israeli composer Joseph

Gruenthal. *Deborah and Jael* is a fine opera by Ildebrando Pizzetti, Joram is the hero of an oratorio by Ben-Haim, and three Biblical episodes figure in Frederick Jacoby's *Hagiographa.* Michael Gnessin composed an opera-poem, *The Youth of Abraham,* and a dramatic song, *Ruth;* Idelsohn wrote a "Jephtha" opera; a tone poem by Rubin Goldmark has Samson as its hero; and Rudi Stephan set to music the story of Adam and Eve (*Die ersten Menschen*). Aaron Copland wrote a choral work, *In the Beginning,* the Esther story figures in operas by Mariotte and Milhaud, and Henry Hadley composed a "Belshazzar" oratorio. The prophetic books form the basis for Frederick Shepherd Converse's *Prophecy* (on words from Isaiah), David Stanley Smith's *Vision of Israel,* and Randall Thompson's *Peaceable Kingdom.* Wayne Barlow, one of the younger Americans, wrote a cantata, *Zion in Exile.* In the symphonic field (with voices) the outstanding works are Stravinsky's *Symphony of Psalms, Jeremiah* by Leonard Bernstein, the *Biblical Symphony* by Nikolai Nabokoff, a *Biblical Symphony* by Juan José Castro, and *The Song of Songs* of Lukas Foss. Abraham Wolfe Binder wrote a children's oratorio on the story of Judas Maccabaeus and a dramatic narrative, *Esther, Queen of Persia.* David, the royal singer and poet, appears in an opera by the modern American composer Adolph Weiss, in a piano work by Mario Castelnuovo-Tedesco, in a French ballet by Henri Sauguet, in Florent Schmitt's "Danse d'Abisag," and in two Israeli works: Karl Salomon's little opera *David and Goliath* and Menahem Mahler-Kalkstein's symphonic work on the David theme. King Solomon is portrayed in Ernest Bloch's rhapsody for violoncello and orchestra ("Shlomo"); Lazare Saminsky has composed a "Jephthah" opera and a ballet, "Rachel's Lament"; and a "Samson" opera, *The Warrior,* was written by the American composer of Jewish descent, Bernard Rogers.

Although of necessity incomplete, our bird's-eye survey lists an amazing number of subjects and composers, and while no detailed analysis has here been attempted, the general trends in Biblical composition have been shown. But these trends differ in Jewish and non-Jewish composers. While for Christian composers the Bible mediates between their own creed and the ancient world with which education and imaginative thinking have made them familiar, the Bible is for the Jews the only great spiritual heritage that is quite unmistakably their own. For the Gentile in the Occidental countries there remains something strange, exotic, unexplained in the Biblical Orient; by painting sacred scenes and by giving them new lyrical, epic, dramatic, or musical expression, Occidental masters attempted to give tangible form to the hidden and mystic and to impart to mankind their own notion of antiquity. For the Jew there is nothing strange in the Biblical world, even if he is most remote from traditional Judaism; creating a work of art in the spirit of the Bible conjures up for him the past splendors of his history and inspires him with hopes for a bright future for his people. It is thus that in spite of many characteristic traits common to the Biblical works of non-Jewish and Jewish artists, we can find one distinctive trend of evolution in the purely Occidental works of Gentile masters inspired by the Bible and quite another in the creations of Jewish composers. In the present chapter we have tried to show the development from the devotional Biblical work by early Christian composers to the Orientally colored compositions of romanticism and the exotic dramas of our times; the contemporary Jewish contributions to Biblical music have been mentioned in this general survey, but their singular position in Jewish music history demands a more detailed discussion in the chapter devoted to the Hebrew music of the present century.

Chapter
NINE

New Trends in Liturgical Music

*I*T WAS IN THE SYNAGOGUE that Israel's tradition lived
on throughout the two millennia of dispersion, and it was on
the high holy days that even the assimilated Jews of the nineteenth and twentieth centuries took part in the sacred service
and were impressed by the cantor's songs, which were so different from the music heard in the western world. For though the
period of emancipation also brought about a far-reaching westernization of the liturgical songs and their performance, enough
characteristic traits remained to distinguish the music of the
synagogue from that of the West and many stylistic features
strike the ear as common in the Jewish synagogal music of communities that are otherwise greatly separated geographically
and culturally. Much of the choral singing in the European and
American synagogues of today is reminiscent of Mendelssohn's
oratorios and romantic opera, and the hazan falls back for his
chant on Italian operatic virtuosity; but complete assimilation

could never be achieved and was indeed rarely aimed at. And though musically the Occidental harmonic and polyphonic arrangement of the originally Oriental chant proves satisfactory only in the rarest cases, the essentially "foreign" (Oriental) character of Hebrew synagogue music is obvious to the musician and the non-musician alike and has been noted by non-Jewish and Jewish observers throughout the ages.

The synagogue chant developed differently in the eastern European countries and in western Europe and America. When eastern Europe came under the influence of the Ashkenazic civilization, the hazanim introduced the Ashkenazic song into their synagogue but had retained in their music the melodic and rhythmic freedom that had characterized their earlier, largely Oriental, chant. The spirit of improvisation was never abandoned in eastern Jewish music; it created a special type of coloratura which combined a most brilliant virtuosity with the expression of an exalted emotion. While in central and western Europe the hazanim molded their song under the influence of the highly developed musical culture around them, the eastern Jewish communities were as isolated in their music as in their life; for until well into the nineteenth century there was no flourishing musical culture in the countries in which they lived.

The eastern European precentor held a prominent position in his community, and the emotional character of his singing became the greatest inspiration for the people. Seventeenth-century sources tell of hazanim whose singing had a profounder influence on the minds and hearts than the preaching of the rabbis, and who moved the worshipers to tears. It is interesting that one such source added that in other countries the hazanim "have neither melody nor emotion"; and it is also reported that at the time of the Chmelnitzki pogroms in 1648 a hazan, Hirsch of

Ziviotov, chanted the memorial prayer "El Mole Rachamim" in so touching a manner that he was able to move the Tartars to save three thousand Jews from the hands of the raging Cossacks.

The Jewish communities in eastern Europe suffered decline in the eighteenth century after a period of pogroms and persecution, and many scholars and singers migrated to the West; yet enough hazanim remained to preserve the tradition of the liturgical style. The East disdained all the contemporary reform and assimilatory movements of the West and saw in them a destruction of the traditional values of Judaism. Emotional depth and vocal virtuosity remained the foremost requirements for the Eastern hazan—in contrast to the musical technique and craftsmanship exercised by his western colleague—and they must have been found marvelously combined in the art of one of the first precentors whose tunes have come down to us, Salomon Kaschtan (1781–1829). Kaschtan was hazan at Dubno but traveled throughout the eastern countries all the year round, returning to his own city only for the high holy days; his influence on the communities he visited must have been overwhelming. His style of performance and composition served as a model to an entire school of hazanim in the East, while his most gifted pupil, his son Hirsch Weintraub, came under the spell of western reform when he occupied a position at Koenigsberg. Other famous nineteenth-century hazanim were Dovidl Brod Strelisker (1783–1848), Bezalel Schulsinger (ca. 1790–ca. 1860), Sender Polatschik (1786–1869), Joseph Altschul (1840–1908), Yoel Dovid Levinsohn (1816–1850)—a pupil and friend of the Polish composer Moniuszko—Boruch Kaliner (died 1879), Yeruchom Blindmann (1798–1891), and Nissan Spivak (1824–1906). The last-named hazan, who became famous under the name of Nissi Belzer, is a characteristic example of one peculiar trend in eastern European hazanuth. While touring the eastern countries he lost his voice through an accident, but his remarkable talents as a choral leader and liturgical composer let the community forget his vocal defects: though it would have been impossible for an eastern community to employ a musician as conductor and composer only (as often happened in the western sphere, where in the field of art music the separation of the creative from the performing artist had meanwhile asserted itself) even a voiceless hazan was able to maintain his position in the eastern synagogue. Nissi Belzer made a virtue out of necessity. He limited his solos to a minimum, making more use of the choir instead, and thus became the founder of a new musical style in eastern synagogue service: virtuosity and solo expression gave way to a well-planned responsorial performance in which the solo parts played only a secondary role.

The ancient tradition was never forgotten in the eastern communities, though toward the end of the nineteenth century—when the work of the reform composers of the West became widely known and the musical culture of the eastern countries rose to great heights—the eastern hazanim absorbed much of the classical and romantic trends of western synagogue music. Among such hazanim were Nisson Blumenthal (1805–1903), David Nowakowsky (1848–1921), Wolf Shestapol (ca. 1832–1872), Boruch Schorr (1823–1904), Elieser Gerovich (1844–1913), Boruch Leib Rosowsky (1841–1919), and Samuel Alman (1877–1947). The last-named introduced the eastern synagogal style into the English service.

While in the eastern synagogue the traditional bonds were so strong that they could inspire the Jewish renaissance movement in music (the hazanic chant, in fact, formed the root of all early Jewish art music) the assimilatory movement in the

West led to a complete change in the religious services and rendered the Oriental origins of synagogue music almost unrecognizable. The translation of the prayers into the vernacular, the stricter rhythmization and melodic symmetrization of the ancient tunes, and the choral arrangement of the psalms and prayers mirror the gradual estrangement of the western Jew from tradition and the appeal the European church music exercised upon him. Classical and romantic harmony is applied to the ancient chant, songs of other people find entrance into the synagogue, and the organ is employed to accompany the singing. The introduction of the organ—and of other musical instruments—into the synagogue had already been tried in Prague in 1594, at the time when Salomone Rossi created in Italy the first synagogue music in the style of his time, and we have already recorded the abortive attempt to establish an organ in the synagogue in Renaissance Venice. But it was only in Germany, in the nineteenth century, that the "organ synagogue" gained ground and was able to defend its place against orthodox opposition.

The reform movement, which reached its first height of development about 1810, had started in Germany in the eighteenth century, and its earliest signs had been choral arrangements in the classical style and the organized employment of musical instruments in the synagogue. The admission of the latter had been stressed by the cabalistic writer Isaac Luria (sixteenth century) and his pupils, and in addition the cantatas sung to instrumental accompaniment in the Protestant churches during the service on Sundays exerted great influence on the Jews. The musicians who had so far only preserved the tradition of the popular ghetto music performed at weddings and other ceremonies put their talents at the service of the synagogue and also influenced the hazanim by the popular style of their music. On

the other hand, the institution of synagogue choirs, which became a common practice at the beginning of the eighteenth
century, was largely due to the Protestant example; many of
the Jewish hymn melodies sung by these choirs were—again
following Protestant precedents—adapted from folk songs, Jewish or German.

The hazanim of the West generally had a good musical background and spent much labor—even research—on their synagogal compositions, much in contrast to the eastern singers, who
drew their inspiration from the emotional mood of their prayers
and left most of their creative work to improvisation; some of
the German cantors are said to have been accomplished players
of musical instruments as well. Of their earliest representatives
the name of Solomon Lifshitz (died 1758) is worthy of note;
among the important cantors about 1800 are Ahron Beer (1738–
1821), Leon Singer (died 1800), and Israel Lovy (1773–1832).

It is only natural that the general assimilation and westernization of Judaism should have found expression in the synagogue
as well as in Jewish life and thought; but the reform movement
did not originate with the officials of the synagogue or other
Jewish dignitaries, though among them there were many to
join the preachers of enlightenment and progress. On the contrary, the keepers of the synagogal tradition and the learned
rabbis were as fervently opposed to change and reform as had
been their ancestors at the time of Salomone Rossi's modernization of the synagogue song. The first men to work for the reform
of the liturgy were enlightened burghers who had been drawn
into the process of emancipation and had lost much of their
spiritual contact with ancient Judaism, and who now tried to
establish a form of Jewish worship acceptable to modern society. They could not go to the extreme of creating an entirely
new service and having original melodies composed for the

prayers; but the prayers were translated into the vernacular, the chant was transformed into simple declamation, and the choral song was based on popular songs or on those of the traditional melodies that seemed to possess the qualities most suited to adaptation. These reforms strove to give Jewish worship a place in modern life and to make it attractive for those that tended to turn their backs on Judaism; they were also part of the general eighteenth-century trend to liberate society from clerical bonds and the feudal order.

The reform movement started in earnest with the translation into German of the prayer book by David Friedlaender, a wealthy Berlin merchant, whose version of 1787, though not immediately accepted, by its very idea exerted a far-reaching influence. In 1810 there was built in Seesen, in Westphalia, the first Reform Temple; it was dedicated by Israel Jacobsohn, a rich and influential merchant who enjoyed the support of the French government of the province and who had tried out his first reforms in the frame of a children's service. Jacobsohn did away with the hazan and introduced a reader instead, and the choir sang hymns on German chorale tunes. In 1815 he opened a similar Temple in his private home in Berlin, and his example was followed by Jacob Herz Beer, Meyerbeer's father, who also had a Temple at his house. His son arranged the music for him; but Beer did not want to do without a cantor, for the Berlin community was accustomed to his singing and would have missed it greatly. He engaged as a hazan Ascher Lion, and among the preachers officiating in his Temple was Leopold Zunz, a brilliant scholar, creator of the "Science of Judaism." Meyerbeer had ideas of his own regarding the musical part of the service and opposed the introduction of the organ, which he regarded as a typically Christian instrument: "I consider it my merit," he writes in a letter to the secretary of the Vienna community, "that, in accordance with Mendelssohn-Bartholdy, I arranged in Berlin an a capella choir only. The praying man should approach God without any intermediary. The Jews have maintained that opinion since the destruction of the Temple, and we should not introduce any innovation. But, if any music is required, then—according to my opinion—flutes and horns should be used, similar to those used in Solomon's Temple. However, the human voice is the most moving."

The German reforms brought forth stormy debates throughout the European Jewish world, and some of the younger rabbis —among them men like Abraham Geiger and Samuel Adler, of the elite of nineteenth-century Jewish scholars—arduously defended the innovations. But it took considerable time before the reforms met with general acceptance, for only singers and composers who could successfully blend the traditional values and the classic-romantic style were able to convince the Jewish worshipers. Such men rose in central European Jewry in the persons of Salomon Sulzer in Vienna, Samuel Naumbourg in Paris, and Louis Lewandowsky in Berlin; their Europeanized Jewish liturgical music greatly impressed their communities, and it was similarly admired by non-Jewish musicians, who frequently adapted their religious tunes—a famous example being Max Bruch's "Kol Nidre" for violoncello.

Salomon Sulzer (1804–1890) was a singer and composer of undisputed talents, and Franz Liszt, who heard him sing, was "deeply stirred by emotion, . . . so shaken that our soul was entirely given to meditation and to participation in the service." Though arranging his liturgical music in the choral style of the period, Sulzer did not discard the traditional tunes which —in his own words—had only to be "improved, selected, and adjusted to the rules of art." Sulzer felt it his duty "to consider, as far as possible, the traditional tunes bequeathed to us, to cleanse the ancient and dignified type from the later accretions of tasteless embellishments, to bring them back to their original purity, and to reconstruct them in accordance with the text and with the rules of harmony. For obvious reasons, this could be more easily achieved with the songs of the Festivals than with the Sabbath service, because for the latter there were frequently employed profane tunes which desecrated the holiness of the service . . . whereas the songs of the High Festivals have an inwardness and depth, a gripping and moving power, which they have preserved through the centuries." Sulzer's music avoids all virtuosity and emotional emphasis; it is always dignified and serious and tends not so much to impress the worshipers as to create the spirit of holiness proper to a house of worship. Nothing is preserved in Sulzer's choral songs of the ancient Oriental and of the traditional eastern European style of hazanuth, but some elements of ancient Hebrew chant remained evident nevertheless—above all to non-Jews—though the classical style of choral harmony frequently covered its Oriental quality.

Two hazanim-composers of German descent were instrumental in reviving the musical heritage of southern German Jewry, whose melodies had been preserved since the early Middle Ages; but they, too, gave their liturgical music contemporary dress. They were Maier Kohn (1802–1875), who worked in Munich, and his most gifted pupil, Samuel Naumbourg (1815–1880), who went to Paris and created there a synagogal style that was influenced by the operatic tendencies of his time; to his two-volume synagogue service famous composers contributed—such as Jacques Fromental Halévy and Meyerbeer.

Sulzer's counterpart in Germany was Louis Lewandowsky, who was born in 1821 in the east German province of Posen but came to Berlin, the future place of his activities, at the age of thirteen (he died there in 1894). He enjoyed a thorough musical training and became familiar with the trends of reform of which Berlin had become the center. A decisive experience for him —as for the entire Berlin community—was the visit of Hirsch Weintraub, who was then hazan at Koenigsberg, and his cantoral performance in the eastern emotional style but to the background of European choral arrangements. Apprenticed to Ascher Lion, the cantor of the Reform Temple, and later to his successor Abraham Jacob Lichtenstein, young Lewandowsky learned all aspects of hazanuth before he tried his hand at cantoral composition himself. Sulzer's music at that time exerted a great influence on the choral song everywhere, but Lewandowsky succeeded in making his own an independent contribution to synagogue music. His work—a complete service for the entire year being his main achievement—is distinguished by the fine melodious lyricism that permeates not only the choral songs but also the recitative based on traditional tunes. His musical settings soon conquered the synagogues, and Lewandowsky himself became the idol and leader of an entire generation of hazanim and synagogue composers; indeed, few others succeeded as he did in blending the traditional and modern, the eastern European and western elements.

Lewandowsky's music proved to have a universal appeal. The service contained in his collection was accepted by cantors all over the Jewish world, and his hymns were sung by Christian communities as well; the style of his music was imitated and elaborated by later composers of liturgical music. Though the famous hazanim of the later nineteenth century and of our own time—such as Joseph Rosenblatt, Mordecai Herschmann, Zavel Kvartin, and others—have shown a preference for the emotional virtuoso style of eastern character, Lewandowsky's music has provided the foundations for the synagogal choral style; together with the works of Sulzer and Naumbourg his compositions still occupy a commanding place in the service of both eastern and western Europe and of the Americas and are even sung in the synagogues of Palestine.

With the development of music in the late nineteenth and early twentieth centuries there rose new synagogue composers who sought to utilize for the liturgical service what was best in contemporary musical art. In the nineteenth century Lewandowsky, Sulzer, and Naumbourg had written their music in the classical choral style; these were followed by other classicists and some composers in the romantic vein, such as Israel Meyer Japhet, Mombach, Wasserzug, Moritz Deutsch in Europe, and Alois Kaiser, William Sparger, and Edward Starck in America. As these composers added nineteenth-century contributions to the service, so twentieth-century composers sought to apply to the liturgy the achievements of modern harmony and counterpoint. At the same time composers tried to strip synagogal music of its romantic cloak and to give it a background more appropriate to its original ancient, Oriental character. They reconstructed the ancient modes and underlined the foreignness of the service, and they reduced the harmonic accompaniment to a minimum. Their work is closely connected with the contemporary renaissance of Hebrew music and the compositions "in Hebraic style" by the Jewish composers of our time. Ernest Bloch, Frederick Jacoby, Lazare Saminsky, Isadore Freed, Jacob Weinberg, Abraham Wolfe Binder, Heinrich Schalit, and Chemja Winawer are among those who have written completely new services for practical or concert performance; Jewish and non-Jewish composers like Roy Harris, Bernard Rogers, Darius Milhaud, Arnold Schoenberg, and in Israel Mordecai Starominsky have enriched liturgical music by original works in which the ancient spirit is expressed in modern terms.[1] Their liturgical style has exerted its influence, in turn, both on the modern masters of Hebrew music and on the composers inspired to independent works by the world of the Bible.

[1] Of musical leaders in contemporary American synagogues Lazare Saminsky, at the Temple Emanu-El, and Cantor David Putterman, at the Park Avenue Synagogue, both New York, must be credited with having commissioned, and performed, the largest number of new liturgical works by non-Jewish and Jewish—American, European, and Israeli—composers.

Chapter
TEN

The National Movement in Eastern Europe

Wʜɪʟᴇ ɪɴ ᴛʜᴇ ᴡᴇꜱᴛᴇʀɴ countries the Jews eagerly sought admission into society and renounced the traditional unity of religion and life for the sake of the liberty, equality, and fraternity preached by the French Revolution, the ideas of emancipation and of "liberal" Judaism and reform remained entirely foreign to their eastern brethren, whose number exceeded theirs manyfold. The very conditions—and restrictions —of life in the eastern states forced the Jewish population into isolation, and the development of an autonomous Jewish state in sixteenth-century Poland, the Messianic movement of the seventeenth century, and eighteenth-century Hassidism had greatly contributed to strengthening the bonds with traditional Judaism from within. With the assimilatory movement in the West a sharp dividing line was drawn between western and eastern Jewry: the emancipation was regarded by eastern Jewry as a betrayal of the spirit of Judaism, and when, on the other hand, the pogroms and massacres of the nineteenth century compelled masses of eastern Jews—who had kept their dress and customs of old—to migrate to the western countries and to America, the assimilated communities saw in them strangers from foreign lands.

The gulf between western and eastern Jewry was widened in the nineteenth century by the nationalistic trends which set in everywhere as a reaction against the cosmopolitanism of the idealistic period. In western Europe the assimilated Jews often espoused the nationalistic feeling and became fervent patriots for the cause of the countries in which they lived. In the East, where the greater and smaller nations rose to independence in the course of the nineteenth century and where the greatest emphasis was laid on the evolution of a national life and culture, the Jews were also much impressed by the renaissance movements around them; but there it led to a strengthening of the *Jewish* national idea. Just as the poets and composers of the eastern countries revived their national lore in the form of works of art, so did the Jews cultivate their own spiritual values and try to give them artistic expression; the national idea which in the countries of their dispersion expressed itself in political strength, inner unity, and national expansion inspired the Jews with a new longing for a homeland and cultural center of their own. The terrible sufferings of the Jews in Poland and Russia only strengthened their national bonds, and all attempts to convert them by ridiculing and suppressing their religious and cultural life were doomed to failure. The yearning for a return to Zion, which had hardly ever ceased in the souls of the eastern Jews, now developed a national as well as a religious character.

George Gershwin paints Arnold Schoenberg in Hollywood. (*Merle Armitage*)

Darius Milhaud discusses one of his piano compositions with Menahem Pressler. (*Ben Greenhaus*)

Aaron Copland. (*Victor Kraft*)

Ernest Bloch. (*Anne P. Dewey*)

It is thus that the important contributions made by the eastern Jews to literature and the arts were not those created in a spirit of emancipation but were works designed to serve the Jewish national renaissance. Only a few assimilated artists can be found in the entire history of eastern Jewry, most of them flourishing at the time of Czar Alexander II (1855–1881), when some Jewish scholars, writers, and musicians tended to a more cosmopolitan and universal art. In the field of music these artists characteristically joined the western trends—and not the national schools—in Russian composition. Outstanding among them was Anton Rubinstein (1829–1894), who achieved world fame as a pianist, composer, and pedagogue; Tchaikovsky was among his pupils. Rubinstein was an influential figure in the musical life of St. Petersburg, where he founded the Conservatoire in 1862 (the Moscow Conservatoire was founded by his younger brother Nikolai [1835–1881] in 1864). The long list of Anton Rubinstein's compositions includes a number of operas and stage oratorios inspired by Jewish themes: *The Maccabeans, The Tower of Babel, The Shulamite, Moses,* and *Hagar in the Desert.*

Two different spiritual movements were styled "enlightenment" in the nineteenth century: the one the "enlightenment" of the West, which led to the declaration of equal rights for all men and opened new vistas for the relations between the Jews and the world around them, and the other—the *Haskala* (Hebrew for "enlightenment")—which originated in the East and was intended to make Judaism a living force by reviving its language and culture. The western emancipation had obliterated the boundaries between Jew and Gentile, and the Jews tended to forget their religious and national heritage while rising to great heights of achievement in cultural fields; exactly the contrary happened in eastern Europe, where the Jews also endeavored to adopt as much as possible of the general knowledge and culture but did so in order to enrich their own spiritual experience. The Jewish-national character of the eastern enlightenment—which was strongly opposed by the orthodox scholars and the hassidim on account of its inherently worldly character—expressed itself foremost in the renaissance of the Hebrew language. The revival and cultivation of the national language and lore had been the first step in the renaissance movements of all the eastern people in the nineteenth century. The Jews, too, soon recognized how strongly a common tongue and folklore distinguish a nation from its neighbors; they realized also that for a people that lived in dispersion throughout the countries of the earth the uniting bonds could become even more powerful. The revival of Hebrew soon showed its first results. Poets and writers cultivated the ancient-modern language in their works: in Abraham and Micha Josef Lebensohn the Jews got their first modern poets, while Abraham Mapu wrote the first novels in modern Hebrew. But as the new Hebrew literature began to flourish, Jewish writers also continued to cultivate the Yiddish language—that derivation from medieval German which the Jews had taken with them to the east on their migrations and which had become in the course of the centuries the language of millions of Jews.

We have to know the sociological and cultural conditions of nineteenth-century eastern Jewish life and of the background of the Jewish national movement in order to appreciate the efforts of those pioneers that have laid the foundations for a renaissance of Hebrew music. The first steps in this field mirror all the different trends characterizing the revival of the Jewish spirit, the Hebrew language, and the national idea: the music reflects the traditional lore of the Yiddish dialect as well as the restoration of Hebrew, it expresses religious contemplation or national enthusiasm, it revives ancient melodies and acknowledges the trends in general nineteenth-century musical art.

All national renaissance movements in music begin with the collection and practical arrangement of folk tunes. The singing, playing, and dancing of the people, their rural and urban life, and their festivals inspired masters like Weber in Germany, Smetana in Bohemia, Grieg in Norway, Gade in Denmark, and especially the Russian composers from the times of Mikhail Glinka. Characteristically it often occurred that foreign musicians kindled the interest of composers in their own national folklore; thus Glinka received his first impetus to write national operas from an Italian in St. Petersburg, Catterino Cavos, whose operas in popular style—making frequent use of Russian folk tunes—exerted a decisive influence on the Russian master; similarly Russian composers inspired Jewish musicians to devote their attention to the treasures of Jewish folk song and folklore. Balakirev and Rimsky-Korsakov, the leaders of the national movement in Russian music, were the first to recognize the qualities of Jewish folklore, and Taneiev and Ippolitov-Ivanov were the teachers of Yoel Engel, the pioneer of the Jewish national renaissance. The Imperial Ethnographic Society invited this critic and scholar to deliver a lecture before the leading musical writers of St. Petersburg, and in 1900 the thirty-two-year-old musician exhibited to them the first fruits of his research into Jewish folk song. For the first time the wide public became interested in the world of Jewish music, and a lively discussion in the Jewish as well as in the non-Jewish field followed Engel's first lectures, publications, and concerts. Engel himself continued his work: he collected and arranged folk tunes, propagated his idea in the spoken and printed word, and organized concerts of Jewish music in the capital and the provinces. He gained a considerable number of ardent followers, collaborators, and friends.

Out of Yoel Engel's circle came the men who founded in St. Petersburg in 1908 the "Jewish Folk Music Society"—with Ephraim Schkliar, Michael Gnessin, Salomo Rosowsky, and Lazare Saminsky as its leading spirits. In the ten years of its activities (which were brought to an end with the Russian Revolution) thousands of songs were collected by the members of the society all over the Russian countries, in Latvia, Poland, Galicia, and elsewhere, and a large number of folk tune arrangements and of compositions based on folklore were actually published. Branches of the society were established in other Russian cities, among them one in Moscow under the leadership of David Schorr in 1913. The circle of writers, composers, and musicians supporting the idea of the society quickly grew: in 1912—the fifth year of its existence—it could boast of some 400 members, of whom almost two-thirds were active in St. Petersburg alone. Apart from the men already named, the society attracted Joseph Achron, Moses Milner, L. Schitomirsky, and the brothers Gregory and Alexander Krein as composers, the pianist Leo Nesviski-Abileah, the engineer and enthusiastic music lover Israel Okun, and the collector N. Kisselhoff. Musicological research recieved a great stimulus through the expeditions of Baron Ginsburg and, later, through the monumental work of Abraham Zvi Idelsohn, who collected ancient Hebrew and medieval Jewish melodies in the countries of the Orient and in eastern Europe and who was instrumental in imparting to comparative musicology the tools for proving the similarity of ancient Temple music and early Christian chant.

The activity of the Russian society met with great interest in all Europe centers and in America, and Palestine gained its decisive contact with the Jewish musical renaissance through the permanent settlement there of some of the leaders of that organization, among them David Schorr, Salomo Rosowsky, Abileah, and Yoel Engel himself. Saminsky and Achron continued their work in the United States, while Gnessin and the Kreins remained in Russia after the Revolution.

The pioneers of Jewish music went different ways in their desire to give a Jewish or Hebraic flavor to their musical expression. Yoel Engel (1862–1927) conceived all his works in the popular idiom. Besides his piano arrangements of folk tunes proper (in which no new harmonic style was created to suit the peculiar features of the eastern Jewish melos), he composed fine lyrical songs on poems by Bialik, Tchernichowsky, Perez, and other modern Hebrew poets; his best-known work is the stage music for Ansky's dramatic legend *The Dybbuk*, which the Hebrew Theater "Habima" performed with enormous success all over Europe and America. Engel's great achievement lies much less in his musical creations than in the fostering of the idea of the Jewish musical renaissance and in his unswerving struggle for the cause. There is nothing new in the stylistic foundations of his music, and his works possess no great inventive originality; but their theme, their spiritual content, and their emotional background give them a character entirely their own. The texts of his early songs are partly Yiddish, partly Hebrew, but his entire work is based on the Yiddish folk songs of Russia, the foundations of which have such widely different sources as the Russian and White Russian song, Rumanian elements, and old German tunes which had been preserved by the Jews in their migration from West to East and adapted by them in the same way as the old German language. In Palestine, where Engel settled in 1924 after a sojourn of two years in Berlin, the composer experienced yet another decisive influence: that of the Oriental atmosphere. The maturing artist achieved a characteristic folk style that united the many heterogeneous elements into a harmonious whole. Many of Engel's songs have become real folk tunes in modern Palestine.

While Engel had never regarded it as his primary task to create musical art works, new tendencies began to take shape in the compositions of his younger colleagues in Russia. These composers also started their way as arrangers of folk tunes or liturgical music, but they soon utilized the traditional melodies for musical works on a larger scale. Moreover, when giving free rein to their own melodic invention they attempted to re-create in their themes the melos of the Yiddish or Hebrew song. Among the older leaders of this school is Salomo Rosowsky (born 1878; emigrated to Palestine in 1925), whose style strongly resembles Engel's and who has contributed to our knowledge of Biblical cantillation—which also plays an important role in his compositions—by lifelong research. The other composers of the Russian school—above all Lazare Saminsky, Alexander Krein, Michael Gnessin (all three born in 1883), Moses Milner, Joseph Achron (1886–1943)—sought contact with the new developments in western music; they tried, each in his own particular way, to elaborate Jewish melos and Hebraic themes by means of contemporary musical technique.

Numerous characteristic features recur in the works of all these composers, and this fact (to be explained by their common background of education in the Jewish as well as in the Russian sphere) justifies our speaking of a "Jewish school in music" just as we talk collectively of the "German romanticists"

or of a "national Russian school." But the composers of the Jewish school, though perhaps more closely resembling one another in purpose, content, and style than the masters of other
European schools, do not lack individual traits either. Lazare
Saminsky—who made his second home in the United States and
there became a leading figure as a lecturer and writer, conductor
and composer—has written "general" as well as "Jewish" compositions and attempted to imbue with Hebraic traits works
conceived in a modern musical style. Alexander Krein found
contact with the Jewish national movement at a comparatively
late stage of his creative development; his symphonic works are
full of sensuous emotion, while his melodic invention clearly
shows the imprint of Hebrew liturgical melos and ornament. His
elder brother, Gregory, has written music that is more meditative and profound in content but lacks the emotional passion that impresses the listener in Alexander Krein's work.
Michael Gnessin's music is characterized by a cooler, more re-
strained temperament; he often shows feeling but rarely strong
emotion, and he emphasizes the national traits much more than
Alexander and Gregory Krein, whose style never denies the
influences of Scriabin and the French impressionist school. Moses
Milner is the composer most rooted in the soil: his music mirrors
little of contemporary developments; it always remains folk-
like, lyrical, and of an immediate emotional appeal. Joseph
Achron, finally, the youngest of these Russian Jewish musicians, was perhaps the greatest creative talent among them;
beside the somber Gnessin, the passionate and colorful Alexander Krein, the meditative Gregory Krein, and the naïve Milner,
he stands out as a most original and vital personality. As a virtuoso of the violin Achron has written a great many works of
virtuoso character: his violin concertos and the smaller pieces
for his instrument combine Jewish melos, refined instrumental

technique, and a novel style of elaboration. In his last phase the composer came much under the spell of Arnold Schoenberg and his music, and his last works are accomplished examples of a modern distinctively Jewish art that can vie with the creations of twentieth-century musical geniuses.

The composers of the Russian Jewish school prepared the ground for widespread activities in the field of Jewish music. In Russia a considerable number of Jewish musicians—and non-Jewish artists as well—became interested in Jewish folklore; a chamber music ensemble organized in 1918 and consisting of a string quartet (Jacob Mistechkin, Gregory Besrodney, Nicholas Moldavan, Josef Cherniavsky), the clarinetist Simon Bellison, and the pianist Leon Berdichevsky toured Europe, America, China, Japan, and Siberia, and finally Palestine, with a repertoire of Jewish music; and publishing companies printed arrangements of Jewish folk songs.

Alexander Veprik (born 1899) belongs to the younger generation of Russian Jewish composers influenced by the Society's work. While Prokofiev's *Overture on Jewish Themes* is among the earliest compositions in a Jewish vein from the pen of a non-Jewish master; Ravel's "Deux Melodies Hébraïques" is another outstanding example. In the western European countries a number of musicians and composers took up the idea of Jewish music and propagated it by collection, performance, and composition. The most active leaders were Léon Algazi in Paris, Joachim Stutchevsky in Vienna (now in Palestine), Mario Castelnuovo-Tedesco in Italy (now in the United States), Alice Jacob-Loewensohn in Berlin (now in Palestine), Marko Rothmüller in Yugoslavia (now in Switzerland), and two composers who have done much to popularize Jewish folksong—Janot S. Roskin and Arno Nadel.

Composers who were attracted by the exotic charm of Jewish liturgical or popular music, which became available in print everywhere after the first World War, can be found in almost all countries; at first they turned to the eastern Jewish folk song which had shaped the Russian composers' Jewish works, but then they went further back to the genuine roots of Hebrew music and its Oriental foundations. The movement which had started in a circle locally and spiritually confined to the eastern Jewish sphere spread throughout the musical world, and when the tragic history of European Jewry reached its heights with the pogroms and mass murders in the years of the second World War many composers were deeply stirred by the ghastly tragedy and inspired to profound musical works in which the Jewish melos found personal expression.

Some of the work of the Russian pioneers was continued in the United States, where a few of the original members of the Jewish Folk Society actually settled and exerted great influence on younger musicians. The National Jewish Music Council, sponsored by the National Jewish Welfare Board, has been organized there to foster composition and research in the Jewish field and to propagate and distribute new material. Among the musicologists and writers in America Dr. Eric Werner and Joseph Yasser have been foremost in new research in the field, and of the many composers especially interested in Hebrew composition the outstanding names are Abraham Wolfe Binder, Jacob Weinberg, Julius Chajes, Herbert Fromm, Gershon Ephros, Max Helfman, Isadore Freed, Harry Coopersmith, Reuben Kosakoff, Rabbi Israel Goldfarb, Hugo Adler, and Zavel Zilberts. The traditional element is strong in all works of these contemporary composers, who belong stylistically—with few exceptions—in the world of late nineteenth-century and early twentieth-century Jewish music as created by the Russian school of Jewish composers.

Of the many compositions by the original Russian pioneers of Jewish music, perhaps only a few have an intrinsic musical value, yet they must all be credited with having drawn the attention of the world's musicians to treasures that without their initiative might have been irretrievably lost with the destruction of the eastern Jewish communities.

The influence exerted by the eastern national school on the composers of the West expressed itself in many ways. The assimilated western musicians found the Jewish folk material as strange to them as it was to the non-Jews, and in their arrangements—made for performers and for a public that demanded Jewish music—they did not always strive for a true realization of the spirit that had created the original songs. The Jewish folk tunes had for them an exotic charm similar to that of Greek or Negro or Chinese songs: they approached them from without, as the national significance of the renaissance movement had not touched them so far. While the national Jewish school in the eastern countries had attempted a synthesis of Jewish melos, traditional song, and national expression, many western composers now introduced the Jewish tunes into musical works that had little to do with the national foundations. In the Germany of the twenties and early thirties there worked a number of composers whose music showed a peculiar blend of Jewish melos and a modern musical language, while a typically French style permeates the Jewish works of composers in France —with Darius Milhaud as their foremost representative. The composers of the West also gave their Jewish music a stronger formal planning and toned down the emotional exaltation dominating the eastern song; it is thus that the music created by the Jewish composers of the West derived more inspiration from the ancient Hebrew melodies and hymns—which had helped to shape the earliest Christian music—than from eastern Jewish folk music, which was made up of a great variety of ingredients, both Slavonic and Jewish.

Two main trends can thus be discerned in the field of modern Jewish music as a result of the Russian Jewish pioneers' decisive initiative: the eastern Jewish school, whose composers create their works on the soil of folklore and try to give musical expression to the life and sentiment of the Jewish people, and the composers of the old musical nations of the West—not united in a school proper—who add Jewish traits to the central European style of the time. The Jewish character is the most important concern of the eastern composers, whose musical language follows the characteristics of Jewish folk music without any attempt at an original or novel contribution to the world's musical literature; the composers of the assimilated sphere struggle for an adequate incorporation of their Jewish spiritual experience into musical works conceived in a novel and progressive idiom. Both trends reverberate in the Hebrew music of our time; the first synthesis of the various traditional and modern elements has been achieved by a genius of Hebrew music, Ernest Bloch.

Chapter
ELEVEN

Hebrew Music of Our Time

AMONG THE MUSICIANS for whom the national renaissance movement proved a decisive experience in their early development the outstanding figure is that of Ernest Bloch. Born in Switzerland in 1880, educated and musically trained in Belgium, France, and Germany, strongly influenced in his later career by the American atmosphere, Bloch could not but imbue his creations with a cosmopolitan and universal style. His career as a composer began, after an early attempt at writing an *Oriental Symphony,* with large-scale symphonic works and with an opera after Shakespeare's *Macbeth*—compositions that continue in the nineteenth-century European musical tradition. But shortly before the first World War, when the waves of the Jewish renaissance movement reached the central European countries, Bloch was apparently caught by its spirit, and he turned out a number of significant Hebrew works in quick succession: two psalms for soprano and orchestra in 1912, three Jewish poems for orchestra in 1913, another psalm—for baritone—in 1914, the rhapsody "Schelomo" for violoncello and orchestra in 1915, and the "Israel" symphony in 1916 (this large-scale work for voices and orchestra had been begun in 1912). It is interesting to reflect that Bloch seems to have been predestined as a composer of Hebrew music, for strange orientalisms had already puzzled the critics at the time of the first performance in Paris of his "Macbeth" opera. "This music is an indecipherable rebus, rhythmically as well as tonally . . . ," was the verdict of one of France's foremost music critics; ". . . as to harmonic sequences, they are no less extraordinary, and one can qualify them as savage. . . ." This was in 1910, when the world had already experienced the operatic dramas of Richard Strauss, who, by the way, exerted a profound influence on the compositions of the young Ernest Bloch.

Bloch's Hebrew music has little in common with the works of the eastern Jewish national school of composers, for he rejects their fundamental tendency to incorporate actual folk tunes in musical works of art. "It is not my purpose, nor my desire," the composer himself has said, "to attempt a reconstruction of Jewish music, or to base my work on melodies more or less authentic. I am not an archeologist. I believe that the most important thing is to write good and sincere music—my own music. It is the Jewish soul that interests me, the complex, glowing, agitated soul that I feel vibrating throughout the Bible: the freshness and naïveté of the Patriarchs; the violence of the Prophetic Books; the savage Jewish love of justice; the despair of Ecclesiastes; the sorrow and the immense greatness of the Book of Job; the sensuality of the Song of Songs. All this is in us, all this is in me, and it is the better part of me. It is all this that I endeavor to hear in myself and to transcribe in my music: the venerable emotion of the race that slumbers way down in our souls." And somewhere else Bloch has stated: "In my works termed *Jewish* . . . I have not approached the problem from without—by employing melodies more or less authentic (frequently borrowed from or under the influence of other nations) or oriental formulae, rhythms, or intervals, more or less sacred! No! I have listened to an inner voice, deep, secret, insistent, ardent, an instinct much more than cold and dry reason, a voice which seemed to come from far beyond myself, far beyond my parents—a voice which surged up in me on reading certain passages in the Bible, Job, Ecclesiastes, the Psalms, the Prophets . . . ! It was this entire Jewish heritage that moved me deeply, and it was reborn in my music. To what extent it is Jewish, to what extent it is just Ernest Bloch, of that I know nothing—the future alone will decide."

Bloch's own words clearly show that his must be a purely emotional music, music born out of glowing passion and inner pathos, of lyrical contemplation and spiritual strength. Bloch indeed is a romantic at heart, and while his musical language reflects twentieth-century tonal developments in his own personal way he is essentially heir to the confessional style of Gustav Mahler. In his late-period compositions—particularly the second string quartet [1]—he comes very near to Schoenberg's expressive twelve-tone melodic invention, and the synthesis between Blochian exoticism and Schoenbergian twelve-tone influence produces a stimulating proof of the latent Oriental roots of the twelve-tone technique. Yet while Schoenberg can hardly have been conscious of the Oriental heritage of his theory at the time of its formation, Bloch would possibly deny an inner contact between his Oriental emphasis and Schoenberg's music; for fundamentally he stands as far from the new attempts at a strict tonal organization made by Schoenberg as from Hin-

[1] See Example 20(a) and (b), p. 246.

demith's revival of communal music and polyphony and from Bartók's artistic sublimation of folklore; he has perpetuated—in a way quite different from Schoenberg's—Mahler's *ethos* and search for truth, and he summarized his own faith when he composed the Twenty-second Psalm and said that he saw in the Biblical text the embodiment of an idea to which he had himself long wanted to give expression—"the idea of the suffering of humanity and of justice and happiness to be realized on earth— the vital cosmic element in the prophetic soul."

Almost all of Bloch's works are conceived in an essentially contemplative mood; they are imbued with a somber spirit of resignation in the beginning but turn to hope and confidence toward the end; only his rhapsody on the Vanity of Vanities concludes on a pessimistic note, the only rays of light and hope coming after a lyrical meditation of the royal preacher and philosopher Solomon. "I discovered its true sense fifteen years after I had written it," said the composer of this passage in "Schelomo" in 1933, "and I have used it to illustrate a page of my Sacred Service, where the words express the hope, the ardent desire, that one day men may at last recognize that they are all brethren and may live in harmony and peace." [2]

To the works that have already been named Bloch added more Jewish compositions in later years, among them "Baal Shem: Three Pictures of Hassidic Life" (for violin, 1923), "Abodah: A Melody for the Day of Atonement" (for violin, 1929), "From Jewish Life—Three Sketches" (for violoncello, 1925), "Méditation hébraïque" (violoncello and piano, 1925), and "The Voice in the Wilderness," a symphonic poem for orchestra with violoncello obbligato (1936). His crowning achieve-

---

[2] The quotations from Bloch are taken from M. Tibaldi-Chiesa's article on the composer in *Musica Hebraica* and G. Gatti's biography in Thompson's *Cyclopedia of Music and Musicians.*

ment in the field of Hebrew music is his Sacred Service (1932). But it seems that his works of the greatest intrinsic musical value are those written without a specific intention, the compositions in which Bloch forgot his role of prophet or preacher and gave free rein to his fertile invention and orchestral fantasy; his Hebraisms—evident in the rhapsodic lyricism of his asymmetric melodies, the variety of his rhythmic schemes, and the exotic coloring—are no less distinct in the works of pure and absolute music than in the compositions inspired by the Bible or by Jewish life. The two string quartets (1916 and 1945), the quintet for strings and piano (1924), the piano sonata (1935), the violin concerto (1938), and the *Suite Symphonique* (1945) are genuinely great music conceived in the entirely personal idiom which is unmistakably Bloch's on the one hand and apparently Hebraic on the other. In the purely Jewish works the struggle for adequate expression often produces disagreement between purpose and artistic result; the abstract works, on the other hand, show Bloch's individual romantic talent at its best, with his musical invention unhampered by philosophical meditation.

In speaking of the Hebraic character of Bloch's music we must not forget that it is the artist who creates a specific musical language and that the musical Hebraisms in Bloch's works are as much a personal creation of his own mind as the Czech flavor is Smetana's characteristic contribution to music and the Russian idiom Mussorgsky's. It is difficult to argue that there exist such things as national Russian or Bohemian or German musical traits: it is the great composers that have given musical expression to their people's character in the frame of works firmly rooted in their national soil; no national music was found by them ready-made for use. In the life of Diaspora Jews the place of national soil was taken by the traditional spirit of

Judaism as preserved in worship and custom, prayer and popular life; the eastern Jewish composers had given tonal form to the more popular aspects; and Ernest Bloch created a Hebraic idiom to express in music the awe-inspiring spirit of Israel's most ancient heritage. He thus holds in the history of Hebrew music the place Smetana and Dvořák hold in Bohemian, Grieg in Norwegian, and Mussorgsky in Russian music: he is the originator of a musical language which identifies his people's own character. Unlike the nineteenth-century masters, however, he has created not a *national,* but a purely *spiritual,* musical idiom —in accordance with the western nineteenth-century conception of Judaism as a spiritual force devoid of a national existence.

Ernest Bloch has taught a great number of disciples in the United States, his second homeland: the most prominent composers among them are Roger Sessions, Douglas Moore, Bernard Rogers, Randall Thompson, Frederick Jacoby, Quincy Porter, Isadore Freed, Mark Brunswick, and George Antheil. In the works of many of these musicians, even the non-Jewish ones, the rhapsodic and Hebraic elements of Bloch's music are further elaborated. His characteristic style has also greatly influenced the work of other musicians who, consciously or unconsciously, have come under his spell. Moreover, by pointing out the deep spiritual significance of the Scriptures and particularly of the Psalms and the Prophetic Books, he has inspired a good many of the contemporary compositions discussed in our survey of Biblical music (Chapter Eight). His is as great and singular an influence in the sphere of music embodying ethical and spiritual ideas as is Schoenberg's in the renovation of purely musical values; he has created a tonal language which has come to be regarded as the most congenial expression of the Biblical spirit and which continuously proves its great influence on the creations of Jewish and non-Jewish composers alike.

A number of important works of contemporary music are particular testimonies to the influence of Bloch. One of them is the "Jeremiah" symphony of Leonard Bernstein (born 1918), the versatile pianist-conductor-composer whose meteoric ascent startled the musical world in the early 1940's. The many-sidedness of his talents, his temperament, and his creative facility are strongly reminiscent of Felix Mendelssohn. Like the early romanticist, the young American composer also showed early interest in the religious sphere; but while Mendelssohn's thoughts were devoted to Christian religious music, Bernstein was concerned with the world of Hebrew thought and wisdom into which he was thoroughly introduced in his youth. His symphony does not follow any fixed program, for the composer's intention is "not of literalness but of emotional quality," and its three movements—"Prophecy," "Profanation," and "Lamentation"—are an epic, rhapsodic symphonic movement of profound depth, a grim scherzo, and a symphonic song for contralto and orchestra. The motto of the work is a broad lyrical theme of a Blochian Hebraic flavor: it gives the entire symphony a characteristic imprint and appears in various guises and variations in all three movements. The Scherzo is based on a traditional liturgical phrase which is most freely elaborated; its queer and exotic rhythms betray the influence of contemporary American jazz. The "Lamentation," based on a song Bernstein had put down on a Biblical text at the age of seventeen, makes an impressive finale which opens in a spirit of resignation and despair but ends on a note of hope and confidence. The student of contemporary music in general and of modern Hebrew music in particular cannot fail to discern that in spite of the composer's romantic leanings this is a work of the 1940's as well as the creation of a composer belonging to a younger generation than Bloch's. The Hebraic idiom shaped by the older master appears

now in modern melodic, rhythmic, and harmonic dress. No wonder, too, that a work written in the years of the second World
War is stronger and more concentrated in its emotional content
than any similar composition of an earlier period.

The "Jeremiah" symphony (which was completed in 1942)
is the only large-scale work among Bernstein's early compositions, but the characteristic style of this music has found an
outlet even in his compositions in a lighter vein; the plaintive
lyricism of the "Lamentation" often recurs in the more tender
moments of his ballet or stage music and in the opening pages
and the "Dirge" of his work for piano and orchestra after
Auden's "The Age of Anxiety" (1948–49).[3] In his lyrical and
contemplative mood Bernstein resembles another great Jewish
composer of America, Aaron Copland (born 1900), whose contributions to Jewish music are a chamber music trio, "Vitebsk"
(1929), and a choral work, "In the Beginning" (1947). Eastern
Jewish and Blochian-Hebraic influence meet in these works of
a master whose scores for theater, film, and ballet have come
to be regarded as the most typically American compositions so
far created and whose stylistic influence on the younger generation of composers cannot be exaggerated.

Works derived in some way or other from Bloch's Hebraic
music abound in contemporary music literature. Most important
among them are Randall Thompson's "Peaceable Kingdom"—a
sequence of sacred choruses, text from Isaiah (1936); Frederick
Jacoby's "Hagiographa for String Quartet and Piano"—three
Biblical narratives: Job, Ruth, Joshua (1938); and the "Song
of Anguish"—after Isaiah—for baritone and orchestra and "Song
of Songs" for mezzosoprano and orchestra by Lukas Foss (born
in Germany in 1922, now in the United States), the last a work
that was counted among the most impressive new symphonic

[3] See Example 22, p. 246.

compositions introduced in 1946. The style of expression and
texture in this "Biblical Cantata" comes very near indeed to the
"Eastern-Mediterranean" style sought by modern Israeli composers. Lukas Foss captures something of the Oriental atmosphere without having experienced its immediate impact. A
singular figure among the older generation of contemporary
composers in America is Leo Ornstein (born 1895), who has
written music in most daring and experimental idioms and
occupies a position between the Yiddish and the Hebrew composers of our times. Other works by composers of eastern
European origin who came under the influence of Ernest Bloch
are the Biblical symphonies of Nikolai Nabokoff, Jacobo Ficher,
and Jacobo Kostakowsky. The profound impression of Bloch's
Hebraic style can also be found in the music of Bernard Rogers,
who studied with Bloch for a number of years and who has
written a number of works with Biblical themes.

A cross section of the trends in Hebrew and Biblical composition of our times is given in a singularly interesting work
which was written by seven contemporary composers of great
individuality—six Jewish and one non-Jewish: a seven-part
symphonic suite based on passages from the early chapters of
Genesis. It had been the idea of the conductor and composer
Nathaniel Shilkret to commission a number of composers to
contribute to a work that was to interpret the story of the Creation and of the first men, and the suite was completed at the
end of 1945. The words are spoken by a narrator, and choral
and orchestral music supplies the musical and interpretative
background to the Biblical narration. Nathaniel Shilkret himself wrote the opening piece, "Creation"; a miniature suite by
the Polish Jewish composer Alexander Tansman follows as illustration of the tale of Adam and Eve; a dramatic piece by

Darius Milhaud tells the story of Cain and Abel; the episode of Noah's Ark is told in music by the Italian-Jewish composer Mario Castelnuovo-Tedesco; the Covenant is the theme of Ernst Toch, the composer of German Jewish descent. There follows a cantata, "Babel," for chorus with orchestra and narrator, by Igor Stravinsky—an impressive work by the composer of the powerful *Symphony of Psalms;* the *Genesis Suite* is brought to an end by a contemplative postlude from the pen of Arnold Schoenberg. The composers were completely free in their treatment of the Biblical material and wrote their contributions entirely independent of each other. The work is of special interest as it unites musical masters of great individual note who had at one time or another treated Jewish or Biblical subjects in compositions of general concern, and it thus mirrors a variety of trends in contemporary music.

The Jewish masters of the western world, the pioneers of the national idea in eastern Europe, and Ernest Bloch as the creator of a Hebraic idiom in music represent the characteristic contemporary trends in the music of Israel—but they all lack the firm roots without which an art of national aspirations can never flourish. Music conceived in complete freedom purely for the sake of art can rise to great spiritual heights and will be universal in character, while the artistic creations of composers inspired by national values may well elevate men throughout the wide world; but no man and no artist, however much a citizen of the world he may feel himself to be, can achieve a happy and sublime expression in art without having his place in society and a land he can call his own. It is thus that the Jewish features of the national Jewish music of eastern Europe and the Hebraic idiom in the works of Ernest Bloch and his

Ex.18 "Kol Nidre" by Arnold Schoenberg

Ex.19 Largo from Schoenberg's Fourth String Quartet

Ex.20a Second String Quartet by Ernest Bloch

Ex.20b V.II mezza voce
New Motif

Ex.21 "In the Beginning" by Aaron Copland

(Mezzo-Sopr.
Solo) In the be- gin-ning ___ God cre- a- ted ___ the
hea-ven and the earth and the earth was with-out form and void ___.

Ex.22 "Lamentation" by Leonard Bernstein

[Mezzo-Sopr. Solo] Ei- cha Jash- va ba- dad ___ ha- ir ra- ba- ti am

Ex.23 "In Memoriam" by Oedoen Partos

Ex.24 First String Quartet by Erich-Walter Sternberg

Ex.25 First Symphony by Paul Ben-Haim

Ex. 18. From "Kol Nidre," by Arnold Schoenberg (1938). The traditional prayer melody of the Day of Atonement service in the woodwinds (lower voice). (Copyright 1948. Used by permission of Bomart Music Publications, Long Island City, N.Y.)

Ex. 19. Largo (third movement) from Schoenberg's Fourth String Quartet (1936). The main theme, played by all strings in strict unison, shows a remarkable likeness to the "Kol Nidre" tune. (Copyright 1939, by G. Schirmer, Inc., New York. Reprinted by permission.)

Ex. 20(a). Beginning of Second String Quartet by Ernest Bloch (1947).

Ex. 20(b). New motif, derived from main theme, in 13th measure of first movement. Schoenberg's influence as well as certain melodic turns characteristic of Hebrew prayer can be noticed in the excerpts. (Copyright 1947. Reprinted by permission of the copyright owner, Boosey & Hawkes, Inc., New York.)

Ex. 21. Aaron Copland: "In the Beginning" (Genesis I), for mixed chorus a cappella with mezzo-soprano solo (1947). (Copyright 1947. Reprinted by permission of the copyright owner, Boosey and Hawkes, Inc., New York.)

Ex. 22. "Lamentation" (third movement) from Leonard Bernstein's "Jeremiah" Symphony (1942). (Copyrighted 1943 by Harms, Inc. Used by permission.)

Ex. 23. Opening of "In Memoriam" by Oedoen Partos (1946) for solo viola and string orchestra. (Copyright 1948, Israeli Music Publications, Tel-Aviv.)

Ex. 24. Opening of First String Quartet by Erich-Walter Sternberg (1924). (Copyright by the composer.)

Ex. 25. Beginning of second movement from Ben-Haim's First Symphony (1939–40). (Copyright by the composer.)

Ex. 26 Psalm 23 by A. O. Boscovich

Ex. 27 "Six Sonnets" by Joseph Gruenthal

Ex. 28 Sonatina by Herbert Brun

248

Ex. 26. Beginning of Psalm 23 by A. U. Boscovich (1947). (Copyright 1948, A. U. Boscovich and Central Cultural Department, Tel-Aviv.)

Ex. 27. Beginning of the first of the "Six Sonnets" for piano by Joseph Gruenthal (1948). (Copyright 1949, Israeli Music Publications, Tel-Aviv.)

Ex. 28. Beginning of second movement from Sonatina for violin alone by Herbert Brun (1948). (Copyright by the composer.)

school have something of a spiritually abstract and remote character and seem to lack ultimate inner satisfaction and happiness. With the return of the Jews to the ancient Land of Israel, the conditions were created for a new national and cultural center that not only is the homeland for the new dwellers of Zion but has already become in the first decades of its renewed existence the greatest source of inspiration for Jewish culture and art all over the world.

Chapter

TWELVE

The Return to Zion

THE POLITICAL AND ECONOMIC conditions prevailing toward the end of the nineteenth century had demanded decisive resolutions from the central European and eastern Jews, as the (voluntary) cultural assimilation in the West and the (enforced) isolation in the East provoked sharp reaction in the Jewish as well as in the Gentile world. The national renascence was borne by the strong belief in the living values of Judaism; and while the first *ideal* aims led to a recognition of the latent qualities of the folk life and customs and to a gathering of forces, there soon also began attempts at a *real* centralization and a re-orientation of Jewish life. In Leo Pinsker's treatise *Auto-Emancipation* (1882) it is for the first time frankly declared that the Diaspora is the cause of all evil; and the author demands that the Jews concentrate in two great countries: in America, which had already become a great center of Jewish settlement, and in Palestine—primarily the country of future

251

potentialities, where the Jews would have to take real possession of the soil, the cultivation of which they would have to
learn anew. Pinsker's treatise preceded by fourteen years that
other famous book of identical purpose—Dr. Theodor Herzl's
Jewish State (1896). The author of the latter work was also
undecided at first what country would prove most suitable for
large-scale Jewish settlement: he proposed Argentina in addition to Palestine. It is significant that the call for centralization should have come from two completely different camps:
Pinsker's from the east of Europe, where oppression and persecution made the life of the Jews miserable, Herzl's from the
assimilated circles of the West. And though both men at first
failed to recognize that the creation of even an autonomous
Jewish colony among other people could never provide a completely satisfactory solution in face of the traditional love and
longing for Zion, it soon became clear that only one country
offered both the material and the spiritual conditions for the
foundation of a Jewish state. Only in the ancient Land of Israel,
the Holy Land of their ancestors, could a new community prosper; for throughout the two millennia of its dispersion Jewry
had never forgotten the ancient splendors of Zion and had never
ceased praying that the coming year would find them in a newly
built Jerusalem. The religious authorities turned against the
purely national zeal of the new movement; but Zionism derived
its great impact from the very promise of a political, national
gathering of the dispersed people in the ancient beloved land
of the Bible.

The first pioneers set out for Palestine in 1882, the very year
in which Leo Pinsker's treatise was published, and since then
many waves of immigration have brought settlers to the Land
of Israel from all parts of the globe. Colonization was begun
by the pioneers of the "Bilu" and "Hovevei Zion" groups, which

came from the countries of the European East in the 1880's, and the same Jewish centers provided the bulk of settlers till in the 1930's there set in the large-scale immigration from central Europe. The settlers not only hailed from different lands and had diverging notions of how to realize the national life; they also differed greatly in their cultural standards, their languages, their forms and ideals of life, and their educational and professional backgrounds. But all groups and individuals were united in their wish to create a new community and to become a people tied together by the bonds of land, creed, language, and common work—and the first step to achieve their goal was the recognition of Hebrew as the common tongue in the old-new country.

The beginnings of the new national home are mirrored in the development of the country's cultural life and thus in its early music history as well. With their language and literature, with their customs and ways of life, the pioneers brought along their songs, their music. The early pioneer songs, sung in the hours of sweat and toil, some surviving to this day, were songs in a Russian, Polish, Ukrainian, Rumanian, or Caucasian idiom; central and western European, Turkish, Egyptian, and Yemenite influences mingled with them freely at a later stage, and the folklore collected by the Society for Jewish Folk Music formed an important part of the early song repertoire. The first working songs, dance tunes, and nursery rhymes that were actually created in Palestine were modeled on those melodies which the immigrants had brought with them, but they soon showed the first signs of an independent character with the beginning of an amalgamation of European and Oriental traits. It is interesting to note that this amalgamation was much more quickly arrived at by the eastern European immigrants than by western European Jewry, the explanation being that eastern European music had generally greater affinities with the Oriental character than the creations of central and western European masters of music, and that the old Jewish tradition was much more alive in eastern countries than in the assimilated western world.

The first function of the new Palestinian center was that of a vast melting-pot in which—much as in the early history of the United States of America—cultural heritages and traditions were recast to form raw material for a new and independent civilization. The Yiddish-Jewish Diaspora song, Hebraic expression, Oriental elements, and modern musical techniques became the foundations of Palestinian music; and the process of amalgamation and crystallization is still going on—more than sixty years after the first settlers set foot on Palestinian soil.

The songs sung by the pioneers while working in the fields or paving the roads, the tunes accompanying the merry dance, the ditties sung by the children in kindergarten and school provide everywhere the foundations of community life and form the starting point for the creators of art music. In Palestine, as in other countries during a period of colonization, they remained the only means of musical expression for many decades. It is with the growth of the villages and the foundation of urban centers that art music gained a foothold in the country and that the Palestinian soil was prepared for artists as well as for composers of music reaching beyond the popular sphere.

Early musical life in the Land of Israel followed European patterns as much as the songs of its settlers. The larger rural communities and the inhabitants of the first Jewish city, Tel-Aviv (founded in 1909), felt the desire to enjoy organized public performances of music as they knew them from European concerts. Musically gifted settlers were the artists for the earliest musical evenings, but with the growth of the communities it soon became worth the while of international artists touring the Mediterranean countries and the East to halt in Palestine and to sing or play for its naturally enthusiastic audiences. Music schools had in the meantime sprung up in the cities and prepared the youth to appreciate good music, and in the twenties the country could boast of a many-colored musical life—with music institutes and concerts in the towns, choirs and popular instrumental groups active in the villages and settlements, and a general enthusiasm for music that astounded visiting artists.

Palestine's first school of music was established in Tel-Aviv in 1910, a year after the city had been founded as a suburb of the ancient Arab town of Jaffa. The initiator of the school was Mrs. Shulamith Ruppin, wife of the noted Jewish sociologist, and it was named Shulamith School after her; M. Hopenko was appointed to lead the affairs of the institution. After one year, seventy-five pupils were studying at the institute, and Tel-Aviv's first concerts were the "public examinations" of its youth in the hall of the first Hebrew grammar school, the Herzliah Gymnasium. A school orchestra was later organized to give concerts in Tel-Aviv as well as elsewhere in the country and to entertain the British forces there in the first World War. A second music school was opened in Tel-Aviv in 1914 by Miriam Levit. Jerusalem got a music institute through the initiative of its first British governor, Sir Ronald Storrs, in 1918, while Haifa followed in the early twenties with an institute led by Mrs. Dunia-Weizmann.

The conditions of life in those early years did not allow of any but rather primitive musical entertainment, as contact with the great world was still limited and the endeavors of an enthusiastic few did not yet find the soil as fertile as it became after the mass immigrations of the twenties and thirties. The Jerusalem governor himself encountered these difficulties when he attempted to introduce music to his people by arranging concerts at Government House. On one occasion he had invited two pianists from Jaffa to play classical piano duets. Though the performers had made a journey of many hours on donkey-back to give the concert, the audience was apathetic; Storrs records in his memoirs (*Orientations*) that the only item that was applauded and had to be encored was the buffet provided during the intermission. For the Music Institute Storrs selected an interconfessional committee and himself procured the teachers as well as the musical instruments. In the ranks of the army he found the violin virtuoso Tchaikov and appointed him principal of the school; the first funds were collected by Tchaikov on an Egyptian concert tour. The institute was open to Christians, Jews, and Moslems alike, but as 90 per cent of the pupils and 75 per cent of the teachers were Jews, and as the Christians and Moslems did not actively support the venture, Storrs handed the school over to the Jewish authorities; they assumed responsibility for its affairs for a short interim period till, after Tchaikov's departure, it became an independent establishment under the directorship of Sidney Seal, a British pianist on active service in Palestine at that time and its principal ever since.

The first large-scale musical organization came into life in 1923 with Mordecai Golinkin's foundation of a Palestine Opera. A year before, attempts at forming an opera company had already been made by Storrs in Jerusalem, but nothing had come of the plan. Golinkin was a conductor who had dreamed of a national opera for Palestine while he was still in Russia and who now realized his vision with the support of an en-

Toscanini and Hubermann after the general rehearsal for the opening concert of the Palestine Orchestra, December 26, 1936. (*R. Weissenstein*)

Folk-dance festival at Dahlia in the Ephraim Mountains, summer, 1947. (*Z. Kluger*)

Yoel Engel.

Joseph Achron. (*Maurice Goldberg*)

Paul Ben-Haim. (*Nachmani*)

Erich-Walter Sternberg. (*G. Sternberg*)

thusiastic troupe of singers and musicians. The Palestine Opera
was opened in Tel-Aviv on July 28, 1923, with a performance
in Hebrew (translated by Aaron Aschmann) of Verdi's *La
Traviata*, and in the course of the four years of its existence
the Opera presented some twenty works in Hebrew versions
by Aschmann, Meir Freidmann, and Abraham Schlonsky. The
company performed in Tel-Aviv, Haifa, and Jerusalem; Golinkin
also used its orchestra and chorus for separate symphonic and
choral concerts. In 1927, when the Opera had to cease activities for lack of funds, a symphony orchestra was founded by
Fordhaus ben-Tsissy, who later devoted most of his time to
oratorio and became musical director of the "Habima" Theater, which in 1932 permanently settled in Palestine. A truly
remarkable feat was the Beethoven Centenary celebration in
1927 under the auspices of the Hebrew University: the symphony orchestra performed the *Eroica* and Fifth symphonies
at the 2,000-seat amphitheater of the University in Jerusalem,
and a series of chamber music evenings was also arranged. In
the same year the Institute for New Music was founded in
Jerusalem by Mordecai Sandberg. In 1929 a smaller instrumental ensemble made its appearance under the baton of Zvi
Kumpaneetz, who stayed in the country till 1932 and gave some
sixty concerts during the three years of its activities. But Palestine did not remain without an orchestra once the beginnings
had been made in the concert field, and in 1933 a Philharmonic
Society was founded which gave regular concerts under the
conductors Golinkin (who also tried at various times to revive
his Opera), A. D. Jakobsohn, Wolfgang Friedlaender, and
Michael Taube, who instituted subscription concerts in December 1934. Other important musical groups of the early
thirties were a Chamber Opera founded by Benno Fraenkel;
a Chamber Orchestra and Academic Choir conducted by Karl

Salomon, and a Musical Society in Jerusalem; and the first organized String Quartet, led by Emil Hauser, who had in 1933 established the Palestine Conservatory of Music and Dramatic Art in collaboration with the Department of Education of the British Administration in Palestine and with the Extension Department of Music then operated by the Hebrew University.

The artists—conductors, musicians, and composers—who visited Palestine in the early years of its musical development make a long and impressive list. They include the composers Michael Gnessin (who spent many months composing in a small wayside house fifteen miles from Jerusalem), Lazare Saminsky, and Joseph Achron; the conductor Oscar Fried; the violinists Jan Kubelik, Henri Marteau, Jascha Heifetz (after whom Tel-Aviv called the concert hall in the Shulamith Conservatoire), Jacques Thibaut, Joseph Szigeti, and Bronislaw Hubermann; the singer Joseph Schmidt; the pianists Leopold Godowsky, Emil von Sauer, Artur Schnabel, Artur Rubinstein, Alexander Borowsky, Imre Ungar, Alexander Brailowsky, Bruno Eisner, and Franz Osborn; the Casadesus family; and the cellists Arnold Földessy and Emanuel Feuermann. For most of these artists their sojourn in Palestine proved a singular experience, and many returned to the country several times. The settlers received their concerts enthusiastically, and large audiences greeted their appearances in the towns. Their programs were the same as those they presented to their listeners in New York and London, Paris and Berlin, Rome and Moscow, Cairo and Tokyo. Western middle-class concert life was thus transplanted to a country in which pioneer spirit and labor reigned foremost, and the musical organizations and the symphonic and operatic groups also imparted to the urban and rural communities the foundations of musical art taught and appreciated all over the western world. The activities of the local groups and the visiting performers thus combined in linking Palestine with the outside musical world; the evolution of a musical culture rooted in the soil and in the atmosphere of the land began in entirely different quarters.

The cultivation and composition of specific Jewish or Hebrew music was furthered by various factors. Concerts devoted solely to Jewish composers or to popular works were instituted in Jerusalem by the composer Jacob Weinberg—who in October 1924 completed the first opera on a Palestinian subject, *The Pioneers* (first performed in New York, where the composer later made his home)—and in Tel-Aviv by Yoel Engel; in the colonies and among the workers united in the Labor Federation ("Histadruth") since 1920 there were organized choruses and instrumental groups; a "Popular Music Institute" was founded by David Schorr; and in 1929 a musical form that became most popular with the Palestinians—community singing in the frame of Sabbath festivals—was launched by Menashe Rabinovitz (Ravina) with the support of the Hebrew poet laureate H. N. Bialik. In 1925 a first gathering of the country's choirs was held in the Jesreel Valley; the meeting gave a great stimulus to choral singing and choral compositions, and the distribution of suitable material to the many groups, especially in the settlements, became the concern both of the Popular Music Institute and of the cultural divisions of the national organizations. Yehuda Shertok, conductor and composer at Yagour settlement, was the first to publish sheets and booklets regularly for the use of the choirs; this task was taken up on a large scale in the forties by the Cultural Department of the Labor Federation.

Another stimulus to composers and at the same time to the

possibility of a widespread distribution of specifically Jewish music was given by the Hebrew theaters, particularly by the Workers' Theater "Ohel" ("Tent") and by the "Habima" ("The Stage"), both of which specially commissioned music for their plays from famous Jewish composers and from local musicians. As many of their early performances—apart from the Hebrew versions of world literature—depicted scenes from Jewish Diaspora life, it was mostly the Yiddish trend in music that dominated the compositions; only gradually did Palestinian plays come to be written, confronting the composer with the problem of an adequate expression in music of the old-new country's re-creation. This theater music—contributed in the early years especially by Yoel Engel, Salomo Rosowsky, Verdina Schlonsky, and Yedidya Gorohov—represents the second stage in the evolution of Palestinian music, for here the composer was forced by the substance of the play to search for a new style breathing something of the Palestinian atmosphere.

The decisive year in Palestinian music history was 1936. In April of that year the British administration opened the Palestine Broadcasting Service—operating an English, Hebrew, and Arabic section—and put at the head of the Music Division a musician of many talents and interests, Karl Salomon. In December 1936, the greatest and artistically most perfect musical organization yet created was launched when Arturo Toscanini raised his baton—in the largest hall on the Levant Fair Grounds in Tel-Aviv—for the first concert of the Palestine Orchestra (which in 1946 was renamed the Palestine Philharmonic Orchestra and became the Israeli Philharmonic Orchestra with the foundation of the State of Israel in 1948). The establishment of a first-class symphony orchestra had been the vision of an artist who, like many others, had paid concert visits to Palestine and had taken away with him the deep impression of an unusually enthusiastic audience and a most fertile soil for good music. This was Bronislaw Hubermann, who devoted many months of organizational work, auditioning, and fund-raising to realize his idea, and whose own enthusiasm infected musicians and conductors all over the world. After the ensemble had had several months of preparation under the guidance of Hans Wilhelm Steinberg, Toscanini offered his services to the new venture, and his concerts with the Palestine Orchestra have gone down as historic events in the upbuilding of the country.

The foundation of a first-class symphonic ensemble attracted a number of outstanding musicians to settle in the country, and their orchestral concerts as well as their chamber concerts and their pedagogic activities raised the standard of music appreciation and music making to high levels. Masterpieces of old and modern music, virtuoso concertos, and chamber works could be enjoyed by audiences all over the country, and special care was taken that the workers were given concerts of their own. The youth of the country could rely for their musical training on teachers of highest standing and were now able to get a first-hand knowledge of the world's great music. The results were soon felt with the rise of a generation of young artists who mounted Palestinian concert platforms side by side with world-famous performers and who could also hold their own before the critical audiences of Europe and America.

The Palestine Orchestra invited a great number of conductors and soloists to visit the country, and many followed the call without asking for remuneration. Among the conductors who appeared in the first ten years of the Orchestra's existence were Felix Weingartner, Malcolm Sargent, Issai Dobrowen, Eugen Szenkar, Hermann Scherchen, Jascha Horenstein, Bernardino Molinari, Charles Münch, Leonard Bernstein, Manuel Rosenthal, Izler Solomon, Ignaz Neumark, Josef Rosenstock, Eduard

Lindenberg, and Simon Parmet. Of the conductors resident in Palestine Michael Taube, Georg Singer, Otto Selberg, Jonel Patin, Karl Salomon, Marc Lavry, Otto Lustig, Paul Ben-Haim, Bronislaw Sculz, and Wolfgang Friedlaender (Youth Concerts) have appeared regularly. Among the soloists of the first decade were Adolf Busch, Ignace Friedmann, Alice Ehlers, Magda Tagliafero, Harriet Cohen, Sabine Kalter, Oda Slobodskaya, Simon Goldberg, Stefan Aschkenase, Jacob Gimpel, Imre Ungar, Shulamith Schafir, Monique Haas, and Nicole Henriot. Many soloists were drawn from the ranks of the orchestra, and young artists took their bow with the organization before embarking on an international career—foremost among them the pianists Pnina Salzmann, Ella Goldstein, Sigi Weissenberg, and Menahem Pressler.

The broadcasting station began its musical programs with modest chamber music offerings and solo appearances but gradually enlarged the scope of its activities till it founded a small-scale symphony orchestra of its own—with Karl Salomon and H. Schlesinger as permanent conductors. The tri-lingual structure of the service was from the very beginnings instrumental in imparting to the many communities in the country the music of the Oriental and European spheres and thus greatly contributed to the mutual knowledge of the Palestine people. With the years the Palestine Broadcasting Service became the greatest consumer of music in the country and offered a hearing to every composer who had something to say. Competitions and commissions gave an additional stimulus to the creators of music. While the Palestine Orchestra was slow in recognizing the importance of furthering the Palestinian composers, the music division of the broadcasting station encouraged them to create and present their music; in November–December 1947 it presented a "Month of Jewish Music" for the first time. With

Israel becoming a state in May 1948, a State Broadcasting Service—named Kol Israel ("The Voice of Israel")—took over the organization and musicians from the British-administrated service.

Various musical organizations utilized the possibilities given by the permanent settlement in the country of the great number of artists serving the Palestine Orchestra. The Tel-Aviv Museum instituted regular chamber music evenings on Saturday nights. Musical societies sprang up in Jerusalem, Haifa, and some of the colonies—notably Rehovoth. The idea of concerts of Jewish music was revived by Joachim Stutchevsky. The Palestine Section of the International Society for Contemporary Music (first recognized in 1928) renewed its activities. The Cultural Department of the Labor Federation developed the concerts in the settlements. Interest in ancient music was aroused by the concerts of the harpsichordist Frank Pelleg. Youth orchestras and workers' ensembles came into existence to provide training centers for future members of the Philharmonic. Even the dream of a Palestine Opera materialized again. After a number of short-lived attempts in the field, the Palestine Folk Opera was founded in 1941, with Georg Singer, Lev Mirsky, Mordecai Golinkin, and Wolfgang Friedlaender as operatic conductors and Marc Lavry as leader of operetta and ballet, and with Gertrud Kraus as choreographer. A considerable number of serious and light musical stage works were produced in the five years of this group's existence, and in 1945 it produced a work especially written for the organization, an opera from Palestinian folk life, *Dan the Guard,* with a libretto by Sh. Schalom and Max Brod and music by Marc Lavry. After a two-year break, opera came to the fore again in the early months of 1948.

With the steep rise in the standard of performance and appreciation the popular movements got an impetus of their own. Larger choruses were organized in the urban centers—foremost among them the United Choruses under Shlomo Kaplan and the Workers' Chorus under Israel Brandmann—to cultivate the Palestinian and classical, traditional and socialist song in contrast to the large-scale oratorios and classical and modern chamber-choral music offered by the Palestine Oratorio (conductor: Fordhaus ben-Tsissy) and the Tel-Aviv Chamber Chorus (conductor: Otto Lustig), respectively. Composers were stimulated to write works for the various organizations. Some of them also wrote symphonic music in spite of the limited opportunities for performance. Encouragement and first recognition came with the Tel-Aviv Municipality's institution of a Yoel Engel Prize in 1945. The first composers receiving the prize were Mordecai Starominsky, Alexander Uriah Boscovich, Erich-Walter Sternberg, Paul Ben-Haim, Menahem Mahler-Kalkstein, Oedoen Partos, and Marc Lavry.

The Palestinian song achieved a character of its own, and in 1942 the first convention could be held to demonstrate and to discuss its various aspects. In 1944 twenty-four choirs formed a chorus of one thousand at the Choir Festival of Ain-Harod in the Jesreel Valley, and in the same year the folk-dance movement was launched on its way; when the second Folk Dance Festival was arranged at Dahlia in the Ephraim Mountains in the summer of 1947, some five hundred dancers presented their popular creations—accompanied by new Palestinian folk music—to a public of some twenty thousand spectators. The Palestine Broadcasting Service had meanwhile greatly developed its technical possibilities, and many important musical performances and festive occasions could be broadcast throughout the country. Music festivals were arranged in various places, the most memorable occasions being the Bach-Handel Festival in Jerusalem (twice arranged), the Passover Chamber Music Weeks (held annually) at Ein Gev on the shores of Lake Kinnereth, the Folk Festivals sponsored by the Artists' Colony at Zikhron Jaacow, and festive performances on Mount Scopus.

The musical enthusiasm of the masses and the steady development of musical organizations provided a most fertile soil for the composers of Palestine. Concert, theater, the dance, choirs, radio, and popular festival offered manifold opportunities for the creative musician; the high standard achieved in musical performances raised the demands of the public as well as the aims the artist set himself. At the same time the transplantation of European musical organization and western concert music confronts the composer with serious problems. In the sphere of folk music the melting-pot process, already far advanced, has created the foundations for the new Palestinian folk music. Musicological research, too, has revealed priceless treasures to the student of folklore—both in the sphere of Bible cantillation (Salomo Rosowsky) and in the Oriental field (A. Z. Idelsohn's collections and studies, which were continued in Jerusalem by Robert Lachmann; since this scholar's premature death in 1939, Dr. E. Gerson-Kiwi has continued recording, transcribing, and studying Oriental music). The composer of art music, however, must build up a new idea—the idea of Palestinian music—out of a background of knowledge based on centuries of European music.

The composers of the Jewish national school in eastern Europe and their followers had tried to derive a typical Jewish musical style from the folk tunes of the Jewish Diaspora; their idiom was closely bound to that of their environment. The

Hebraic idiom of the Bloch school had been inspired by the spirit of Judaism as preserved in the Bible and the prayers; there was no connection in this music with actual contemporary Jewish life. In new Israel the composer lives in a newly formed society and in an environment full of historical and sacred associations and pregnant with promises of the future, he sees a landscape he loves, he feels the pulse of his own people's life, and he speaks the language of the land—which is a modern form of the Hebrew of the Bible. Living has achieved a meaning for the Jew who has become a master of his own life on his own soil but who has to start shaping his existence anew from the very beginnings. The immigrant must learn to cultivate the fields that will yield their harvest to his people and to conquer the spirit of the language in which he will speak to his neighbors; the creative artist must likewise acquire the roots of a new language and attempt to absorb the spirit and atmosphere of the country. In judging the first efforts of Israeli composers in the various fields of music we must not forget that only civilizations boasting of a long and unbroken tradition and supported by strong national foundations have been able to produce sublime, lasting works of art, and that composers who are creating under conditions new to them and in a country that only gradually reveals its singular beauty must needs overcome a stage of struggling, experimenting, and search before achieving the first heights of artistic expression.

Many different tendencies might be observed in the output of the country's composers. A great number are utterly unconscious of the influence exerted by the new medium, yet their music mirrors the Palestinian atmosphere in one way or another; one group pretends that no truly Palestinian music can ever be created without the elaboration or imitation of the melodies typical of the old Orient or the new country; yet another opinion is expressed by those saying that not the melodic material but the spirit of the country should characterize the new compositions—that is to say, the spirit of the glorious Biblical past or of the modern pioneer work. It need not be stressed that great music has never developed by way of "tendencies" and that the composer's success depends not so much on his material, his sympathies and ideas, and his artistic desire as on the greatness and originality of his invention and the craftsmanship underlying the presentation of his musical inspiration. But young nationalistic communities do not always heed such deliberations, and very often a poor work is applauded on account of its national trends or the appearance of a favorite tune. In fact, such a work might even inspire composers of stature to better and greater music. Many Israeli musicians have been led to believe that a "set of variations on a Palestinian folk song" must needs represent Palestinian music, or that musical craftsmanship is less important than national enthusiasm clad in sounds. Yet the country has also to its credit a great number of composers in whose creations a faithful and natural musical expression is found—in the frame of a purely musically conceived composition—of the work and feast, the sorrow and mirth, the song and dance, the tradition and youth of the country.

As in all national renascence movements, the most important composer in early Palestine music is "Anon." His songs and dance tunes appear in kindergarten and schools, in the fields, on the village green, and at rural festivities, and he inspires the song writers throughout the country. Nursery song literature in Hebrew had its origin in the works of Yoel Engel, who based the bulk of his children's songs on texts of H. N. Bialik; modern writers of popular tunes include Mordecai Zeira, Daniel Sambursky, Yehuda Shertok, Shalom Postolsky, Emanuel Pugatchov, Menashe Ravina, Nahum Nardi, Ephraim Ben-Haim, Moshe Wilensky, Zvi Kaplan, Yariv Esrahi, Yoel Walbe, Sarah Levy, Izhaq Edel, David Sahavi, Nissan Cohen-Melamed, Benjamin Hatulli, Marc Lavry, and Yedidya Gorohov. The songs of the last-named show a particularly interesting synthesis of East and West. The genuine folk songs and those attempting to become such are being collected and published at intervals, and choral arrangements are made for the sake of settlement choruses.

Some of the composers mentioned above have also created works on a larger scale: they have written art songs, folk-tune arrangements and variations, and instrumental works of merit. Based on music by Engel and on tunes of the country are instrumental compositions by Israel Brandmann (born 1901). His "Variations on a Theme by Engel" for piano and string orchestra (1934) and his "Variations on a Hebrew dance tune" for strings (1928) have been widely played, and his violin sonata of 1927 is the first valuable work in an abstract form with distinctly Palestinian traits in its thematic invention. Izhaq Edel (born 1896) has pondered much on the possibilities and necessities of modern Hebrew music and has come to the conclusion that European scales and harmonies should have no place in the work of the Palestinian musician but that the structural forms of sonata, rondo, and aria are the highest achievements that can possibly be reached and can well be filled with entirely new contents. He thus uses them as frames for his oboe sonatina (1943) as well as for his two string quartets, while his themes are based on synagogal or ancient modal scales. His "Capriccio" (1946—in a version for piano and in an orchestral arrangement) elaborates a Jewish dance theme in rondo form.

The atmosphere of the country is the most important aspect in the two suites for string orchestra and the variations for string quartet by Yariv Esrahi (born 1904) and in Israel's most popular orchestra work, the light-hearted symphonic poem *Emek* by Marc Lavry (born 1903). Lavry is also the composer of the Palestinian opera already mentioned, *Dan the Guard* (1944–45), of an oratorio, *Song of Songs*, of a symphonic poem, *Stalingrad*, and of a *Tragic Symphony* (commemorating the martyrs and heroes of the Warsaw Ghetto); in addition he has written songs, choruses, music for the theater, and works for various other media. In a purer form he has introduced folk material and folk spirit in his concert overture *From Dan to Beersheba* (1947) and in his two piano concertos (1945, 1947).

Though the composers so far mentioned have enriched Palestinian music with a number of fine works, their contributions cannot in any way be regarded as "contemporary music," strictly speaking, derived as they are from traditional and conventional forms and means of expression. The same holds true with regard to a number of composers hailing from the sphere of influence of the Russian Jewish Folk Song Society, such as S. Rosowsky, Gabriel Grad, Moshe Rapaport, Shalom Aharoni, and—to a lesser extent—of Aviassaf Bernstein and Joachim Stutchevsky. The former has composed concertos for piano (1944) and violin (1945), variations for violoncello and orchestra (1944), a suite of musical pictures inspired by the scenery and moods of the Lake of Tiberias (1945), and some piano and chamber music. Stutchevsky has done much for the study and arrangement of eastern European folklore music, but has absorbed something of the Palestinian atmosphere in his latest works, which include a charming suite for flute and piano, a duo for violin and violoncello, and piano music.

The picture becomes different when we approach the composers who have come to Israel from western European countries or those who have deliberately sought contact with modernism. Even when they occasionally take a folk song or dance motive as basis of a musical creation, these composers attack their material from a purely formal, abstract point of view. Karl Salomon (born 1897), for instance, has written a set of orchestral variations on a well-known Palestinian folk tune (1937) and given the work the scope and form of a symphony, each theme of which presents a new variation of the folk theme, with the theme in its original form heard only in the last stages of the work. An ingenious conceit is a set of variations in virtuoso style for violin and orchestra composed on a children's song. In a suite of Greek dances Karl Salomon has demonstrated the affinity of the folk music of two Mediterranean countries. The same composer's piano concerto is a successful attempt to blend popular influence and symphonic principles, while much individuality is felt in his choral suite on texts by John Donne.

Most of the composers hailing from central and western European spheres of influence have paid more attention to the originality of style and the transplantation of contemporary principles of composition than to folklore; they let invention work freely for them, and little of their music suggests historical, geographical, or national problems. Biblical subjects or Palestinian impressions have nevertheless often given food to their inspiration.

The leading figures among the composers of Palestine in the "symphonic era" are Erich-Walter Sternberg and Paul Frankenburger, who has assumed the Hebrew name of Ben-Haim. Sternberg (born 1898) was a well-known figure in contemporary German music before he settled in Palestine, and his independent style has changed little if at all in his Palestinian years. Sternberg has no sympathy with borrowings from folk music, but a prominent feature of his creations is the preponderance of Jewish subjects, which already prevailed in some of his pre-Palestinian compositions. Sternberg has written a large number of songs, two string quartets, and choral music. Among his works are "Song of Praise" after Yehuda ha-Levy and "Inferno," an anti-war cycle, a children's opera based on Hugh Lofting's "Dr. Dolittle" stories, a piano trio, a quintet for wind instruments, and a symphonic overture; his most important works so far are the "Praise Ye," the suite for string orchestra *Joseph and His Brethren* (1939), and the large-scale symphonic work *The Twelve Tribes of Israel* (1942). In the last-named composition, each of the Biblical tribes is characterized by one variation of the basic theme, which—in the composer's own interpretation—represents the common root and the common belief of the Israelite tribes. There is firm strength in the theme of the work, and the variations draw their character and mood from the descriptions of the tribes in the Holy Scriptures. The final variation, dedicated to Benjamin, the chosen tribe, the "ravenous wolf" according to Gen. 49:27, takes the form of a mighty quadruple fugue to crown an impressive and finely conceived work. In the suite *Joseph and His Brethren* each of the short movements depicts a scene from the legend which at all times has attracted painters, writers, and musicians, and the thoughts, feelings, and experiences of the principal characters are transformed into musical ideas. Yet in spite of the programmatic character of the composition, form and thematic development are musically conceived for each of the eleven movements. In 1947 Sternberg completed a symphonic poem, "Hearken, O Israel," in which a traditional prayer chant is the foundation for a symphonic song of praise in elaborated rondo form.

The music of Paul Ben-Haim (Frankenburger—born 1897), like Sternberg's, stems from central European modernism; but while Sternberg speaks an ardent, sometimes even acid, musical language, the themes and moods of Ben-Haim tend to the soft and pastoral. No wonder, then, that Ben-Haim's Palestinian compositions show a stronger influence of the rural, pastoral atmosphere of the countryside. The composer's pre-Palestinian works include an oratorio, *Joram,* a *concerto grosso,* and *Pan*— a symphonic poem for soprano and orchestra. In Palestine, Ben-Haim has completed two symphonies and a number of fine songs, in addition to chamber music, which seems to be the composer's very best medium of expression. His four-movement string quartet (1937) is the first of his chamber works written in Palestine, but it is already permeated with the singular atmosphere of the land. A characteristic pastoral theme of the viola opens the quartet and may be said to dominate all of its movements—a sonata movement, a puckish scherzo, a short air-like andante, and a delicate rondo. Ben-Haim's second Palestinian chamber work is a set of variations on a Hebrew folk song for piano, violin, and cello (1939), the theme of which is of Bedouin origin; and this was followed by the composer's finest chamber music composition of this period, a quintet for clarinet and strings (1941) which contains a pastoral sonata-form molto moderato, a capriccio-like scherzo, and a set of variations on a quiet and melodious original theme.

The two symphonies of Ben-Haim offer complete contrasts. The first (1939–40) contains two dramatic movements of tragic quality, while the second of the three movements is a contemplative, lyrical piece of rare beauty, possessed of an inner calm that can leave no listener unimpressed. The second symphony (1943–45), in four movements, is pastoral throughout and bears the stamp of folkloristic influence; contemplation of landscape and the beauties of nature have occupied the composer's mind, and the opening theme of the flute sets the pastoral mood of the first movement as well as of the entire symphony. The work is delicately scored, especially in the Notturno, which forms the third movement. A symphonic work on a smaller scale is Ben-Haim's poem for violin and orchestra, "In Memoriam" (1942), a requiem without words that takes the shape of a one-movement piece in three interlinked parts: an introduction, an invocation, and a dramatic allegro ("Remembrance"), after which an epilogue calls back the theme of the introduction and brings the work to a solemn conclusion. A concerto for strings (1947) and a piano concerto (1948) followed the style of the composer's Second Symphony.

Of great originality is some of the work of Joseph Kaminski (born 1903), violinist and conductor of Russian-Polish origin. This includes a concertino for trumpet and orchestra (1940–41), in which the first movement is a travesty of a hackneyed Vivaldi theme (it is styled "Un poco Vivaldi"), after which there follow a slow and lyrical movement with a liturgical touch, and a boisterous tarantella; *Ha-Aliyah* (*The Ascent*), a set of variations on a popular Jewish melody (sung at the Feast of Lights) symbolizing the characters of the nations with whom the Jews lived before their ascent to Palestine and closing with a Zion's Hymn of the medieval poet Yehuda ha-Levy; and a comedy overture, in which the middle section was inspired by Oriental singing and dancing. Smaller-scale works are a "Legend and Dance" for strings and a ballad for harp and orchestra (1945), while in the realm of chamber music Kaminski has written an interesting string quartet. It begins with a many-colored allegro which leads without break into a variation movement. The theme of the variations is a songful theme of delightful simplicity; it is elaborated in five "character variations" ending in a quiet epilogue. The last movement of the quartet is dominated by gay dance rhythms, but a quotation of the main theme from the beginning of the work ushers in a contemplative, almost mystic mood, and the work closes in delicate pianissimo sounds.

Though reared in musically different surroundings, Verdina Schlonsky (born 1905), Palestine's foremost woman composer, shows in her works a spiritual affinity with Kaminski's music. Her works include a three-movement symphonic poem, *Jeremiah—David—Heroic March* (1937); a suite for string orchestra (1937), compiled from her music for the Hebrew theater; and a symphony in four movements. They culminate in the piano concerto (1942–44), a two-movement composition in which polyphonic, playful, dramatic, and virtuosic elements are molten together. Most characteristic in this effectful concerto is the presentation of the main themes in two-part texture and their subsequent separate development. In 1948 Verdina Schlonsky completed her second symphony and a symphonic cantata.

An intellectual of many interests is Max Brod (born 1884), critic, novelist, poet, composer. His music includes a violin sonata, two rustic dances for piano and for orchestra, and a Hebrew requiem composed in memory of his wife. European memories and great interest in the Oriental foundations of Palestinian music characterize his works.

The compositions of Joseph Gruenthal (born 1910) and Heinrich Jacoby (born 1909) are works of absolute music that show little influence of Palestinian or general Oriental character; this may be due to the fact that the composers are residents of Jerusalem and have less contact with rural life and atmosphere than their colleagues in the coastal towns or country villages. Jacoby's works include concertos for viola (1939) and violin (1942), a four-movement symphony (1944), a series of miniatures for small orchestra (1945), two string quartets, and a piano trio—the latter containing the material out of which the composer derived the third and fourth movements of his symphony. Jacoby is a descendant of the Hindemith school, and the German composer's playful polyphony as well as his later romantic trends is mirrored in the Jerusalem musician's works. While on active service in the Israeli army (1948–49) Jacoby turned to a simplified idiom in his songs, string music, and a variation work for small orchestra, "David Had a Lyre." He also wrote a symphonic prologue for orchestra. Gruenthal's orchestral compositions culminate in the choreographic poem "Exodus" (1945–46) in which tonal form is given to one of the most dramatic incidents in ancient Jewish history—Israel's deliverance from the serfdom of Egypt and the miraculous passage of the Red Sea. It is a composition deeply imbued with the Biblical spirit but interpreting the ancient texts in the contemporary musical idiom and in the frame of a form that is purely musically conceived; relevant Biblical passages are sung by a baritone soloist in the five interlinked sections of the poem. Gruenthal has also written a piano concerto (1944), the four movements of which are full of dramatic developments and interesting pianistic problems; his chamber music includes suites and sonatas for unaccompanied cello and viola and a duo for cello and harp. In a work described as a symphonic cantata (1948–49) for piano, solos, chorus, and orchestra, the Jerusalem composer revives an ancient legend from the Maccabean period, in which a heroic mother rejoices over the steadfastness of her sons although their refusal to bow before the Cross costs them their lives. Hannah, the mother, takes her own life in an exalted spirit, praising the one and only God. Gruenthal's work re-creates the episode in stark concentration and in dramatic colors; the piano solo part serves as a kind of narrator and commentator. The composition ends in a jubilant "Hallelujah," at the climax of which two boys' voices join the chorus to intone an ancient Oriental psalm tune.

A spiritual force of decisive interest was the work and teachings of Stefan Wolpe (born 1902), a composer who was himself greatly impressed by the Palestinian surroundings during the five years he stayed in the country, and whose influence is still being felt in the work of some of his former students, such as Zvi Kaplan, Wolf Rosenberg, and Herbert Brun. Wolpe, now a resident of the United States, continued his occupation with Palestinian and Biblical themes in his new country. The many-coloredness and vivacity of his rhythms lend to his music, especially his choral works, which are widely sung by Palestinian choruses, a flavor and character quite of his own. A conspicuous place among his large-scale works is occupied by the Moses ballet, "The Man from Midian" (1943).

Among the composers of European modernist tendencies, there must still be named Abraham Daus (born 1902), who has written a "Legend and Scherzo" for string orchestra, an *Overture to a Cantata* (1942)—being the elaborated version of the Prelude to the *Sea-Gate Cantata* celebrating the Tel-Aviv Port —and a number of chamber works, among them songs with flute and viola accompaniment and a set of variations on a Yemenite theme for flute and piano; Oedoen Partos (born 1907), a musician of highest stature, who has written "In Memoriam" for viola and string orchestra, a concertino for string quartet, a choral fantasia with orchestra employing Oriental tunes in an ingenious way, a viola concerto, and songs with instrumental accompaniment; Yehuda H. Wohl (born 1904), whose two symphonies and chamber music were influenced by Paul Ben-Haim's music; Berthold Kobias (born 1895), a prolific composer of chamber music for various combinations; Hans Hurtig (born 1907), who wrote songs and piano music; Bernd Bergel (born

1909), who puts his great talent almost exclusively to the service of the children's choruses; and Peter Gradenwitz (born 1910), who has written a *Symphony of Variations* for solo instruments and orchestra (1941), a serenade for violin and small orchestra (1941) in one movement, a chamber trio for flute, viola, and cello (1939), and *Four Palestinian Landscapes* for oboe and piano (1946) in four movements.

One of the most interesting compositions produced by Palestinian composers is the *Sabbath Cantata* by Mordecai Starominsky (born 1916), written to psalm texts and passages from the Song of Songs. The work is set for chorus and instrumental accompaniment; the composer develops his counterpoint on a modal basis, but the impression is not archaic at all, since plain-chant and synagogue music were derived from a common source. A *Folk-Chorus Suite* by the same composer did not quite reach the standard of the earlier work, though it contains many novel choral effects and an authentic Hebrew touch. Starominsky has written little for instruments.

In the middle forties Palestine composers began to talk of a "Mediterranean school," taking up the term "Mediterranean music" coined by Nietzsche almost a century before when he opposed the singular charm of Bizet's "southern" music to the heavy strains of German—particularly Wagner's—tonal art. Paul Ben-Haim belongs to the group tending to incorporate something of the Oriental-pastoral-Mediterranean spirit in their music—for which "eastern Mediterranean music" would be a more proper term. Max Brod is one of the proponents of the school, and Marc Lavry's works of the later forties likewise have much affinity with this style. M. Mahler-Kalkstein (born 1908) has turned, after composing modernistic music in the

French style, to "Mediterranean" composition and has gained success with a five-movement *Folk Symphony* (1945); in his string quartet (1945) he has tried to give expression to Palestinian-Oriental elements in the frame of a classically shaped chamber work and has continued in a similar way in two sonatinas for piano, a concertino for strings and flute, and his songs. His second symphony (1947–48) has a Biblical theme: in its center stands King David, and the four movements are described as "Childhood," "Heroism," "Exile," "Splendor."

The most ingenious composition in the early development of the "eastern Mediterranean style" is the concerto for oboe and orchestra (1943) written by Alexander Uriah Boscovich (born 1908). This work was the first effort of a composer to introduce genuine Oriental elements not only into the melodic and rhythmic foundations of a musical work but also into instrumental expression and scoring. The three-movement concerto culminates in the second movement, in which a monotonous melody conjures up the world of an endless desert colored by slowly moving caravans. This singular stroke of genius was followed by a less successful attempt at orientalizing music, a *Semitic Suite* (1946) of little song- and dance-pieces for orchestra in which the orientalisms breathe too much of descriptive effect. Boscovich's only other large-scale work so far is a violin concerto (1942, revised 1944).

The youngest generation of composers active in the later forties is less concerned with the problematic sides of Israeli music than the musicians of the older generations, for many of them were born in Palestine or at least received their education and training there and absorbed the Palestinian way of living and the spirit of the country in a much more immediate way

than the immigrants of former generations. Among the talents
of this younger generation are Moshe Lustig (born 1922),
among whose compositions there stand out a sonata for harp
and French horn (1943–44), a quintet for flute and strings
(1945), a piano piece (1946), and "Kinnereth"—an orchestral
fantasy on two Palestinian tunes (1946); Herbert Brun (born
1918), who combines in his works clear-cut formal design and
concise expression with a singular freshness of attack and
rhythm, and who has written *Five Piano Pieces*, some chamber
music, a concertino for orchestra in three movements (1947),
and a sonatina for violin alone (1948); Robert Starer (born
1924), whose strikingly individual works—characterized by
fresh melodic invention and lyrical swing—include a three-
movement violin sonata (1945), a suite for strings with violin,
viola, and cello solo (1945), a *Rhapsodie Orientale* for orchestra
(1946), a *Divertimento* for five instruments (1946), a string
quartet (1947), and a piano concerto and an orchestral overture (1948); Ben-Zion Buschel (born 1928), who has composed
a song cycle after Tagore for high voice and flute (1946), a
choral motet (1947), a ballad for violin solo, piano works,
"Movements" for orchestra (1947–48)—a three-movement
suite—a "Prayer" for baritone and small orchestra (1948), and
a four-movement symphonic composition with vocal solo
(1948–49) based on David's mourning over Jonathan's death
(II Sam. 1:19); Yehoshua Lakner (born 1923), whose first
suite for piano has interesting color; and the young Jerusalem
composers Heinz Alexander (born 1915), Zvi Ben-Josef (1918–
1948), Gideon Olsvanger, and Abel Ehrlich. Of great promise
was Daniel Friedlaender (1918–1936), to whose memory a rest
house for artists—nucleus of an artists' colony—was dedicated
in Zikhron Jaacow by his mother.

New problems were presented to the Jewish composer with

the actual foundation of the Jewish State of Israel in 1948. For the first time in modern history a Jewish army was formed, which needed its own stirring songs and marches; the larger musical institutions assumed representative character, though in its early struggles the new state could not be expected to accept state sponsorship of opera, theater, and orchestra; and Jewry all over the world looked to their brethren in the Land of Israel for works of art as strong and as elevating as the defenders of the country had shown themselves to be against its aggressors. These developments imbued the Israeli composers —and the artistic institutions—with a new sense of responsibility, for their country suddenly stood in the limelight of the news and of world interest; and they were confronted with new tasks that had to be solved in new ways.

Composers on active service during Israel's war reacted to the exigencies of the time mainly in three ways: they tried to contribute new songs to the folk repertoire—which had not hitherto included marches and soldiers' songs; they wrote choral and instrumental works in a simplified medium; and they turned in an increasing degree to the books of the Bible, especially to those episodes offering parallels between Israel's struggles and victories of old and the fight of the new State of Israel. New strength and confidence permeates the musical works created under the impact of the latest events; not only the compositions of the younger men but also those of the older composers reflect the spirit of the times, and the entire future development of Israeli music will be decisively influenced by the trends formed in modern Israel's greatest period.

The student of music in modern Israel will note the rather curious lack of interest on the part of modern Israeli composers in religious music—the field which constituted the main branch of Jewish musical and creative activity throughout the centuries of Diaspora life and which still largely occupies Jewish composers in Europe and the Americas. The reason lies in the very structure of Israeli Judaism. The bulk of the youth is organized in the Labor Federation and lives in socialist settlements in which the traditional feasts assume new forms of celebration, while the Jewish orthodox tradition finds itself in a state of opposition. In order to perpetuate the law as it has guided world Jewry for thousands of years, the Israeli authorities have to contend with many obstacles; and in his fight to preserve the very existence of tradition and traditional law the religious leader cannot be expected to adopt progressive views and to develop synagogue service and liturgical forms as they were developed in all countries of the Diaspora. Thus the liturgical style in Palestinian synagogues still presents a rather chaotic mixture of tendencies and forms, and no real attempts at unification and modernization are evident. The composer has thus no interest in contributing to its literature, and the Israeli musician is not drawn to the liturgy at all. In a wider sense this was also the reason why he found the way to Biblical texts and poetry much later than his colleagues in other countries, a paradoxical situation that only a new order in Israel's religious life—which will surely develop in the new state—can be expected to improve. On the other hand, the new forms of ceremonial and celebration developed in the rural settlements and villages—in the early state still independent in their ways and means—are important musically, for the composers of the country are eager to contribute their share to the musical life of the communities and have often written elaborate works—for whatever choral and instrumental forces are available in the settlements that needed them—that revive the spirit of the ancient feast born out of the cycles of nature and of national elevation. Yehuda Shertok, Matthityahu Weiner, and Nissim Nissimov—all active in rural settlements—were the first to compose musical "services" for the community feast. In the oratorio-like works of this kind, in which all solo singers, chorus, and instrumental players that are locally available are the actual performers of the music in addition to speakers or narrators, the bulk of the community is generally asked to participate in the choral singing at the climaxes of the service, ancient practice is thus revived in the struggle for new forms of life and expression. It may well be that these rural "services" will become the nucleus for a new organization of communal life in the entire Land of Israel and greatly influence the reorganization of religious life as well as the musical forms to be developed by Israeli composers.

Two generations of composers have so far devoted their talents to the upbuilding of a musical culture in the Land of Israel, but impressive though their contemporaries may find their best contributions to Palestinian music, they will most certainly be viewed by future historians as no more than modest beginnings in a new field. The future of Israel's musical art depends on a great many factors—on the development of the country and its resources, on the degree to which the new State of Israel will recognize and further the work of its creative artists, and on the acknowledgment on the part of the composers themselves of the task allotted to them. The composer of modern Israel not only serves his own newly created nation; his may be a historic position. Throughout their ancient and modern history the Jews have played a role of mediator between the civilizations—from the time of the Patriarchs down to the most recent centuries; with his return to Zion the Jew has brought the modern West to the ancient East and performs a twofold mediation. Israeli artists and composers may play a decisive part in the age-long and ever-topical search for a synthesis between East and West; taking his task seriously, he may by his own work and imagination exert a far-reaching influence throughout the world on the ways and means of a new art and on the great masters of music to come.

EPILOGUE

Between East and West

AFTER ALMOST TWO THOUSAND years of dispersion
the Jews have begun to create a new national and cultural center on the very same spot that once saw their most splendid
achievements in national life, science, and art. They have
brought Occidental civilization to their Oriental brethren; they
have applied modern agricultural technique to a soil that had
been plowed in the same way since time immemorial, they have
irrigated the desert and made it bloom again by means of modern
scientific knowledge, and they have imported the rich heritage
of European art into a country that had preserved a most ancient
tradition.

Under the influence of European music, Oriental musicians
are rapidly adapting their tunes to western harmonization and
abandoning their own instruments in favor of the piano and
the modern orchestral instrumentarium. Comparative musi-

cology and Oriental music research have to make great strides
to record the last remnants of ancient Oriental (Near Eastern)
musical culture. The song of the Bedouin, the shepherd, the
Muezzin, and the teller of epic tales, the synagogue chant of
the Yemenite, Samaritan, and Persian Jews—all of them preserved since Biblical times with probably little variation, if any
at all—will soon be irretrievably lost; for communities that have
lived in seclusion and isolation since the beginning of the Christian Era are now exposed to the influence of western civilization
through their direct contact with the western world as well as
through listening to broadcasts from all over the globe.

In the song of the Oriental-Jewish communities the new settlers of Palestine meet the last echoes of the ancient Hebrew
tradition, while the actual sounds of the Oriental world are ever
present in the music of their Arab neighbors and of other Oriental
communities. Arab music in this area is in a state of flux, too,
and no truly great musician seems to have arisen as yet to give
expression to the impact of East and West. The Arab Orchestra
—brought into being by the Palestine Broadcasting Service and
continued independently by the Trans-Jordan–owned station
after the end of the British mandate—has been experimenting
widely in this direction, and a number of Arab school choruses
of remarkable standing cultivate Occidental as well as Oriental
music. The considerable Armenian community, with a venerable
tradition of religious music of its own, has produced a number
of interesting musicians, and so have other Oriental groups. In
the midst of this world the composer of modern Israel sets to
work—burdened with the heritage of the great musical tradition of Europe, disturbed by the twentieth-century changes in
the social status and artistic creed of the composer, haunted by
nostalgic memories, and placing all his faith in a new and hope-
ful future. Commanding a musical technique based on the prin-

ciples of harmony and counterpoint, he is confronted in the new country with melodic patterns that do not naturally lend themselves to harmonization or polyphony. To him, Oriental melodies at first seem monotonous, lacking in variety, primitive; and he is inclined to forget that the Oriental, on his part, can as little tell the difference between a Bach chorale, a Mozart symphony, and a Schoenberg quartet—thinking all of these monotonous, lacking variety, primitive—as the Occidental can distinguish among an oriental Call to Prayer, a shepherd tune, and an ecstatic dance. Yet the unique atmosphere of the country, the continuous contact with rural life of all those who do not confine themselves within the walls of the cities, and the feeling that only with difficulty could the musician continue to create as he has done in a radically different world make themselves felt in the works of almost all serious composers—pioneers all in their own particular way.

It is interesting to compare Jewry's position in Israel today with that of thousands of years ago. Today, as then, immigrants are coming from many different countries, bringing along with them the habits and customs, the civilizations and tastes of their former surroundings. Today, as then, Palestine represents a large crucible and its inhabitants nourish great hopes of a culture and art of their own. In early times, Jerusalem was a spiritual center and a center of philosophy, art, and science that fed not only Judaism alone but all surrounding cultural centers. The Temple, symbol of ancient Judaism, has not been rebuilt, and Jerusalem has become an international city claimed by many creeds and nations all over the civilized globe. But the Hebrew University on Mount Scopus overlooking venerable old Jerusalem as well as the width of the Jordan Valley and the Dead Sea, the stony vastness of the desert and the Judean Mountains, is rapidly developing into a new spiritual center of the Middle East. Authors, poets, and novelists, scientists and research workers are active all over the country, and Israel's musicians and composers are regarded wherever they appear in the wide world as "musical ambassadors" of a rising culture.

East and West meet in the works of the composers of modern Israel, and not all of them may be conscious of their position in musical history. The need for a fresh musical impetus has long been felt in contemporary music in general, and composers have, from the times of Debussy, looked to the East or to the song and dance of the "primitives" for new inspiration. From the exotic elements in Debussy and in Mahler to the eastern European sources of Béla Bartók's great works and to the Schoenbergian twelve-tone scale with its ancient *maqam* = character, from the earliest invasion of Spanish, African, and American rhythms into art music to the influence of jazz and swing elements on the masters of today, there is an unbroken chain of musicians who are dissatisfied with the highly developed musical art of the West. It is thus that the example of Israel—whose modern city of Tel-Aviv has been aptly described as a "show-window to Europe"—may prove of benefit to western music one day, as an example of possible ways to infuse new elements into the art of contemporary music. It is thus that the time may not be too distant when textbooks of musical history will devote a special chapter to "Contemporary Music in the Land of Israel," just as they now carry in their first pages a survey of "The Music of the Ancient Hebrews." It is thus that a fascinating story unrolls before the eyes of the historian who visits that Eternal Land and listens to the song of its shepherds in the deserts and the newly plowed fields and greening meadows, to the exquisite music carried by the light breeze over the Sea of Galilee, and to the sounds of the many-voiced chorus and orchestra reverberated by the mountains of Judea. . . .

Appendix
ONE

Chronological Table of
Jewish General and Cultural History

Approximate dates are enclosed in parentheses.

GENERAL HISTORY	CULTURAL HISTORY

Chapters One and Two: From the beginnings to the destruction of Jerusalem and Israel's dispersion

Before the Common Era:

3761 Beginning of the Jewish calendar (fixed in 344 of the Common Era)	
(2000–1600) The Patriarchs (2000: Abraham)	
13th Century Moses	
1200–1050 The Judges	(1150) Deborah's Song
1050–586 The Kings (1000) David (950) Solomon	1000–450 The Prophets

GENERAL HISTORY

933 Partition of the Kingdom
722 Assyrian Exile
587 Fall of Jerusalem to Nebu-
    chadnezzar
    Babylonian Exile—to 538

538–332 The Persian period
332–166 The pre-Maccabaean
    Greek period
331 Foundation of Alexandria

320 Judea passes under Egyptian
    rule
203 Antiochus takes Jerusalem
    Judea under Syrian rule

167 Maccabaean revolt, headed
    by Mattathias
165 Victory of the Jews at Beth-
    Zur
    Rededication of the Temple
104 Kingdom of the Hasmoneans
63 Pompey conquers Jerusalem
    and puts an end to Jewish
    independence
48 Death of Pompey
37–34 Herod "the Great," King of
    Judea

The Common Era:
6 Judea becomes a Roman prov-
    ince
4 B.C.–39 A.D. Herod Antipas
    ruler of Galilee and Pe-
    raea
29 (?) Crucifixion of Jesus
30 (or 35) Conversion of St.
    Paul
37 Birth of Josephus

CULTURAL HISTORY

(725) Isaiah
(600) Jeremiah
(575) Ezekiel
(700) The earliest Hebrew script
    known: The Siloah in-
    scription

(621) The discovery of the Torah
(450) Completion of the writing
    of the Torah (Ezra)

(300) The Greek version of the
    Scriptures: "Septuaginta"

(450–250) The "Sofrim"—
    learned writers
(250) Simon the scholar
(180) The Book of Ben-Sira writ-
    ten (Hebrew)
30 (to 10 A.D.) Hillel the Great
    (from Babylon) teaches
    in Jerusalem
(300–100 A.D.): Influence of
    Hellenism on Jewish cul-
    ture

40 (to 20 A.D.) Philo of Alexandria

10–220 The Tannaites, whose
    teachings are collected in
    the Mishna

38 Persecution of Jews in Alexandria
41–54 Claudius Emperor
54–68 Nero Emperor
64 Burning of Rome and persecution of Christians
66 Jewish revolt in Palestine
69–79 Vespasian Emperor
70 Titus destroys Jerusalem and
   the Temple

70 Jochanan ben Zakkai estab-
   lishes a Rabbinical School
   at Jamnia (Yavneh)

Chapter Three: The Jews under Hellas and Rome

79–81 Titus Emperor
81–96 Domitian Emperor
96–98 Nerva Emperor

98–117 Trajan Emperor

117–138 Hadrian Emperor
117–118 Jewish revolt in Palestine
132–135 Revolt of Bar-Kochba
138–161 Antonius Pius Emperor
161–168 Marcus Aurelius
(180–250) Soldier Kings and decline of the Roman Em-
   pire
(250) and 303 Persecution of the
   Christians on a large scale
(250–650) Babylon under Persian
   rule
284–305 Diocletian Emperor
323–337 Constantine the Great
   who makes Christianity
   the state religion (325
   First Church Council at
   Nicaea)
330 Constantinople (formerly Byzantium) becomes capi-
   tal of the Roman Empire
(350) Jewish revolt in Galilee

76–79 Josephus completes his history of the "Jewish War"
93–94 Josephus completes his "An-
   tiquities"
(100) Synod of Yavneh; Old Testament canon finally fixed
(125) Rabbi Akiba

(135) Martyrdom of Rabbi Akiba
140–175 Revival of the Jewish
   schools in Palestine
(190) Official text of Mishna fixed
   by Rabbi Yuda ha-Nassi
219 Babylonian schools founded at
   Sura and Nehardea by
   Rab and Samuel respec-
   tively, later at Pumbeditha
220–500 Period of Amoraim, the
   interpreters and teachers
   of Scriptures and Mishna
   after the Tannaites
320–370 Decay of the Palestinian
   schools; completion of
   Palestinian Talmud; fix-
   ing of the Jewish calendar
   by Hillel II

GENERAL HISTORY

361–363 Julian the Apostate

375 Beginning of the great Migration of People

395 Partition of the Roman Empire after the death of Theodosius:

    395–1453 Byzantine (Eastern) Empire

    395–476 Western Empire (conquered by the Goths)

614 Persian troops conquer Palestine

629 Restoration of Byzantine rule in Palestine

CULTURAL HISTORY

499 Completion of the Babylonian Talmud

589–1038 Period of the Ge'onim (heads of the Babylonian schools at Sura and Pumbeditha)

Chapters Four and Five: The Settlement of the West and Medieval History

321 The first Jews in Cologne

711 The Arabs conquer Spain

8th–13th Century The Jews flourish in Islamic Spain

640 Bostanai, founder of the Dynasty of the Babylonian Exilarchs

1096 The first Crusade, followed by persecution of Jews

    The first Privileges for the Jews in Germany: Speyer and Worms

1236 Privileges for the Jews in all German countries

1296 Expulsion of the Jews from England

1298 Expulsion of the Jews from Franconia

1306 Expulsion of the Jews from France

761 Rise of Karaite sect

892–942 Sa'adyah ha-Gaon

998–1038 Hai, the last of the Geonim

(800) Massora

900–1400 Flourishing of Jewish philosophy of religion

1075–1105 The commentaries of Raschi

1050 Gabirol

1080–1145 Yehuda ha-Levi

1135–1204 Maimonides

1165–1173 The travels of Benjamin of Tudela

1200–1600 Flourishing of the Cabala

1233 The writings of Maimonides burned at Paris

1242 Copies of the Talmud burned at Paris

1348–49 "The Black Death" in Europe

1394 Second expulsion from France

1453 Constantinople falls to the Turks

1492 The Arabs driven from Spain, expulsion of the Jews

1497 Expulsion of the Jews from Portugal

1525 Josel von Rosheim defends the Jews in his writings

1591 Spanish Jews settle in Holland

1500–1700 The Messianic movement

1657 Resettlement of the Jews in England

(1310) Publication of the "Zohar," the Cabalist compendium

1340 "Turim" Law Code completed by R. Jacob ben-Asher

1437–1509 Don Isaac Abarbanel

1455–1522 The humanist Reuchlin

1475 The first Hebrew books printed

1492 First printed edition of Mishna with commentary of Maimonides issued at Naples

1520–1523 First complete edition of the Babylonian Talmud in 12 vols. folio

1523–1524 First printed edition of the Jerusalem Talmud in one volume

(1560) Shulchan Aruch compiled

1626–1676 Sabbatai Zvi, the Pseudo-Messiah

1632–1677 Baruch Spinoza

Chapter Six: Renaissance Italy

1516 The Ghetto of Venice

(1600) Privileges for Jewish scholars and artists in Renaissance Italy

1513–1578 Asarja dei Rossi, the Jewish humanist

1571–1648 Leone da Modena

(1587–1628) Flourishing of dance and music in the golden age of Italian music. Salomone Rossi and other Jewish musicians at the Court of Mantua

1629 A Jewish music academy in Venice

GENERAL HISTORY   CULTURAL HISTORY

Chapters Seven to Ten: A Century of Emancipation and the National Movement in Eastern Europe

1740 Israel Baal Shem, Hassidic movement

1787 Declaration of freedom of religion in America

1790 Declaration of equality of the Jews by the French National Assembly

1812 The Jews recognized as citizens in Prussia

1869 Conclusion of the European emancipation: the "North German Union"

1840 Pogroms in Damascus

1881 (and after) large-scale pogroms in Russia

1729–1786 Moses Mendelssohn

(1800) Beginnings of the reform movement

(1823) Science of Judaism

(1800–1933) Flourishing of the Jews in European culture and the arts

(1800–1918) Flourishing of the cantoral art in the eastern European countries

1877 Abraham Goldfaden founds his Jewish (Yiddish) Theater in Jassy

1908 Foundation of the "Society for Jewish Folk Music" in St. Petersburg

Chapter Twelve: The Return to Zion

1882–1905 First wave of immigration into Palestine

1905–1914 "Second immigration" and creation of a labor movement in Palestine

1914–1918 First World War

1917 Russian Revolution

1917 Balfour Declaration: England supports the building of a National Home for the Jews in Palestine

1919–20 Pogroms in the Ukraine

1919–1924 "Third Immigration"

1922–1948 England's mandatory power in Palestine

1924–1927 "Fourth Immigration"

1874 Chaim Weizmann born near Pinsk

1882 Pinsker: "Auto-Emancipation"

1896 Herzl: "The Jewish State"

1897 First Zionist Congress (in Basle)

1916 "Habima" Theater founded in Moscow

1924 The first Hebrew opera in Palestine

1925 Opening of the Hebrew University in Jerusalem

1927 Beginning of "Fifth Immigration," growing after 1933 and including children's and youth immigration on a large scale

1933 Rise of the National-Socialist regime in Germany and growth of Fascism in all central Europe

1936–1939 Arab riots in Palestine

1939–1945 Second World War and destruction of Jewish communities in central and eastern Europe—pogroms and mass murders till the fall of the Nazi regime

1947 The United Nations decree the partition of Palestine and the establishment of an independent Jewish State

1933 (and later) Emigration of Jewish artists from the central European countries

1936 Opening of Palestine Broadcasting Station and inauguration of Palestine Orchestra (Toscanini)

Appendix
TWO

Biblical References to Music
and Musical Instruments

OLD TESTAMENT (HEBREW)

Genesis—4:21 (Kinnor, 'Ugab)
    31:27 (Kinnor, Tof)
Exodus—15:20 (Tof)
    19:17, 19; 20:18 (Shofar)
Leviticus—25:9 (Shofar)
Numbers—10:2, 8, 9, 10 (Hazozra)
Joshua—6:4, 5, 6, 8, 9, 13 (Shofar, Keren)
Judges—3:27; 6:34; 7:8, 15, 18, 19, 20 (Shofar)
    11:34 (Tof)

I Samuel—10:4 (Nevel, Tof, Halil, Kinnor)
    13:3 (Shofar)
    17:17, 23 (Kinnor)
    18:6 (Tof, Shalishim)
II Samuel—2:28 (Shofar)
    6:5 (Kinnor, Nevel, Tof, Mna'anim, Zelzelim)
    6:15; 15:10; 18:17; 20:1 and 22 (Shofar)
I Kings—1:34, 39, 41 (Shofar)

[1] The instruments are discussed in Chapters One and Two.

I Kings—1:40 (Halil)
    10:12 (Kinnor, Nevel)
II Kings—3:15 (Minstrel)
    9:13 (Shofar)
    11:14, and 12:13 (Hazozra)
I Chronicles—13:8 (Kinnor, Nevel, Tof, Zelzelim, Shofar)
    15:16 and 20 (Nevel, Kinnor, Zelzelim)
    15:19–28 (Miziltaim, Nevel, Kinnor, Hazozra, Shofar, Zelzelim)
    16:5–7, 28 (Nevel, Kinnor, Zelzelim, Hazozra)
    23:5 (Players on musical instruments)
    25:1 ff. (Kinnor, Nevel, Keren, Zelzelim)
II Chronicles—5:12, 13 (Zelzelim, Nevel, Kinnor, Hazozra)
    7:5 (Instruments of music)
    9:11 (Kinnor, Nevel)
    13:12, 14 (Hazozra)
    15:14 (Shofar, Hazozra)
    20:28 (Nevel, Kinnor, Hazozra)
    23:13 (Hazozra)
    29:25 ff. (Zelzelim, Nevel, Kinnor, Hazozra)
    35:15 (Singers)
Ezra—2:65 (Singers)
    3:10 (Hazozra, Zelzelim)
Nehemiah—4:18, 20 (Shofar)
    7:44, 67 (Singers)
    10:40 (Singers)
    12:27, 35, 41, 45, 47 (Zelzelim, Nevel, Kinnor, Hazozra, Singers)
    39:24 and 25 (Shofar)
Job—21:12 and 33:31 (Tof, Kinnor, 'Ugab)
Isaiah—5:12 (Kinnor, Nevel, Tof, Halil)
    14:11 (Nevel)
    16:11 (Kinnor)
    18:3 (Shofar)
    23:16 (Kinnor)
    24:8 (Tof, Kinnor)
    27:19 (Shofar)
    30:29 (Halil) and 32 (Tof, Halil)
    50:1 (Shofar)
Jeremiah—4:5, 19, 21; 5:1, 17 (Shofar)
    31:4 (Tof)
    42:14 (Shofar)
    48:36 (Halil)
    51:27 (Shofar)
Ezekiel—26:13 (Kinnor)
    28:13 (Tof and Pipes)
    33:3 ff. (Shofar)
Daniel—3:5 ff. (Keren, Mashrokita, Katros, Sabca, Psanterin, Sumponia)
Hosea—5:8 (Hazozra, Shofar)

Joel—2:1, 15 (Shofar)
Amos—2:2, and 3:6 (Shofar)
     5:23 and 6:5 (Nevel)
Zephaniah—1:16 (Shofar)
Zechariah—9:14 (Shofar)
      14:20 (Zelzelim)
Psalms—33:2 (Nevel-Assor)
     44:8 (Minnim)
     47:5 (Shofar)
     49:4 (Kinnor)
     57:8 (Nevel, Kinnor)
     68:25 (Kinnor)
     71:22 (Nevel, Kinnor)
     81:2, 3 (Nevel, Tof, Kin-
       nor, Shofar)
     92:3 (Nevel, Kinnor)
     98:5 and 6 (Kinnor, Ne-
       vel, Shofar, Hazozra)
     108:3 (Nevel, Kinnor)
     137:2 (Kinnor)
     144:9 (Nevel-Assor)
     149:3 (Tof, Kinnor)
     150 (Shofar, Nevel, Kin-
       nor, Tof, Minnim,
       'Ugab, Zelzelei-Shema,
       Zelzelei-Truah)
Ben-Sira—9:4 and 32:5–8

NEW TESTAMENT (GREEK)

Matthew—9:23 Aulos (oboe)
I Corinthians—13:1 Kumbalon
         (cymbals)
I Corinthians—14:7 Aulos, Kithara
Revelation—1:10; 4:1; 9:14 Sal-
       pinx (trumpet)
Revelation—5:8; 14:2 Kithara
Revelation—18:22 Kithara, Aulos,
       Salpinx

Appendix
THREE

"Hatiqvah," The Jewish National Anthem

IN 1897 the song named "Hatiqvah" (Hebrew for "The Hope") was adopted as the Jewish national anthem. The author of the poem is Naphtali Herz Imber (born 1856 in Zloczow, died 1909 in New York), a poet and writer who had much interest in music and who also published some essays on musical folklore and on music in the ghetto. The poem "Hatiqvah" appeared in 1886 in a collection *Barkai* published by Imber in Jerusalem (this was in the very first years of Jewish recolonization in Palestine). Tradition has it—but the authenticity of the story is difficult to prove—that Imber wrote the poem in the colony Rishon-le-Zion (one of the first new settlements on the coastal plain) and that a farmer of Bohemian descent adapted for the song an old Bohemian folk tune (sung today as in No. 10 of the music table). Another possibility is that Imber used phrases of the traditional "Yigdal" prayer melody (one version of which is given in No. 7). Rabbi Israel Goldfarb, Brooklyn, New York, who when he was still a young student knew Imber, says in a communication to the author of this book: "I feel that Mr. Imber borrowed it (the music) from a Cantorial composition by the famous Cantor Nissan Belzer

No. 1. Beginning of the hymn as sung in Israel today.

No. 2. A tune contained in the Prayer for Dew ("Tal") of Sephardic Jews (Noskowski Collection, p. 218—after Idelsohn).

No. 3. Beginning of a Polish folk song (after Idelsohn).

No. 4. Basque folk song (after Salaberry, *Chants populaires du pays basque*, 1870, p. 260).

No. 5. Basque folk song (after Salaberry, *op. cit.*, p. 236).

No. 6. Spanish cancio (Felipe Pedrell, *Cancionero popular español*, Vol. II, p. 186).

No. 7. Beginning and cadence of the "Yigdal" tune as composed by the English singer and composer Leon Singer at the end of the eighteenth century; it inspired Thomas Olivers, a Welshman and Wesleyan minister, to write a hymn, "The God of Abraham, Praise," on the same melody (this hymn became very popular after its publication in 1772). See Idelsohn, *Jewish Music*, New York, 1929, pp. 220 ff.

No. 8. The form given to the ancient Bohemian folk tune in Smetana's symphonic poem "Vltava" (1874): it first appears there in the key of E minor, later in E major; for purposes of comparison it is here noted in G.

No. 9. Part of the beginning of Mahler's "Song of a Wayfarer" (1884); Mahler hailed from a small Bohemian town.

No. 10. A Bohemian folk song (after Martinowski, *Böhmische Volkslieder*, No. 22, quoted by Tappert, *op. cit.*, p. 18).

No. 11. A German nursery song.

No. 12. A German nursery song.

of Odessa. Imber, who was contemporaneous with that well-known Hazzan, must have heard the composition sung and took over the part which begins with 'We'Havi'ēnu leZion Irĕcha' (—and bring us to Zion, Your City). I examined that composition in manuscript and found the music to tally note for note with the Hatiqvah melody. It is not likely that Nissan Belzer copied from Imber because it was the custom in those days to borrow Synagogue melodies for secular songs. We have many such examples of Goldfaden borrowing from well-known Cantorial compositions for his Yiddish operettas when the Yiddish stage was young." (Letter from Rabbi Goldfarb, dated July 16, 1948.) The author has not been able to examine the said composition himself, but it must clearly be of the "Yigdal" type (No. 7).

The words and music were adopted as the Jewish national anthem by the First Zionist Congress in Basel in 1897, following the suggestion of the Zionist leader David Wolffsohn, which was unanimously accepted by the assembly.

The tune of the "Hatiqvah" is one of the so-called "wandering melodies," which appear in many forms and variations as folk songs of many peoples and which have consciously or unconsciously inspired composers to melodic invention of their own (see Wilhelm Tappert: *Wandernde Melodien. Eine musikalische Studie,* Berlin, 1889, from which some of the examples illustrated have also been taken).

The "Hatiqvah" melody can be found in a great number of folk tunes and musical works: our selection of twelve tunes—transposed for the purpose of easier comparison—lists only the most characteristic examples.

Bibliography

THE SUBJECTS discussed in this book have attracted many hundreds of scholars and writers throughout the centuries, and a complete bibliography of Hebrew music and kindred themes would fill a volume by itself. The following selection lists the most conclusive books and articles and those which have been especially helpful to the present author in his work and which contain detailed biographies and lists of sources. We have not included in the present bibliography the—sometimes quite remarkable—material contained in the large encyclopedias, general, musical, and Jewish, the most reliable of which are those in the *Jewish Encyclopedia, Jüdisches Lexikon, Dictionary of the Bible, Encyclopedia Britannica, Grove's Dictionary of Music and Musicians, Oxford Companion to Music, Harvard Dictionary of Music, H. J. Moser's Musiklexikon,* Lavignac's *Encyclopédie de la Musique, Encyclopédie de la musique et dictionnaire du conservatoire,* etc. Nor have we listed biographies of musicians which are included in every musical book of reference. The Biblical sources (listed in Appendix Two and throughout the book itself) and the Talmudic sources (frequently quoted in Chapter Three) are not given in the bibliographical list either.

For the historical part of the book the author has used the works of

Simon Dubnow, H. Graetz, Josef Kastein, Josef Klausner, and Arthur Ruppin (*Sociology of the Jews*).

The following list opens with general books and with those containing much bibliographical material. The books on special periods follow in chronological order (following the chapters of the book), and a bibliography of Hebrew books on the subject and of antisemitic literature concludes the survey of a literary field plowed by so many authors.

HISTORICAL SURVEYS: HEBREW AND JEWISH MUSIC, GENERAL MUSICAL HISTORY

Berl, Heinrich. *Das Judentum in der Musik*. Berlin, 1926.

Cohen, A. Irma. *An Introduction to Jewish Music*. New York, 1923.

Cohen, Maxwell T. *The Jews in Music*. New York, 1939.

David, E. *La Musique chez les juifs*. Paris, 1873.

Ewen, David. *Hebrew Music*. New York, 1931.

Haywood, Charles. "The Gentile Note in Jewish Music," *Chicago Jewish Forum*, 1946.

Idelsohn, A. Z. *Jewish Liturgy*. New York, 1934.

———. *Jewish Music in Its Historical Development*. New York, 1929.

———. *Thesaurus of Hebrew Oriental Melodies*. 10 vols., Leipzig, 1914–1932.

Landau, Paul. "Das Orientbild des modernen Europa" (MS).

Lang, Paul Henry. *Music in Western Civilization*. New York, 1946.

Lauko, D. *Die jüdische Musik*. Pressburg, 1926.

Levy, S. *Das Judentum in der Musik*. Erfurt, 1930.

Rothmüller, Aron Marko. "Die Musik der Juden" (MS).

Sachs, Curt. *The Commonwealth of Art*. New York, 1946.

———. *The History of Musical Instruments*. New York, 1940.

Salesky, G. *Famous Musicians of a Wandering Race*. New York, 1927.

Saminsky, Lazare. *Music of the Ghetto and the Bible*. New York, 1935.

CHAPTERS ONE TO THREE

Ackermann, A. *Der synagogale Gesang in seiner historischen Entwicklung*. Trier, 1894.

Arends, L. A. F. *Ueber den Sprechgesang der Vorzeit*. Berlin, 1867.

Bevan, E. R., and Singer, Charles, eds. *The Legacy of Israel*. London, 1927.

Cook, Stanley. *An Introduction to the Bible*. London, 1945.

Delitzsch, Franz. *Physiologie und Musik in ihrer Bedeutung für die Grammatik, besonders die Hebräische*. Leipzig, 1868.

Engel, Carl. *The Music of the Most Ancient Nations, Particularly of the Assyrians, Egyptians, and Hebrews*. London, 1864.

Finesinger, S. B. "Musical Instruments in the Old Testament," *Hebrew Union College Annual*, 1926.

Friedländer, Arthur M. *Facts and Theories Relating to Hebrew Music*. London, 1924.

Friedmann, A. von. *Der synagogale Gesang*. Berlin, 1904–1908.

Gressmann, H. "Musik und Musikinstrumente im Alten Testament," in *Religionsgeschichtliche Versuche und Vorarbeiten*, II, Giessen, 1903.

Hemsi, A. *La Musique de la Torah*. Alexandrie, 1929.

Idelsohn, A. Z. "Der jüdische Tempelgesang," in *Handbuch der Musikgeschichte*, Guido Adler, ed. Berlin, 1922.

Imber, Naphtali Herz. "The Music of the Psalms," *Music Magazine*, 1894.

Lachmann, Robert. *Jewish Cantillation and Song in the Isle of Djerba*. Jerusalem, 1940.

——. *Musik des Orients*. Leipzig, 1929.

Leitner, F. *Der gottesdienstliche Gesang im jüdischen und christlichen Altertum*. Freiburg, 1906.

Pfeiffer, A. J. *Ueber die Musik der alten Hebräer*. Erlangen, 1779.

Praetorius, F. *Die Herkunft der hebräischen Akzente*. 1901.

——. *Die Uebernahme der frühmittelalterlichen Neumen durch die Juden*. 1902.

Pulver, Jeffrey. "Israel's Music-Lesson in Egypt," *Musical Times*, London, 1915.

——. "The Music of Ancient Egypt," *Musical Society Proceedings*, London, 1921.

Reese, Gustave. *Music in the Middle Ages*. New York, 1940.

Rosowsky, S. "The Music of the Pentateuch; The Tropes and Their Musical Analysis," *Musical Society Proceedings*, London, 1934.

Saalschütz, Joseph Levin. *Geschichte und Würdigung der Musik bei den Hebräern.* Berlin, 1829.

Sachs, Curt. *Die Musik der Antike,* in Ernst Bücken, *Handbuch der Musikwissenschaft.* Potsdam-Wildpark, 1928.

——. *Musik des Altertums.* Breslau, 1924.

——. "The Orient and Western Music," *The Asian Legacy and American Life,* A. E. Caristy, ed. New York, 1945.

——. *The Rise of Music in the Ancient World.* New York, 1943.

Schneider, P. J. *Biblisch-geschichtliche Darstellung der hebräischen Musik.* Bonn, 1834. (Contains a very valuable discussion of the early musicological literature on the subject.)

Sellers, Ovid R. "Musical Instruments of Israel," *The Biblical Archaeologist,* 1941.

Stainer, John. *The Music of the Bible.* London, 1879; new edition (F. W. Galpin, ed.), 1914.

Til, Salomon von. *Dicht-, Sing- und Spielkunst sowohl der Alten als insbesonders der Hebräer.* Frankfurt, 1706.

Wagner, Peter. *Einführung in die gregorianischen Melodien,* I–III. 1901–1923.

Weiss, J. *Die musikalischen Instrumente des Alten Testaments.* Graz, 1895.

Werner, Eric. "The Conflict between Hellenism and Judaism in the Music of the Early Christian Church," *Hebrew Union College Annual,* 1947.

——. "The Doxology in Synagogue and Church, A Liturgico-Musical Study," *Hebrew Union College Annual,* 1946.

——. "Leading Motifs in Synagogue and Plain Song," *Papers of the American Musicological Society,* Detroit Congress, 1946.

——. "The Oldest Sources of Synagogal Chant," *Proceedings of the American Academy for Jewish Research,* 1947.

——. "Preliminary Notes for a Comparative Study of Catholic and Jewish Musical Punctuation," *Hebrew Union College Annual,* 1940.

Wiley, Lulu Rumsey. *Bible Music.* New York, 1945.

CHAPTERS FOUR TO SIX

Abrahams, I. *Jewish Life in the Middle Ages*. London, 1932.

Badt, Bertha. *Die Lieder des Süsskind von Trimberg*. Berlin, 1920.

Berliner, A. *Aus dem Leben der deutschen Juden im Mittelalter*. Berlin, 1900.

Birnbaum, Eduard. *Jüdische Musiker am Hofe von Mantua von 1542–1628*. Wien, 1893.

Chase, Gilbert. *The Music of Spain*. New York, 1941.

Ecker, Lawrence. *Arabischer, provenzalischer und deutscher Minnesang. Eine motivgeschichtliche Untersuchung*. Bern, Leipzig, 1934.

Elbogen, I. *Geschichte der Juden in Deutschland*. Berlin, 1934.

———. *Der jüdische Gottesdienst*. Berlin, 1913.

Farmer, H. G. *A History of Arabian Music*. London, 1929.

———. *Maimonides on Listening to Music*. Bearsden, Scotland, 1941.

———. "Medieval Jewish Writers on Music," *Music Review*, Cambridge, England, 1942.

———. *The Organ of the Ancients: From Eastern Sources*. London, 1931.

———. *Sa'adyah Gaon on the Influence of Music*. London, 1943.

———. *Studies in Oriental Musical Instruments*. London, 1931 and 1939.

Gradenwitz, Peter. "Musik des Ghetto," *Monatsschrift für Geschichte und Wissenschaft des Judentums*, Breslau, 1937.

———. "An Early Instance of Copyright," *Music and Letters*. London, 1946.

Güdemann, M. *Geschichte des Erziehungswesens und der Kultur der Juden in Italien während des Mittelalters*. Wien, 1884.

———. *Das jüdische Unterrichtswesen während der spanisch-arabischen Periode*. Wien, 1873.

Henriques, Rose L., and Loewe, Herbert. *Medieval Hebrew Minstrelsy*. London, 1926.

Imber, Naphtali Herz. "Music of the Ghetto," *Music Magazine*, 1897–98.

Kinkeldey, Otto. "A Jewish Dancing Master of the Renaissance," *Freidus Memorial Volume*. New York, 1929.

Nettl, Paul. *Alte jüdische Spielleute und Musiker.* Prag, 1923.

————. "Some Early Jewish Musicians," *Musical Quarterly,* 1930.

Ribera y Tarrago, Julian. *Music in Ancient Arabia and Spain.* Stanford University, 1929.

Roth, Cecil. *L'Academia Musicale del Ghetto di Venezia.* Firenze, 1928.

————. *History of the Jews in Venice.* Philadelphia, 1930.

————. *The Jewish Contribution to Civilization.* Oxford, 1943.

Sachs, Curt. *World History of the Dance.* New York, 1937.

Schudt, S. *Jüdische Denkwürdigkeiten.* Frankfurt, 1714.

Sola, D. A. de, and Aguilar, E. *The Ancient Melodies of the Spanish and Portuguese Jews.* London, 1857.

Werner, Eric. "Die hebräischen Intonationen in B. Marcello's *Estro poetico-armonico,*" *Monatsschrift für Geschichte und Wissenschaft des Judentums,* Breslau, 1937.

Werner, Eric, and Sonne, Isaiah. "The Philosophy and Theory of Music in Judeo-Arabic Literature," *Hebrew Union College Annual,* 1941.

Wolf, Albert. *Fahrende Leute bei den Juden.* Leipzig, 1909.

Zoller, J. "Theater und Tanz in den italienischen Ghetti," in *Mitteilungen zur jüdischen Volkskunde,* Wien, 1926.

Zunz, M. *Die Synagogale Poesie des Mittelalters.* Frankfurt, 1920.

CHAPTER SEVEN

Bekker, Paul. *Gustav Mahlers Sinfonien.* Berlin, 1921.

Einstein, Alfred. *Music in the Romantic Era.* New York, 1947.

Hensel, Sebastian, ed. *Die Familie Mendelssohn.* 2 vols. First ed., Leipzig, 1879; first English ed., London, 1882.

Kapp, Julius. *Meyerbeer.* Berlin, 1920.

Landau, Anne L. *The Contribution of Jewish Composers to the Music of the Modern World.* Cincinnati, 1946.

Newlin, Dika. *Bruckner—Mahler—Schoenberg.* New York, 1947.

Phillipps, Olga Somech. *Isaac Nathan.* London, 1940.

Reis, Claire. *Composers in America.* New York, 1948.

Sward, Keith. "Jewish Musicality in America," *Journal of Applied Psychology,* 1933.

Werner, Jack. "Felix and Fanny Mendelssohn," *Music and Letters,* London, 1947.

(See also the bibliographical lists published by the Jewish Music Council, New York.)

CHAPTERS EIGHT AND NINE

Breslaur, Emil. *Sind originale Synagogen- und Volksmelodien bei den Juden nachweisbar?* Leipzig, 1898.

Cohen, Francis L. *The Rise and Development of Synagogue Music.* London, 1888.

Schönberg, Jakob. *Die Traditionellen Gesänge des israelitischen Gottesdienstes in Deutschland.* Nürnberg, 1926.

CHAPTERS TEN AND ELEVEN

"Antecedents of Jewish Music," *Musical Courier,* 1913.

Brod, Max. "Jüdische Volksmelodien," *Der Jude,* Berlin, 1916–17.

Kaufmann, F. M. *Die schönsten Lieder der Ostjuden.* Berlin, 1920.

Nadel, Arno. "Jüdische Musik," *Der Jude,* Berlin, 1923.

———. "Jüdische Volkslieder," *Der Jude, Berlin,* 1916–17.

Parkes, James. *An Enemy of the People: Antisemitism.* New York, 1946.

Sabaniev, L. "The Jewish National School in Music," *Musical Quarterly,* 1929.

———. *Die nationale jüdische Schule in der Musik.* Wien, 1927.

Stutchevsky, J. *Mein Weg zur jüdischen Musik.* Wien, 1935.

CHAPTER TWELVE

Gradenwitz, Peter. "Composers of Modern Palestine," *Musicology,* 1947.

———. "Composers of Palestine," *Monthly Musical Record,* London, 1948.

Philipsen, Carl Bernhard. "Musik in Palästina," *Anbruch,* Wien, 1922.

"Popular Music of Palestine," *Musical America,* 1909.

Sachsse, L. "Palästinensische Musikinstrumente," *Zeitschrift des Deutschen Palästina-Vereins,* 1927.

Saminsky, Lazare, and Nolan, P. J. "Governor Storrs and Jerusalem School of Music," *Musical America,* 1923.

Simon, Fritz. "Vom musikalischen Leben in Palästina," *Zeitschrift für Musik*, Regensburg, 1928.

Storrs, Ronald. *Orientations*. London, 1937.

BOOKS IN HEBREW

Bronsaft, M. *The National-Jewish School in Music*. Jerusalem, 1940.

Edel, I. *The Palestinian Folk Song*. Tel-Aviv, 1946.

Gerson-Kiwi, E. *Music of the Orient—Ancient and Modern*. Tel-Aviv, 1949.

Geshuri, M. *Various Writings on Hassidic Music*. Jerusalem, 1931 ff.

Gradenwitz, P. *The Music of Israel*. Jerusalem, 1945.

Idelsohn, A. Z. *Jewish Music*. Tel-Aviv, 1926.

——. "The Song of the Yemenite Jews," *Reshumot*, Odessa, 1914.

Kühn, J. *Music in the Bible, the Talmud, and the Cabala*. Vienna, 1929.

Loewenstein, H. "Jewish Music in Manuscripts before 1800," *Kiryat Sefer*, Jerusalem, 1942.

——. "The Science of Music in the Sources of the Tenth to the Seventeenth Century," *Kiryat Sefer*, Jerusalem, 1944.

Portaleone, Abraham ben-David. *Shiltei Haggiborim*. Mantua, 1612.

Ravina, M. *Jewish Musicians*. Tel-Aviv, 1941.

——. *Letters on Jewish Music*. Tel-Aviv, 1941.

——. *Yoel Engel and Jewish Music*. Tel-Aviv, 1947.

Stock, J. *M. Gusikov*. Tel-Aviv, 1947.

Stutchevsky, J. *Jewish Music*. Tel-Aviv, 1945.

TENDENTIOUS AND ANTISEMITIC PUBLICATIONS

Blessinger, Karl. *Mendelssohn, Meyerbeer, Mahler: Drei Kapitel Judentum in der Musik als Schlüssel zur Musikgeschichte des 19. Jahrhunderts*. Berlin, 1939.

Eichenauer, R. *Musik und Rasse*. München, 1932.

Judentum und Musik. Mit dem ABC jüdischer und nichtarischer Musikbeflissener. Herausgegeben von Christa Maria Rock und Hans Brückner. München, 1936.

Kahl, Willi. "Mendelssohn und Hiller im Rheinland. Zur Geschichte der Judenemanzipation im deutschen Musikleben des 19. Jahrhunderts," *Die Musik*, Berlin, 1938.

Lorenz, Alfred. "Musikwissenschaft und Judenfrage," *Die Musik*,
    Berlin, 1938.

Die Musik, Sondernummer, Berlin, 1936.

Wagner, Richard. *Das Judentum in der Musik*. Leipzig, 1850. (Trans-
    lation: *Judaism in Music*. London, 1910.)

Wünsch, Walter. "Der Jude im balkanslawischen Volkstum und
    Volksliede," *Die Musik*, Berlin, 1938.

VARIOUS

Articles on various aspects of Jewish and Hebrew music in the volumes of the *Jewish Music Journal* (appeared 1934–35); the publications of the Jewish Music Forum and the Jewish Music Council, both
New York; *Musica Hebraica*, Jerusalem, 1938; and the anthologies of
Jewish folklore. For a comprehensive bibliography on near-eastern
and Palestine music see the lists in *Notes*, 1948–49.

Index

A

Aaron, 30, 39

Abimelek, or The Two Caliphs, by Meyerbeer, 175

Abileah. *See* Nesviski-Abileah

"Abodiah," by Bloch, 239

Abraham, 24, 25, 32, 209

Abraham bar-Chiya, 109

Abraham ben Yizhaq, 110

Abramino dall' Arpa Ebreo, 135

Abraham's Sacrifice, by Scarlatti, 202

Abravanel (Isaac ben Yuda), 134

abub, 54

academy in the ghetto of Venice, 154

accents, Hebrew language, 84, 156

Achron, Joseph, 228, 229, 230, 231, 258

Adam and Eve, by Thiele, 206

Adam and Eve theme, *In the Beginning,* by Copland, 209, 240
in work by Stephan; 209
in work by Tansman, 244

Adler, Hugo, 233

Adler, Samuel, 218

Adon Olam, by Salomon ibn Gabirol, 112

"Age of Anxiety," by Auden, 243

Aharonim Shalom, 269

Ain-Harod Choir Festival, 264

Al-Chakam I, Sultan, 114

Al-Farabi, 109

Al-Ghāzali, 105

Al-Kindi, 108, 109

Al-Mansur, 113-14

al mût lab'ben, 69

Alamoth, 51, 52

Albert, Eugen d', opera on the Cain theme, 208

Alexander the Great, 76

Alexander II, Czar, 225

Alexander, Heinz, 279

Alexandria, 77

Alfasi, Isaac, 104

Alfonso IV, King, 114

Algazi, Léon, 232

Alkabetz, Solomon, *L'cha dodi,* 113

Alman, Samuel, 214

Altarpiece at Ghent, 36

"Alte Jüdische Spielleute und Musiker," by Nettl, 140, *note*

Altschul, Joseph, 213

Amasai, 51

Ambrosio Ebreo, 135

American music, participation by Jews, 192, *note*

Amoraim, 81

Amos, 47

315